Race and Criminal Justice

Race and Criminal Justice

Michael J. Lynch
E. Britt Patterson

School of Criminology and Criminal Justice
Florida State University

Harrow and Heston
PUBLISHERS
New York

Harrow and Heston, Publishers
Stuyvesant Plaza
P.O. Box 3934
Albany, N.Y. 12203

ISBN: 0911577-20-3

Library of Congress Cataloging-in-Publication Data:

Lynch, Michael J.

Race and Criminal Justice / Michael J. Lynch, E. Britt Patterson.

      p.   cm.

    Includes bibliographical references and index.

    ISBN 0-911577-20-3 : $17.50

    1. Discrimination in criminal justice administration—United States. 2. United States—Race Relations. I. Patterson, E. Britt.. II. Title.

HV9950.L96   1991

364.3'4--dc20   91-20028

                                       CIP

Contents

To Liz and Laura

Foreword

Daniel Georges-Abeyie

On Monday morning, March 4, 1991, nonblack America awoke to a nightmare all too real and familiar to America's black and Hispanic citizens; the spectacle of a nonwhite male being brutalized by the police. On this occasion, the nonwhite American was named Rodney King, and the brutalization was in the form of a stun-gunned exconvict undergoing a ten to fifteen minute clubbing and kicking by four white officers while another twenty-one stood by and watched (all but one of whom were white).

The Rodney King beating revived a similar incident in my own life. Twenty years earlier a Puerto Rican friend and I (my own racial/ethnic origin is Afro-Carribean) had undergone a similar beating in a South Bronx public housing lockup. Similar to Rodney King our skin was nonwhite, our ancestry nonWASP, and our crime or criminal infraction nonexistent. In the case of Luis and myself, we had played cards on a bench bordering the housing project's basketball court. We had been "warned" not to play cards, much less gamble, in public. We were not gambling, simply playing cards. But we were not in the sanctuary of our low income housing project. The problem was the white "cops" unfamiliarity with our culture, that of the African-Puerto Rican/Virgin Islander. He saw our public display of card playing (we could just as easily have been playing dominos, a favorite Afro-Caribbean game) as a rampant act of disobedience and hooliganism. What the officer did not know or did not care to respect was a culture which called for single sex recreation away from our female siblings, mothers, cousins, etc., By playing cards in the park we were manifesting ultimate respect for younger siblings, male and female, as well as teenage and older extended family members. Afro-Caribbeans were not expected to bring their male compatriots into a crowded apartment for a robust game of cards or dominos, especially if the consumption of alcohol was a possibility. After all, the luxurious apartments of a South Bronx public housing unit or tenement consisted of one bathroom, bedrooms (possibly three), a kitchen with an eating nook, and a rather roomy but not extravagant living room which doubled as an all purpose room.

The police who apprehended Luis and I gave us the choice of going downtown to Youth Hall (and the certainty of a youthful offender record and the likelihood of a brutal weekend of warding off violent homosexual sociopaths and hostile nonVirgin Islander/non-Puerto Rican youth who distrusted or perhaps even hated us for our ethnicity) or a trip to the public housing project lockup for a beating by the boys in blue. For Luis and I the answer was easy, "Hey mon, lets go! This ain't no big deal. Where da lockup!" We were taken to the bowels of a thirteen story building, marched into a celled holding area and told to hold onto the bars while three grinning pink-faced officers in blue retrieved what appeared to us to be small oars (we had not been to college, nor did we know anyone who had; thus fraternity paddles appeared to be canoe or row boat oars. We had also never been in a canoe or row boat). Once the paddles were retrieved the "fun" commenced; a ten to fifteen minute beating by three men in blue. The blows, like Rodney King's, landed primarily on our legs, calves, thighs, buttocks, and the flat of our backs. We saw stars and breathed hatred. Had the officers not had guns we would have turned on them in a murderous rage. Instead, we were beaten to the ground, shrouded in our silence and their racial taunts and laughter.

Unlike Rodney King, neither of us were exconvicts and we both came from solid families that cared. My father was a New York City Transit Authority Police officer (who moonlighted as a security guard at one of the gip joints on the Third Avenue strip below the EL) while my mother, a truly saintly woman, scrubbed floors and walls in a local junior high school. Luis, who like I lived in a public housing unit, lived with his grandparents, usually only his grandmother, a Puerto Rican of light complexion who doted over him and loved me like a son. His father was a minor league baseball player in Puerto Rico, while his mother remained a mystery to me even though I had known Luis for more than eighteen years; family meant secrets shared and kept, something our anglo compatriots did not comprehend.

Although beaten in silence in the bowels of the projects, almost every youth and adult in the projects knew of our beating. I did not tell my father, a muscular Torolano who wore the blue uniform, badge and gun of the New York City Transit Police about the beating because I feared he would turn his gun on the three white housing authority officers (after all, family, race and ethnicity were stronger loyalties than a blue uniform, shiny badge and nickel plated gun. In addition, the beating of a cop's son, even a black cop's son, was a monumental breach of informal police social etiquette). Thus, when we told our legal guardians about the marks left by this brutal display of New York "Petit Apartheid" violence at the hands of the police, we implied that they resulted from a street fight or "jumping and thumping" at the hands of enemy youth.

For the uninitiated, the police beatings of Rodney King or myself and Luis might appear to be an aberration, an anomaly — but they are not. The anomaly, as Lynch and Patterson suggest in the introduction to this book, was the capture on film of such a beating (e.g., Rodney King). Another example of our hidden Petit Apartheid reality involved a "ride around," i.e., the placement of a youth in the back seat of a police car, the subsequent cuffing, clubbing, punching, pinching, kicking and biting of the suspect (not a formal arrestee) as the cruiser circled the housing project and then deposited its human cargo on the curb where it was first loaded. These ride alongs happen on a weekly basis; nonwhite, Hispanic, Anglo-Caribbean and African American youth were beaten by pale faced men in blue similar to the Rodney King and Georges-Abeyie/Luis cases, while brown and black complexioned men in blue stood in silence and watched, or turned their eyes or backs to the unofficially sanctioned police violence.

Through my own real life experiences I know that the differential treatment of minorities occurs. I also known that it is more widespread than official statistics might indicate.

But why the police violence, and why the public shock and the concomitant rationalization of the violence by nearly twenty percent of the American public in the case of Rodney King? How frequent is the differential treatment of racial minorities, and in fact, who are these minorities? In what form does this differential treatment of blacks and other minorities manifest itself? And, at what points in the system of criminal justice is differential treatment of minorities encountered? These and other questions are asked and answered by my criminological colleagues to my left and right published in this volume. Their questions and answers are much overdue in that American remains one of numerous nation-states in which people know and care little about each other. It remains a nation-state racked by violence and encrusted in a correctional response that gives life to Jeffrey Reiman's (1990) Pyrrhic Defeat thesis, a thesis that acknowledges a class and race based response at great financial and human cost with minimal effect, other than to unintentionally maintain a plentiful supply of Rodney Kings. To put Reiman's claim in perspective, consider the following statistics. In 1990, the California Department of Corrections prepared its Population Projections report for 1990-1991. In that report the Department projected a 1991 correctional population 105,898 and a 1996 correctional population of 125,075. The actual March 31, 1991 correctional population in California was 99,790, of which 35.2 percent is black, 30.3 percent is Mexican-American, 29.6 percent white and 4.8 percent "other." Florida statistics are equally depressing; a black population "comprising a larger proportion of Florida's prison population with almost each passing month, blacks showing a steady increase from 54.5% in March 1989 to 57.6% in March 1991." These statistics cause one to pause and ask: "why are there so many minorities in prison?" And, "why is the race/ethnic distribution in prison so skewed?"

Ours is a nation in which a correctional Pyrrhic Defeat reality for many nonwhites is more attractive than a "free world" reality of minimum wage, no or little health and dental care, mass malnutrition, and substandard housing. For minority residents of the South Bronx, Tallahassee's Frenchtown, Miami's Overtown or Liberty City, prison may mean meat twice or three times a day for the first times in their lives, relatively clean clothes without tears, a room (a cell), regular health and dental care, and the certainty of a place to sleep every night. The slum-ghetto is a violent world very much like the prison or youth facility. Thus "prison ain't no big thing" to many minority youth; in fact, as a youth, my South Bronx compatriots and I referred to the upstate frigid northern correctional barrens as going "upstate on vacation." I do not mean to suggest that there is nothing wrong with prison (e.g., its not a "nice" place) or that prisons need to be made worse. However, prison may be an attractive alternative to some minority community members because society has failed to address the social problems that run rampant in minority communities.

In brief, I trust that this short volume complied by my colleagues Britt Patterson and Michael Lynch will provide the proverbial "food for thought" so often missing when discussing the criminality of nonwhite America and the partiality of the American criminal justice system. The original articles collected for this book reflect both the formal and informal biases encountered by nonwhites at every stage of the criminal justice process. This volume should take its place along side other classic and well received recent works examining racial/ ethnic bias in the criminal justice system. This book, like many others, does an excellent job of exposing the formal and informal biases minorities encounter. The challenge, however, is not only to uncover and understand how these biases disadvantage minorities, but to remedy them.

Introduction

The individual differences between members of the same race are so great that those between races themselves are small by comparison (Willem A. Bonger 1943:9).

Michael J. Lynch and E. Britt Patterson

AS WE prepared this book for press a series of events surrounding the beating of a black man, Rodney King, by several white police officers[1] was unfolding in the media and shocking news-viewers nationwide. The King incident made national headlines when it was captured on video-tape by a nearby resident. We watched in horror as King was repeatedly shot with a stungun and beaten severely (he suffered broken ribs, a broken ankle, a fractured skull and possible brain-damage) while he lay helplessly on the ground. Investigations into this incident and the practices of the Los Angeles Police Department unearthed over one-hundred people who reported being brutalized by Los Angeles police officers. Many were minorities. If not for the fortuitous piece of video-tape, these instances of police brutality and the racial tone of these incidents would continue to be hidden from public view, as is the bulk of racially and ethnically biased criminal justice practices throughout the nation.

For many, the shocking news is that the King incident was not an isolated event. Following its exposure, other incidents in New York, Miami and Charleston, South Carolina (to name a few) made headlines.[2]

Informal Bias

King's treatment by LAPD officers and many other forms of racial bias encountered in the criminal justice system are informal forms of racial bias; that is, they are not officially sanctioned, and are not formal police policy. No one admits to them; no one writes them down as policy; and no one *records* their occurrence. Usually, there are no statistical records for researchers to investigate. For example, without the video-tape, the King incident would not have become evidence for scholars who examine racial or ethnic bias in the criminal justice system.

Informal forms of racial or ethnic bias come in a variety of packages, some of which we might never entertain as biased practice until we confront them face to face. In preparing this book for publication we had the unfortunate opportunity of encountering just such an informal and hidden form of race bias.

Several months ago we contacted a number of scholars about writing a chapter for this book. One scholar we contacted was (and still is) a respected criminal justice researcher who works for a criminal justice agency in a state with a large criminal justice system. He had been researching racial bias in misdemeanor cases, and we asked him to write a chapter on this topic. He agreed and told us that his extensive research revealed that minorities were disadvantaged relative to whites in misdemeanor cases when controlling for a variety of other possible explanations (e.g., social class, offense type, prior record). Accordingly, he concluded that *state-wide* minority race affiliation had a positive and statistically significant impact upon the handling of misdemeanor cases. His supervisors, embarrassed by such findings, requested that he do additional analyses, and he complied. Each time the results were the same: a statistically significant race effect. Only after lengthy delaying tactics, did his supervisors allow the findings to be published as an official state report.

The supervisors' action in this case may be understandable given the political context in which many criminal justice personnel work; but these actions are not ethically or morally justifiable. The informal (and unrecorded) act of racial bias which these supervisors engaged in (repressing publication of findings showing a widespread form of racially-related criminal justice decision making bias) has not only hidden a form of race bias from public view (and in so doing created the idea that race bias is minimal or circumstantial in this state), but has also created an environment in which racially biased practices can flourish. In addition, we are sure that the supervisors who made this decision do not perceive themselves as having acted in a racially biased manner, nor did they *intend* to act in a racially biased manner. However, outcomes may be biased even if there is no intent to act in a racially biased manner. When race or ethnic bias occurs, it may not be consciously engineered; it may simply occur because those involved fail to *consciously design out racially or ethnically biased practices.* Many types of racial or ethnic bias that occur in the criminal justice system occur simply because the consequences of specific policies are not well thought out, or have their historical roots in earlier biased laws and practices (see Bailey, this volume).

Institutionalized Bias

An example of unintended racially biased effects of new laws and policies comes from a drug law recently passed by the Minnesota legislature (though later declared unconstitutional by a county judge). This law set forth the following penalties for first time cocaine users: for crack cocaine a four-year prison sentence; for powered cocaine, probation. On its face such a law does not appear outwardly discriminatory; that is, until the reality behind the law is exposed. The reality: in 1988, 92 percent of those arrested for crack cocaine use were black, while 85 percent of those arrested for powdered cocaine use were white (Raspberry 1991). Thus, under this law, it was more likely that blacks would receive greater punishment than whites. We do not believe that such laws and biases are accidental. Furthermore, we are alarmed by this and similar legal rulings and criminal justice practices.

What explains the types of racial and ethnic biases that occur in the criminal justice system? Different researchers provide different answers. In our view, informal and formalized racial and ethnic bias are symptoms of broader, institutionalized forms of racial and ethnic bias that are a part of everyday life in America. Such a view of American society or the American criminal justice system is certainly not popular. After all, over one-hundred-and-twenty years ago our nation fought a civil war to eliminate a specific type of racial segregation and bias — slavery. A century later, the black civil rights movement was in full swing, bounding hopefully forward in an attempt to eliminate racial bias and create equal rights regardless of skin color. Though these events mark milestones in our growth as an egalitarian and democratic nation, we have failed to purge racism (not to mention other isms) from the American social scene and social consciousness. The Ku Klux Klan still roves the streets of America preaching racial hatred; racially motivated crimes (bias crimes) continue to grab national headlines; pejorative slang, used to devalue and degrade racial and ethnic groups (as well as women), is still heard far too often; and, most recently, a stunned nation watched as a black was beaten on national television by Los Angeles police officers.

During the 1950s similar racist practices were seen as a reflection of bigoted attitudes of individuals from specific regions (e.g., South) and social groups (e.g., the less educated). However, with the ghetto uprisings of the 1960s it became apparent that racial oppression was much more entrenched in American society; it was part of the national culture (Skolnick and Currie 1973). This more pervasive form of racism was recognized as existing in the social and economic fabric of American society; as part and parcel of American institutions.

For example, consider the American institution of education. Researchers have demonstrated that schools attended by minority children receive disproportionately fewer funds on a per pupil basis than schools attended by non-minority children (Espinosa 1982). This inequity in education translates into institutionalized poor school performance by minorities. For example, of 1100 students denied diplomas based on the Minimum Competency Test in Florida as of March 1984, approximately 56 percent were black (Schwartz 1984). A survey of individuals 25 years or older in Chicago indicated that 49.4 percent of blacks and 57.6 percent of Hispanics had dropped out of school (Orfield et al. 1984). It is clear that in the area of education, minority children are taught in public schools that are inferior in quality to those that white children attend. In a society of ever increasing technology and competition, this can be likened to a "death sentence" for minorities; a path to racial destruction and economic exclusion and a path into the criminal justice system where further biases will be encountered.

Given this context of institutionalized racial bias it would be inconceivable for the justice system (which is a product of society) to be immune from racial and ethnic bias. Our impartial system of justice, depicted in popular and legal culture by a robed and blind-folded woman holding the scales of justice, is much less impartial than its imagery.

There are numerous examples of the ways in which racial biases seep into the legal system. This book is intended to provide some insight into the types of racial and ethnic biases that currently detract from our legal system's ability to render an impartial, unbiased form of justice. Given the brevity of this book, we cannot hope to discuss all aspects of racial or ethnic bias in the criminal justice system, and instead focus upon a few select points in the system to illustrate our contention. In addition, there are many broader, more sweeping economic, social and political issues which affect racial and ethnic bias that we cannot hope to cover here in an adequate manner. For example, consider the very concept of race.

Conceptualizing Race and Ethnicity

In 1964 the well known anthropologist, Ashley Montagu, published a book entitled *The Concept of Race*. Montagu's goal was to demonstrate that our conception of race, which was taken from the biological sciences, was unacceptable. The biological conception of race states that there are distinct subspecies within the human species that can be distinguished via "distinctive hereditary traits" (Montagu 1964:xi). This biological depiction of race, Montagu argued, is oversimplified (theoretically inaccurate), methodologically faulty (1964:xii), and impedes rather than facilitates the scientific study and classification of human populations (Montagu 1964:xiii). In Montagu's view, facts about human populations were forced to fit into a preconceived biological notion of race, while, in reality, the facts about race tended to disprove the biological theory of race. Montagu argued that in a scientific view, these facts should have been used to dismantle and eliminate the biological conception of race. What a different world it might be if this had indeed happened!

The term "race" was first used by Buffon in 1749 to describe what he believed to be six groupings of humans (Montagu 1964:3). Two centuries of scientific work have served to cement Buffon's myth (what Montagu calls Buffon's "arbitrary convenience," (1964:5)), and transform it into an objective reality:

> The omelet we call 'race' has no existence outside the statistical frying-pan in which it has been reduced by the heat of the anthropological imagination....
>
> ...[M]any differences exist between different groups of human beings..., but [our]... conception of these [differences] is erroneous, and...unscientific (1964:6,7).

The argument can be reduced to the observation that *race* is a *social construction* or label that is used to differentiate people with outwardly distinct physical characteristics. Consider, for instance, the species of fish *Betta Splendis*. These fishes come in several color varieties, yet they are all the same species. Outwardly they appear different; genetically, they are the same. In other words, the differences between what we perceive as distinct "races" are not objective, biological differences, but socially constructed differences (Montagu 1964:13; Symanski and Goertzel 1979:269). Consequently, as Blauner (1972) points out: "Racism can be defined as a propensity to categorize people who are culturally different in terms of noncultural traits, for example skin color, hair, structure of face and eye."

Such socially prescribed differences can serve a number of purposes. Most importantly, they serve to: (1) devalue a group, making it a cheap source of labor;

(2) and reinforce existing power and class arrangements (Symanski and Goertzel 1979:268-69). In short, "class society is stabilized by racism" (Symanski and Goertzel 1979:270). Others (e.g., Blauner, 1972) point out that racism helps to "fortify the precarious cultures of the racial oppressors" and serves as " 'contrast conceptions' to help define themselves."

The social construction of race includes not only visible, yet meaningless, physical distinctions, but stereotypes as well. Races of people are initially differentiated in terms of visual cues or physical appearances. These differences are broadened and precipitated by attaching stereotypes to them — especially stereotypes which contain the assumption that people who look "different" will behave differently. For example, the common criminal stereotype (e.g., young, black, urban, male) is attached to the more general racial concept "black" or "African American." The result: when we think of blacks or African Americans we generalize from specific cases involving black criminals, to the more general class "blacks;" thus making the logical fallacy of assuming that all blacks are criminals. This is by and large an untrue generalization — a stereotype. Nonetheless, in spite of this logical fallacy, these generalizations are made every day by the media, law enforcement agencies and personnel, as well as court personnel. In short, these generalizations affect how people from different "races" are evaluated and treated by the justice system (e.g., see Lafree 1989)— with information that is prejudicial.

A similar analysis can be applied to ethnicity. However, it is easier to show that ethnicity is a social construction that depends upon distinguishing people through customs and traditions, dress and language, and geographical distinctions. People who speak or act differently, just as people of a different color, can be selected out for unequal treatment quite easily. Unequal treatment of ethnic groups serves the same purposes as those outlined above.

Chapter Summaries

This book is an attempt to explore how racial biases work in actual practice. Various chapters focus on bias in criminal justice decision making, from arrest, to bail and sentencing decisions; the differential application of law to racial and ethnic groups; differences in the legal system's response to racial and ethnic groups, and the meaning and construction of race in the criminal justice system.

From the discussion thus far, it is clear that the issue of race in the fabric of American society is not a new nor transient phenomenon. In "Law, Justice and 'Americans,'" Frankie Bailey provides a provocative historical overview of how "new" minorities (e.g., immigrants) are viewed by the American justice system. The historical perspective supplied by Bailey's piece is of extreme importance because many of the practices and attitudes found in today's justice system have their roots in the past. If one wants to understand the context in which current justice decisions, including possible biases, are constructed, we cannot forget the historical origin of those practices.

In "Minorities and the Police" Smith, Graham and Adams examine several critical issues regarding the police and race such as: 1) citizen ratings of the quality of police services; 2) police officer perceptions of the citizens they patrol; 3) the filing of reports; and 4) making arrests in conflict situations. From their analysis, they conclude that race plays a role in some situations but not in others. Specifically, their data indicate that nonwhites living in nonwhite areas have less favorable views of police. Further, nonwhites who had a prior contact with police were more likely to be arrested, while for whites prior knowledge of the disputing parties had no bearing on the custody decision.

The institutionalization of various criminal justice guidelines were initially undertaken with the intent of reducing disparity and discrimination in the decision-making process. In "Biases in Formalized Bail Procedures," Patterson and Lynch address whether bail guidelines serve this goal. Employing data on suspected felons in a Florida county, they conclude that discrimination continues to exist but in a new form. Although nonwhites were not more likely to be given bail amounts exceeding the guidelines, they were less likely than whites to be given bail amounts lower than those specified in the guidelines. Thus, by virtue of being nonwhite, suspects were not given the same privileges granted whites.

An extensive literature now exists regarding court processing differences between nonminorities and minorities. However, to a large extent, minority status is equated with being black while nonminority status has become synonymous with being white. The Farnworth, Teske and Thurman chapter clearly illustrates the empirical consequences of such a distinction by considering both ethnic and racial disparity at two crucial decision points: charging and the type of sentence imposed. In their data set of individuals charged with felony marijuana possession for sale with a prior record, Hispanic defendants suffered more severe disadvantages. Thus, this important chapter points to the urgent need to consider ethnicity in future criminal justice research.

The role of race in the imposition of the death penalty has a long and controversial past. Robert Bohm thoroughly and thoughtfully examines the past and present state of racial influences on the administration of capital punishment. This informative chapter illustrates that race remains an important factor in executions by the state even in post-Furman America.

The historical over-representation of black juveniles in the juvenile justice system is widely known. It has been estimated that nation-wide 24 percent of referrals to juvenile court are black, while black youths 10-17 make up only 16 percent of the population (OJJDP 1989). In their chapter, Tollett and Close clearly demonstrate this over-representation of blacks juveniles across several decision points in the Florida system. In light of their findings, they provide a unique look at the perceptual differences between minority and nonminority practitioners in regard to the causes and cures of such gross over-representation.

American Indians' status in the system of justice is an area rarely explored. In "American Indians and Criminal Justice", Zatz, Lujan and Snyder-Joy enlighten us to the myriad of concerns revolving around the experience of American Indians in the criminal justice process. From complex jurisdictional considerations to cultural differences in the perceptions of justice, this chapter points the reader in new and exciting directions in the study of uniform treatment for American Indians in criminal justice processing.

In "Ethnic Bias in a Correctional Setting," David Clark sheds light on a neglected minority — the "Mariel" Cubans. In this thought-provoking article, Clark traces the plight of this group of Cuban immigrants from their departure from Cuba to their prolonged "preventive" detention by the U.S. government. Though Clark concludes that bias was not a major factor in the treatment of this ethnic group, this chapter raises many questions about American justice.

The chapter by Jim Thomas reinforces a point we made earlier by examining the social construction and meaning of race in a prison setting. Thomas argues that race is a code which embodies a variety of meanings. The meanings attached to race shape how prison culture is communicated and experienced. In this chapter, Thomas is specifically concerned with how race affects the prison experience for blacks.

Most prisons are characterized by an overrepresentation of minorities. Jim Nelson examines overrepresentation of minorities in New York State's prison system. Nelson notes that 80 percent of the state's prison population is Hispanic or black while blacks and Hispanics make up only 25 percent of the state's population. Through extensive modeling of incarceration following arrest, Nelson skillfuly demonstrates that minorities were incarcerated more often than whites controlling for a variety of other factors.

In his chapter, Jim Garofalo illustrates how interracial conflict is played out on the streets between people of equal power. This article provides a sharp contrast to structural models that examine the institutionalized effects of racial bias which flow in one direction: from the powerful to the powerless. Garofalo argues that in comparison to institutionalized structures, power disparities on the street are not as pronounced and consequently racial conflict tends to reveal itself in a different form: the powerful and powerless are equally likely to be victims and offenders.

Conclusion

Racial biases of the sort described throughout this book will not disappear overnight. It will take a conscious effort on the part of society to eliminate them. We anticipate the day when a book of this nature will no longer be needed. However,

> Those who believe that racial oppression is on its way out, or can be readily eliminated in American life through reforms that guarantee greater equality in living standards and political participation, fail to reckon with the 'integrating' role that racism performs for the society and the depths to which it has penetrated the national culture (Blauner 1972).

Such a conclusion does not provide a happy ending. But, then, racism is not a happy story.

While our book focuses upon racial and ethnic bias in the criminal justice system, we agree with William Julius Wilson (1990:10,12) when he argues that:

> no serious student of American race relations can deny the relationship between the disproportionate concentration of blacks in impoverished urban ghettos and historic racial subjugation in American society....[A] racial division of labor has been created due to decades, even centuries, of discrimination and prejudice....

Thus, in order to eliminate racial and even ethnic bias, we will be required to do more than change attitudes; we will be required to change the economic structure of American society which perpetuates and institutionalizes racial and ethnic bias even in the absence of outwardly discriminatory attitudes.

NOTES

1. Four officers took part in the beating, while approximately fifteen other officers, who are equally guilty in our view, looked on.

2. The Charleston case is particularly interesting, and presented the visual image of a black man, Howard Sims, being held by two white officers while being kneed in the groin. The shocking news here: mistaken identity — Sims was not the man police were after!

Law, Justice, and "Americans": An Historical Overview

Frankie Y. Bailey

THE INVESTIGATION of racial or ethnic bias in the justice system is a complex task. Statistical analyses of current practices are often insufficient indicators of the presence or absence of racial or ethnic bias. Current practices which, on their face, do not appear to be outwardly biased, often hide practices, regulations and laws that emerge directly from racial and ethnic bias. Thus, to fully comprehend the context in which legal decisions are made, and in order to evaluate the presence or absence of racial or ethnic biases, it is necessary to understand the historical origins of processes and attitudes that impinge upon current decision making mechanisms.

This chapter illustrates the importance of historical analysis to studies of racial and ethnic bias and demonstrates how the powerful employ law and justice against emergent minority groups.

The Historical Origins of Bias

Since the colonial period, immigrants to the United States have come in three major "waves." During each wave certain groups have predominated: Irish, Germans, English, and Scandinavians (1820-1889); Italians, Austro-Hungarians, Poles, and Russians (primarily Jews) (1890-1924); and Mexicans, Cubans, Vietnamese, Filipinos, and Koreans (1953-present; McLemore 1983:52). The first to arrive during the colonial period were the Northern Europeans. They were thus able to claim the status of settlers, and thereafter served as the "nativist" hosts to the immigrants who followed them.

By the early 20th century, these nativists were expressing deep misgivings about the "new immigrants." The Young Men's Christian Association (YMCA) articulated the prevailing concern:

> Years ago...immigration was largely English, Irish, German, and Scandi-
> navian—wholesome, earnest, faithful citizens and nation builders. Of late
> years, however... masses of suspicious, clannish people from Southern and
> Southeastern Europe have swarmed to our already congested cities...It is
> not a question of whether we want them or not. They are here and their
> numbers are increasing...Unless we can assimilate, develop, train and
> make good citizens out of them, they are certain to make ignorant, suspi-
> cious, and unAmericanized citizens out of us (Carlson 1975:112).

Actually, in their day, both the Irish and the Germans had been viewed with suspicion by the English immigrants who preceded them. Irish peasants, who had come to the United States in the wake of Ireland's potato famine, settled into overcrowded urban tenements or found work on railroad construction crews or in mines. Wherever they went they were seen as brawlers and ruffians. To those who had arrived before them, the Irish seemed "ignorant practically uncivilized people" who were too fond of saloons (McLemore 1980:55). Similarly, nativists feared that German "radicals" who came to America in 1848 following the revolution in Germany would be as politically disruptive in their new country as they had been in their old one. These German activists disconcerted the old Americans with their advocation of "sweeping reforms relating to the church, the Presidency, the Constitution, slavery, prohibition, and so on" (McLemore 1980:58).

But to the relief of the nativists, both the Irish and Germans proved they could assimilate. After two or three generations in the United States, they had carved out their niches in the political, cultural, and economic substructures of the country. However, with the arrival in the early 20th century of "new immigrants," who had different customs, spoke "foreign" languages, and practiced other religions, the question asked again was: "Can these foreigners be made into 'good Americans?'"

The new immigrants found themselves the focus of programs aimed at their "improvement" that ranged from moral crusades against vice to adult education classes offered in settlement houses (Carlson 1987). During this Progressive Era, criminal justice system workers also geared up to respond to the problems presented by the immigrants. In reformatories and prisons, criminal justice practitioners worked to provide those immigrants who had engaged in deviant behavior with the "self-discipline" that would prepare them to be productive contributors to their new country (see also: Gusfield 1963; Platt 1979).

Yet the fear always remained that newcomers would somehow succeed in "changing" America. This fear spurred recurrent rumors of "alien conspiracies." Woodiwiss (1988:106) describes the "nativist xenophobia" in the years after World War II: "In the immediate post-war years early century images of Sicilians and Italians as 'death-bound assassins' and 'Black Hand' extortionists were refashioned into a catch-all explanation of the country's organized crime problems; something now called the 'Mafia' had taken over!"

Historically, although they were often beset by xenophobic images of lurking threats to American democracy, nativists were always willing to consider the possibility of the assimilation of "aliens" into the population—if those aliens were willing to make the effort required to become "Americans." However, as many would-be Americans discovered, the yardstick by which a "good American" was measured had been fashioned during the Revolutionary period. This was based on a white, Anglo-Saxon Protestant standard—a standard to which some "aliens" would never completely conform.

So it was that in 1879, President Rutherford Hayes wrote: "I am satisfied that the present Chinese labor invasion...is pernicious and should be discouraged. Our experience with the weaker races—Negroes and Indians, for example —is not encouraging...I would consider with favor any suitable measures to discourage the Chinese from coming to our shores" (Miller 1974:38). In 1882, the United States Congress passed the Chinese Exclusion Act. This legislation came in the wake of escalating anti-Chinese violence in the West.

Moreover, in February 1942, President Franklin Roosevelt signed into law Executive Order 9066, which gave the Secretary of War the power "to exclude, remove and then detain U.S. citizens of Japanese descent and their alien parents" (Lauren 1988:132). In *Korematsu v. United States*, 323 U.S. 214 (1944), the Supreme Court upheld this exclusion order. However, in his dissenting opinion, Justice Owen Roberts pointed out that Korematsu, an American citizen, had been convicted because he had refused to consent to "imprisonment in a concentration camp, based [on] his ancestry, without evidence or inquiry concerning his loyalty and good disposition towards the United States." Neither Congress nor the American public were greatly troubled by this situation at the time.

American Justice and the Color Line

As James Oliver Robertson (1988) observes, in the "mythology" which shaped white Americans' sense of themselves and their national identity, the first settlers were said to have found the land "wild, desolate, impenetrable, savage desert." As Christians and bearers of Anglo-Saxon civilization, they "had literally to 'carve out' a place for themselves...building and marking boundaries between civilization and the wilderness, frontiers to keep the savage wilderness and its denizens from encroaching." According to this mythology, Robertson (1988:49-50) explains, "If wilderness survived, then it had destroyed and defeated civilization." This white American mythology—which encompassed a belief in America's "manifest destiny"—was the white Northern European version of "valued" civilization. The idea of "civilization" came to be symbolized by the physical and psychological boundaries that separated white Europeans from "others." Robertson (1988:93) also notes:

> Color and race...gradually replaced class and birth as primary determinants of belonging....By the time of the American Revolution, Indians and blacks...had come to be perceived not only as pagan and savage but as ignorant, inferior, and most importantly, *colored*. Lines were drawn around these peoples of color, frontiers to separate White Americans from other.

White colonialists used legal mechanisms to control members of inferior races who lived among them even before they had won their own "freedom" from England. By the mid-18th century, the colonists had already moved toward the creation of a "peculiar institution" in the South that permitted the legal enslavement of blacks. Furthermore, in the post-Revolutionary period, the new Americans began to look for ways to deal with the "Indian problem."

The Indians

During their earliest encounters with American Indians, some white settlers believed that the more docile Indian tribes could be Christianized and civilized. Within a generation after the settlers arrived, however, their approach to Indian relations had more to do with bullets than Bibles, and created a pattern of "frontier violence." In 1823, President Andrew Jackson seized on an earlier proposal by Thomas Jefferson that the Cherokee Indians be removed from the land obtained in the Louisiana Purchase. Jackson turned this proposal into the official policy of the government.[1] In 1830, after the Indians had refused to take part in a voluntary removal program, Congress passed the Indian Removal Act. Under this Act, southern Indian tribes were forced to move to lands west of the Mississippi. During this period of removal and relocation, tribes which offered resistance were decimated by war and starvation. The superior technology and superior numbers of the whites brought the Indian nations into submission by the late 1880s.

Indians forced onto reservations became dependent on the white government for much of their sustenance. It was during this period that the government also began its program for "Americanizing" Indian youth through education in white boarding schools. Moreover, in a more sweeping effort to civilize the Indians, the General Allotment (Dawes) Act, which was passed in 1887, authorized the allotment of individual parcels of land to Indian "owners." (The concept of private ownership of land was not recognized by the Indians themselves). The Dawes Act was based on the assumption that Indians would become farmers and thereafter adopt the white man's way of life. The Dawes Act also contained a provision that land not assigned to Indians within a twenty-five year time period would be declared as "surplus." The federal government made surplus land available to non-Indiańs, and millions of acres of land formerly held by Indian nations fell into the hands of whites.

During the nineteenth century, the federal government also passed legislation aimed at the problem of crimes committed by the Indians under its guardianship. In 1885, Congress passed the Major Crimes Act (18 U.S.C.A. 1153). This Act allowed the federal government to assume jurisdiction over major felonies committed in Indian Country and removed exclusive jurisdiction over such offenses from the tribes. The passage of this Act was, in part, a political response to public outcry that occurred when an Indian named Crow Dog killed a popular Brule Sioux Chief named Spotted Tail. The Supreme Court, in *Ex Parte Crow Dog*, 109 U.S. 556 (1883), had held that Crow Dog could not be prosecuted by the federal government because the treaty with the Sioux gave the tribe jurisdiction over such offenses. Under traditional tribal law, the preferred response to such offenses was based on a philosophy of reconciliation which required the offender to make compensation to the victim's family. Crow Dog would not be punished by death or imprisonment as he would be under the white man's law. To white observers, Crow Dog seemed destined to get away with murder.

Ironically, Crow Dog became a popular hero in the press, and swayed public opinion in his favor, when he did what no white man would have done by walking through a snowstorm to turn himself in to the federal marshal on the day that had been agreed upon. It was because of his sudden popularity that attorneys volunteered to take a writ of habeas corpus to the Supreme Court (Deloria and Lytle 1983:169). The Supreme Court granted the writ, and Crow Dog was freed. But Congress, feeling the pressure of public opinion, moved to deal with what was considered the Indians' "primitive" form of justice by passage of the Major Crimes Act.

The Major Crimes Act applied to any Indian who committed an offense against another Indian or any other person within the borders of Indian country. The Act provided the federal government with greater control over the tribes and placed further limits on tribal self-government. In *United States v. Kagama*, 118 U.S. 375 (1886), the constitutionality of the Act was challenged. The Supreme Court upheld the Act, reasoning that the Indian nations had a guardianship relationship with the federal government, and therefore the government had a right and an obligation to take such action in order to provide the tribes with adequate protection (Deloria and Lytle 1983:171).

By passing a second piece of legislation, the Assimilative Crimes Act (July 7, 1898, 30 Stat. 717, and later amendments), Congress moved to close another gap in the law as it applied to Indians. Under this Act, "whoever...is guilty of an act or omission which although not made punishable by any enactment of Congress, would be punishable if committed or omitted within the jurisdiction of the State, Territory, Possession, or District in which such place is situated,... shall be guilty of a like offense and subject to a like punishment" (18 U.S.C.A. 13). This Act allowed the federal government "to apply (assimilate) minor state criminal laws to federal enclaves, such as Indian reservations, where no definitive statement on such activity had previously existed" (Deloria and Lytle 1983:173).

In 1953, Congress passed Public Law 280 (67 Stat. 588) which allowed state governments (in California, Minnesota, Nebraska, Oregon, Wisconsin, and Alaska) to assume both civil and criminal jurisdiction over Indian reservations if they wished to amend their constitutions to do so. In 1968, the Indian Civil Rights Act placed procedural restrictions upon tribal courts which handled criminal cases. In effect, most of the guarantees found in the Bill of Rights were made applicable to tribal court proceedings. Critics of the above enactments— the General Crimes Act, the Major Crimes Act, the Assimilative Crimes Act, Public Law 280, and the Civil Rights Act of 1968—point out that these laws not only allow federal and state intrusion into tribal self-government but also force tribes to accept a legal system that violates traditional tribal values and norms. In this way, law has been used to force the Indian Nations to accept the Anglo-American concept of justice.[2]

Blacks

In the post-civil war period, as the federal government was moving to establish greater jurisdiction over the Indian tribes by application of the guardianship theory, it also moved to extricate itself from involvement with the freed slaves in the South. The federal government's involvement with former slaves came about as a result of the War Between the States. The North, as victor in the conflict, found itself faced with the responsibility of protecting black people cut adrift in hostile territory by the Emancipation Proclamation. However, as Carlson (1975:59) points out: "The motivation to end slavery was ideological, not humanitarian." The South—with its outdated concepts of "honor" and aristocracy—was out of step with the "national ideology," and the North sought to bring the region in line with its own "Protestant Republican ideals" (Carlson 1975:60).

In the aftermath of the war, white Southerners faced the task of rebuilding after devastating losses of life and property. As the losers in an ideological conflict, they also found themselves subject to the policies of the victors. The era of Radical Reconstruction with federal military occupation of the defeated South was in effect a policy "instituted to Americanize black and white Southerner alike" (Carlson 1975:66). This Americanization process was intended to bring the agrarian South in line with the industrializing North. After 1877, however, with the end of Radical Reconstruction, the North gradually retreated from its plan for the redemption of the South. It was obvious that the plan was not politically expedient because it was further alienating the ex-Confederates. In addition, because many Northerners shared the Southern perception of blacks as an inferior species, they were sympathetic to the South's pleas that it not be forced to remain at the mercy of black "savages" and the white "radicals" who had joined them. Reports of political corruption and black "crime waves" served to convince Northerners that the South should be allowed to deal with its post-war problems in its own way.

In the postbellum South, whites sought to regain control over the black population. Although the black codes various states enacted shortly after the war had been vetoed by the Radical Republicans in the federal government, they provided a prototype for the creation of legal mechanisms for black control. Through the use of vagrancy laws, blacks were kept on the land as laborers. Through the use of chain gangs and the convict lease system, blacks prisoners were used to rebuild the South and to undergird its economic growth (Adamson 1983, 1984). And when faced with an epidemic of crimes by the new black criminals—"black bad men" or "bad niggers,"—the South responded to the full extent of the law and with extralegal justice (see Rabinowitz 1978; Harris 1973; Hindus 1980; Beck and Tolnay 1990).

These "black bad men," who Southern newspapers described as "savages," were said to be the perpetrators of "brutal outrages" (rape or attempted rape) against white women. Although most studies have discounted any true epidemic of black-on-white rape in the postbellum South, these charges provided the justification for the epidemic of lynchings which reached its peak in the early 1890s. Nevertheless, Ayers (1984:241) provides the following explanation for this lynching epidemic:

> [In the postbellum era] the 'best' whites and blacks seldom had contact with one another, as both races increasingly withdrew into their own neighborhoods and churches...At the time the lynching crisis hit the South no man under 30 years old, white or black, would have any memory of slavery at all—only of racial distrust, conflict, and bloodshed. Since most 'criminals' and most violent men have always been young, and nowhere younger than in the postwar South, it is safe to assume that most lynchers and lynching victims came from this new generation. These men, white and black, feared each other with the fear of ignorance. They saw each other dimly, at a distance.

As blacks migrated to the cities of the North and Midwest to escape Southern violence, they encountered white immigrants who did not welcome their presence. This antagonism was sometimes mutual. Black leaders, such as Booker T. Washington, warned against the use of immigrant labor. These leaders and the black press "pointed to the foreigners as disturbers of the peace and causers of urban crime, and said that increased immigration would result in a loss of status, jobs, and civic recognition for blacks" (Henri 1975: 145). In fact, the New York Age went so far as to claim that immigrants were "teaching black people to be lawless" (Henri 1975: 145). This black xenophobia toward new immigrants was encouraged by those who feared that blacks and new immigrants might "form an alliance against their native white exploiters" (Henri 1975: 146).

Blacks and immigrants were not coming together, however; not even physically. In the cities, they were moving away from each other. In a process of ethnic succession, as blacks moved into urban neighborhoods such as New York's Harlem, their Irish, Jewish, Polish, or Italian neighbors moved out. In the South, "Jim Crow" — a system of legal segregation — had been in place since the late 19th century. It had been affirmed as "American apartheid" (Joseph 1987:155) by the Supreme Court's decision in *Plessey v. Ferguson*, 163 U.S. 537 (1896). In this case, the Court held "separate but equal" was not a violation of the Fourteenth Amendment to the Constitution. It was sixty years later, in *Brown v. Board of Education*, 347 U.S. 483 (1954), that the Court reversed its earlier decision, ruling that "separate" was "inherently unequal." In the intervening years, nevertheless, the status of blacks remained less than that of "full" Americans.

Mexican Americans

The Treaty of Guadalupe-Hidalgo (1848), signed at the conclusion of the Mexican-American War, created the borderlands of the Southwest United States territory. Those Mexican citizens who chose to remain in the area for one year automatically became citizens of the United States. However, throughout the latter part of the nineteenth century and into the beginning of the twentieth...nomadic bands of Indians, Mexicans, and Anglos continually confront[ed] one another in pitched battles. These activities led to the adoption of racial epithets and derogatory stereotypes: The anglos were referred to as gringos (foreigners) and the Mexicans as greasers, while the Indians were condemned by both groups as savages (Bullington 1977:31).

Other stereotypes of Mexicans developed as they either became United States citizens or traveled back and forth across the border as temporary laborers. Mirande (1987:17) points out that the end of the Mexican-American War marked the beginning of hostilities between Anglo-Americans and Chicanos, displaced Mexicans who now found themselves within the territorial boundaries of the United States. As legal and extralegal mechanisms were used to take land and power away from the Chicano, the police, military, and Border Patrol were employed to maintain them in a subordinate position. The 'bandido' image emerged as Chicanos responded to such injustices and to lawlessness on the part of the dominant society.

Mirande describes the behavior of the Texas Rangers toward the Chicanos as "the epitome of police brutality" in that the Rangers "committed numerous abuses, violated the civil liberties of Chicanos, and killed Chicanos and Indians at will" (1987:20). The Texas Rangers reflected perhaps the animosity and prejudice many Anglos felt toward Chicanos. Despite such attitudes, the demand for Mexican labor continued to increase during this period of economic expansion in the United States' industrial and agricultural sectors.

However, as Mirande (1987:21) notes, "the supply of Mexican labor has been likened to a 'faucet' that can be readily turned 'on' and 'off' depending on prevailing economic conditions." During shortages of American labor, such as World War I and II, Mexican labor has been in demand. During the Great Depression, on the other hand, Mexicans were "repatriated" and "a reign of terror ensued in Chicano neighborhoods as they were cordoned off and raided" (Mirande 1987:21).

Like other non-whites, Mexican-Americans were also stigmatized by stereotypical notions about their "inherent" criminality. Bullington (1977:36) notes that one of the first mentions of delinquency among Chicano youths appeared in an article published in 1920. At that time, Chicanos were only beginning to move into large metropolitan areas, although over thirty thousand Mexican-Americans lived in Los Angeles. The images of Chicano delinquency presented during and after this period reflected the fact that Chicano youths were organizing into neighborhood gangs to protect their "turf" from outsiders. This type of organizing was something that other ethnic youths, including white ethnics such as the Irish, had done when they settled in urban areas. The Los Angeles Chicano youth gangs of the 1930s, however, adopted a distinctive style of dress (called "drapes" by Chicanos, "zoot suits" by blacks). These pachucos routinely engaged in minor delinquent acts and social activities. Their activities also included "occasional defense of their territory from alien gangs." Although these gang conflicts were generally between Chicano gangs, during World War II violent warfare between rival gangs brought them to the attention of the public. The Los Angeles Police Department and the Los Angeles Sheriff's Department began to make nightly sweeps in the Chicano community, arresting youths who were dressed in "drapes" (Bullington 1977:39).

When twenty-two Chicano youths were charged with the murder of another Chicano youth in the "Sleepy Lagoon Case," a grand jury investigation of Chicano delinquency was convened. Captain Ed Duran Ayres, Chief of the Foreign Relations Bureau of the Los Angeles Sheriff's Office, was called to testify. He presented a report to the grand jury in which he asserted that the Mexican youths, unlike their "Caucasian" counterparts, were more inclined to use lethal violence during fights because of their "desire is to kill, or at least let blood." Furthermore, the Captain explained: "When there is added to this inborn characteristic that has come down through the ages, the use of liquor, then we certainly have crimes of violence" (McWilliams 1968:234).

Ayres's comments and the case itself received wide attention. Because the Axis powers with whom the United States was at war seized on this evidence of racial discord in the "land of the free" and because the matter was threatening the Good Neighbor Policy with Latin American countries, national political leaders brought pressure to bear to defuse the situation in Los Angeles. However, national and internal attention was again focused on the city in June 1943 when the "zoot suit riots"—conflicts between Chicanos and white servicemen—broke out.

The actions of the sailors received praise from the Los Angeles media. The Los Angeles Times, in its front page account of the violence, said the zoot suiters had learned "a great moral lesson from servicemen" (Bullington 1977:41). The response by the Los Angeles police during the riot was to arrest Chicano youth, sometimes after the Chicanos had been beaten by white rioters. In what Mirande (1987:163) describes as "an excellent example of the mobilization of bias,...Chicano youth were transformed from normal adolescents to 'pachuco killers' and 'zoot-suit gangsters'" who deserved what they got.

While Chicano youths were being characterized as gangsters and killers, Chicano drug use was being described as another indication of the groups "criminal tendencies." By the 1920s, marihuana use had become associated with migrant Mexican field workers. According to Himmelstein (1983:51), "The idea that marihuana use made Mexican laborers violent was well established among upper-strata Mexicans in both Mexico and the United States in the 1900s." Moreover,

> Mexican laborers...often were perceived by Anglos as 'criminal types':
> They were noted for carrying knives and being drunk and disorderly.
> When marihuana was discussed, it was usually associated with Mexicans.
> As a result, marihuana also became associated with violence, a `killer
> weed' (Himmelstein 1983:51).

However, as Bullington (1977:15) argues, "the concern with drug use by persons of questionable character clearly [has] often related directly to deep-seated prejudice against specific minority groups." Musto (1973:7-8) points out that the concern expressed by police officers in the postbellum South about cocaine use by blacks was due to their belief that it made them not only more violent, but fearless supermen. During the 1930s and 1940s, the pachuco gangs were also reported to use marihuana. In the postwar period, heroin use increased in the barrio, and so did the reputation of Chicanos for illicit drug-related behavior (e.g., Moore 1978).

Conclusion

In the report prepared by the Governor's Task Force on Bias Related Violence for the State of New York (1988), the Task Force states: "The idea that being of white, Northern European descent constitutes a normal state of existence from which various groups of people deviate is pervasive in this society." The Task Force goes on to cite the headline in a recent newspaper article, "Cops learn to deal with ethnics":

> This implies not only that one does not have to learn to deal with "non-ethnics" (all of whom apparently behave in a rational, comprehensible, and natural fashion), but also that being White and of Northern European heritage does not constitute an ethnicity. This means that Americans of non-White, non-European backgrounds are seen not only as acting differently, but as being, in some very basic sense, different kinds of persons...(230).

These non-white, non-Northern European "persons" who are seen as acting and as being different are also perceived as the source of a permanent "underclass"—a "dangerous class"—made up of criminals, deviants, and the undeserving poor. Wilson (1990:162) has stated:

> We should note that Western Europe suffered grievously from banditry, gangs of knights errant, criminal syndicates, highwaymen, knaves, vagrants, class tensions and social dislocations, murder and mayhem in its

> royal houses and common hovels—outlawry of various descriptions—for centuries prior to its discovery, conquest, enslavement, decimation, and colonization of non-European populations.

He adds:

> An argument can be made that the latter activities relative to non-European populations permitted Western Europe to 'export' its troublemakers and criminals, and to 'legitimize' the expression of their criminality and homicidal habits on 'savage' populations.

This argument may be too strong for the more conservative "American" to accept. However, what the "underside of American history" does reveal is that the "American myth" of "justice for all" has not been the "American reality." Historically, in America, the reality has been justice for those who are recognized as "Americans."

NOTES

1. See Deloria and Lytle (1983) and McLemore (1980) for discussion of the Supreme Court's reasoning in the Cherokee Nation Cases in which the Court recognized the limited sovereignty of the Indian Nations and their right to protection by the federal government from intrusion by the states. Note that Jackson disregarded this decision by the Court, and in subsequent decisions, the Indian Nations came to be described as having a guardianship-ward relationship with the federal government rather than the status of independent nations—thus opening the door for violations of the treaties made with the Indian Nations.
2. See Comments, "Toward Consent and Cooperation: Reconsidering the Political Status of Indian Nations, *Harvard Civil Rights-Civil Liberties Law Review* Vol. 22(2):507-622 (Spring 1987), for one such critique.

Minorities and the Police: Attitudinal and Behavioral Questions

Douglas A. Smith, Nanette Graham
and Bonney Adams

T HIS CHAPTER presents data on three issues involving minorities and
police. The first issue explores whether citizen ratings of the quality of
neighborhood police services vary by the race of individual citizens and
the racial compositions of communities. The second issue examines police
officers' perceptions of citizens in their patrol areas. Two attitudes are examined:
officers' perceptions of the likelihood of citizen abuse and citizen respect for
police in areas they patrol. We use these data to examine whether variation in
police attitudes is related to the racial composition of the neighborhoods. The
third issue considers whether police actions (i.e., filing official reports of
property victimizations and making arrests in conflict situations) are influenced
by the race of the parties involved and the racial composition of the area in which
these encounters occur.

We selected these issues because of long standing speculation and research which suggests that police officers' actions are structured by the contexts in which they work and their perceptions of those they encounter during routine police work. Ultimately our concerned is whether police decision making is influenced by the race of citizens police confront and the racial composition of the communities in which police work. Thus, in one sense, this chapter shares a goal with much previous work of explaining how race influences police decision making (Black 1976, 1980; Fyfe 1981; Hepburn 1978; Smith, et al. 1984; Smith 1986). However, since police patrol both people and places, we want to know if police and citizens' views of each other vary systematically with individual attributes and spatial characteristics. Moreover, we want to know if and to what extent police officers' perceptions of citizens influence their discretionary choices.

To explore these questions we use three data sets collected as part of the Police Services Study, which contain data from 24 police agencies operating in 60 primarily residential areas. The data used in this chapter include observational information gathered during ride-alongs with police officers on approximately 900 shifts, interview data from the officers observed, and interview data with random samples of residents in the sixty study areas. These data allow us to match officer interview data with observational field data and citizen perceptions at the community-level.

Citizen Evaluations of Police

In an early study of citizen assessments of police, Bayley and Mendelsohn (1969) conducted four surveys of citizens, police officers, and community leaders in Denver, Colorado. One aim of this study was to determine the texture of relationships between police and minority citizens. Using a variety of questions regarding perceptions of the quality and fairness of the job police are doing, Bayley and Mendelsohn found that blacks consistently rated police performance more poorly than whites. In addition, they found that citizen judgments of police were not affected by age, sex, or other background variables and concluded that "the most important factor influencing people's views of the police is ethnicity" (1969:113).

The finding that minorities in general and blacks in particular hold less favorable views of police has been replicated in other studies (see Cohen and Viano 1976). These studies have also shown that attitudes toward police vary with individual socioeconomic status, and age. In particular, persons of lower socioeconomic status and younger individuals hold less favorable assessments of police.

Citizens' perceptions of police are an important element of the environment within which police work, for at least two reasons. First, while police enforce laws, the vast majority of police work involves providing a variety of social services such as handling disputes, or otherwise maintaining order (see Wilson 1968; Reiss 1971; Green and Klockars 1991; Mastrofski 1983). Since the problems police confront are often ambiguous, the manner in which police resolve them are many and varied. Muir (1977) has developed a theory of policing that focuses on police styles of handling ambiguous problems. To Muir, one of the defining characteristics of skilled police officers is their ability to empathize with the suffering and concerns of the people who request their services. It is possible that in environments where citizens hold negative assessments of police, the ability of police officers to empathize with peoples' problems is diminished. This may have implications for how police handle such problems and is an issue examined later in this chapter.

A second reason citizen attitudes toward police may be important involves the current concern with "community policing" (see Goldstein 1987; Sherman 1986; Skolnick and Bayley 1986; Green and Mastrofski 1988). In community policing a major component of the police role is to reinforce informal community norms and values regarding community order and to work with community residents to counteract threats to community order. To accomplish this goal, police and citizens must work collectively in an atmosphere where community residents support police, and where police view community residents as aligned with their initiatives. In sum, the success of community policing depends upon a level of police-citizen reciprocity which may be undermined if citizens hold unfavorable views of police. The issue may become especially acute in poor minority communities where threats to public order abound and police-citizen relationships may be characterized by friction rather than mutual respect and cooperation.

Examining Citizen Perceptions of Police

To identify factors which vary with citizen ratings of police services, individual residents were asked to rate the quality of neighborhood police services on a five point scale from excellent to very poor. Overall, only 10.7 percent of the sample rated police service in their neighborhood as inadequate or very poor. However, black residents' assessments of the quality of police services were more negative than white residents' assessments. While 7.6 percent of white residents rated police services as inadequate or very poor, 18.6 percent of nonwhite residents rated police services as very poor.

With this difference in mind, we examined whether negative assessments of police by black residents could be explained by factors other than race. For example, what impact does living in high crime areas have on citizen ratings of police services? Moreover, since nonwhites are more likely than whites to live in high crime neighborhoods, does this fact account for the difference between blacks' and whites' assessments of police services? Put somewhat differently, it may be that nonwhites and whites who live in high crime areas are equally likely to rate police services as poor or inadequate.

To explore this or similar possibilities, we present results from three regression models of citizen ratings of police in Table 2.2. The correlation matrix for the variables employed in this part of the analysis is provided in Table 2.1. For the regression analysis, the dependent variable is the five point scale of the quality of police services where high values on the scale represent more favorable citizen ratings.

Model 2.1 (Table 2.2) reports standardized regression coefficients and t-ratios for citizen ratings of police, and indicates that citizen assessments of the quality of police services vary with a number of factors. Nonwhite residents have a significantly lower assessment of the quality of police services than white residents. This difference is important because it *cannot* be attributed to differences between nonwhite and white residents on seven other characteristics in this model. This model also indicates that negative assessments of police are held by those who have been victimized in the last year, or personally stopped by police for some matter. Those who view police more favorably include females, persons with higher levels of income, and those who personally know at least one patrol officer in their neighborhood.

While negative assessments of police by nonwhite residents persist when differences between income, education, and victimization are controlled, perhaps racial differences could be explained by the characteristics of the communities in which nonwhites and whites reside. To assess this possibility, Model 2.2 reports results from a regression model that adds three neighborhood characteristics to the equation - the neighborhood crime rate, the percent of households in the area with less than $5,000 annual income and the percent of non-white residents.

Results from Model 2.2 show that while controlling for neighborhood crime rate and poverty level, nonwhites still hold significantly less favorable views of police than whites. However, the size of the relationship is greatly diminished from that seen in Model 2.1, which excluded neighborhood characteristics. It is worth noting that persons living in higher crime areas and poorer communities report significantly less satisfaction with the police.

Perhaps the most informative results concerning the influence of race on citizen's views of police can be found in Model 2.3. This model assesses attitudes held toward police by nonwhites controlling for the percent of the neighborhood population that is nonwhite. The motivation for this model is a quasi-subcultural theory. Much of the literature on minority attitudes toward police allude to a we/

Table 2.1

Correlation Matrix Among Citizen and Neighborhood Characteristics
and Citizen Ratings of Police (N = 8196)

		X1	X2	X3	X4	X5	X6	X7	X8	X9	X10	X11	X12
X1	Citizen Rating	1.00											
X2	Female	.02	1.00										
X3	Non-white	-.18	.02	1.00									
X4	Family Income	.09	-.18	-.25	1.00								
X5	Education	.06	-.09	-.25	.48	1.00							
X6	Age	.15	.03	-.10	-.26	-.27	1.00						
X7	Victim	-.19	.01	.04	.05	.04	-.23	1.00					
X8	Stopped	-.09	-.13	.05	.06	.07	-.23	.11	1.00				
X9	Know Police	.12	-.11	.08	.03	-.01	-.06	.03	.03	1.00			
X10	Pct nonwhite	-.20	.03	.77	-.33	-.29	.00	.06	.03	.10	1.00		
X11	Poverty Level	-.23	.05	.51	-.47	-.37	.07	.06	.01	.02	.66	1.00	
X12	Crime rate	-.21	.01	.42	-.24	-.22	-.05	.15	.02	.02	.55	.41	1.00
	Mean	3.72	.57	.28	3.14	12.42	45.74	.31	.14	.27	28.38	20.82	109.34

Table 2.2

Regression Models of Citizen Ratings of Police (N = 8196)

Independent Variable	Model 2.1		Model 2.2		Model 2.3	
	β	t	β	t	β	t
Female	.051	4.74*	.044	4.12*	.045	4.26*
Non-white	-.141	-12.53*	-.039	-2.40*	.083	3.11*
Age	.127	10.75*	.124	10.60*	.123	10.58*
Family Income	.096	7.70*	.033	2.52*	.037	2.83*
Education	.023	1.89	-.004	-.37	-.005	-.43
Know Police	.144	13.60*	.141	13.48*	.140	13.37*
Victim	-.157	-14.61*	-.134	-12.51*	-.135	-12.58*
Stopped	-.039	-3.54*	-.039	-3.68*	-.040	-3.72*
Crime rate			-.092	-7.30*	-.108	-8.38*
Poverty Level			-.159	-10.73*	-.148	-9.96*
Pct non-white			-.009	-.48	.069	2.90*
Non-white x Pct non-white in area					-.196	-5.73*
Constant	3.227		3.721		3.705	
R-square	.105		.131		.135	

* p < .05

they perspective in which minority group members view police as the "they" and themselves as the "we". To the extent this is true, the attitude of individual nonwhites toward the police should be more negative to the extent that the individual lives in a neighborhood where the majority of residents are nonwhite. A critical mass of persons holding less favorable views toward the police may serve to amplify existing tensions between police and the public.

Results from Model 2.3 are consistent with this quasi-subcultural interpretation. Specifically, the coefficient for the interaction between nonwhite and percent nonwhite in the area is negative (-.196) and significant, indicating that nonwhites living in areas with higher percentages of nonwhites in the population have less favorable views of police than nonwhites living in areas that are more racially mixed.

In sum, the models in Table 2.2 suggest that individual attitudes regarding the quality of police services vary with race. However, this relationship is conditional on the percent of a neighborhood population that is nonwhite. Moreover, this relationship is independent of the other variables included in the analysis such as crime rates, poverty levels and individual characteristics. The implication of this finding is that policing program initiatives that rely upon police-community cooperation and support face an uphill battle in areas where these programs may be most needed.

Police Perceptions of Citizens

The second issue we consider involves police perceptions of citizens who live in their patrol areas. To explore this issue we examine data from two questions asked of 1,116 patrol officers assigned to the sixty study neighborhoods. These questions use a four point Likert scale to measure the officers' agreement or disagreement with the following two questions: "Most people in this community respect police officers," and "The likelihood of a police officer being abused by citizens in this community is very high." Overall, 79.4 percent of patrol officers surveyed either agreed or strongly agreed with the question that most people in the communities they patrol respect police officers. At the same time, almost half (44.2 percent) agree or strongly agree with the statement that the chances of a police officer being abused by citizens in their area is very high.

Police perceptions of citizen respect were examined to determine if officers' perceptions vary with the racial composition of the communities they patrol. The research question is: "do police officers who work in neighborhoods with larger proportions of minority residents regard citizens as more hostile than officers working in areas with fewer minority residents?" To test this issue we employ several variables that measure police officer characteristics (i.e., race, age, education, length of service in the study neighborhood, and supervisory/patrol role), and three community level measures (crime rate, poverty level and racial composition of these areas). The correlation matrix for these measures is shown in Table 2.3.

The correlation matrix reveals that police perceptions of citizen respect and perceived abuse correlate with the percent of nonwhite residents in the neighborhood (.16 for abuse and -.12 for respect). Thus, police working in areas with higher concentrations of minorities perceive their chances of abuse to be higher and the amount of respect they receive from residents to be lower. However, police officer perceptions also vary with community crime rates and poverty levels, which in turn are correlated with the percentage of minority residents. Thus, it is impossible to determine from the correlation matrix whether racial composition, community or officers characteristics are the principle factors influencing police perceptions of citizens.

To clarify these relationships, we estimated a series of regression equations for police perceptions of citizen respect and abuse. The results from this analysis are shown in Table 2.4. Two equations each are presented for perceived levels

Table 2.3

Correlation Matrix Among Police Officer and Neighborhood Characteristics and Officer Perceptions (N = 1116)

	X1	X2	X3	X4	X5	X6	X7	X8	X9	X10
X1 Abuse	1.00									
X2 Respect	-.34	1.00								
X3 Officer Age	-.10	.14	1.00							
X4 Supervisor	-.12	.11	.52	1.00						
X5 Length in Area	.03	.02	.41	.33	1.00					
X6 Officer Education	-.07	.01	-.16	-.00	-.08	1.00				
X7 White Officer	-.00	.10	.05	.05	.06	-.01	1.00			
X8 Pct. N.W. in Area	.16	-.12	-.03	-.01	.07	.04	-.24	1.00		
X9 Poverty Level	.16	-.13	-.03	-.00	.06	-.02	-.10	.67	1.00	
X10 Crime Rate	.25	-.22	-.04	-.02	.04	.04	-.19	.52	.36	1.00
Mean	2.47	2.83	32.0	.19	3.92	14.00	.90	29.00	22.00	108.00

of respect and abuse. Models 4.1 and 4.3 examine police officer characteristics that influence their perceptions of citizen respect and abuse. Models 4.2 and 4.4 add the three neighborhood characteristics to the analysis.

Table 2.4

Models of Police Perceived Citizen Abuse and Respect (N = 1116)

Independent Variable	Respect				Abuse			
	Model 4.1		Model 4.2		Model 4.3		Model 4.4	
	β	t	β	t	β	t	β	t
White Officer	.093	3.13*	.064	2.05*	.001	.005	.049	1.65
Officer Education	.029	.968	.032	1.09	-.076	-2.54*	-.083	-2.82*
Supervisor	.054	1.53	.052	1.53	-.093	-2.64*	-.091	-2.67*
Length in Area	-.061	-1.85	-.044	-1.38	.096	2.92*	.072	2.24*
Officer Age	.140	3.83*	.127	3.53*	-.107	-2.90*	-.089	-2.51*
Pct. N.W. in Area			.077	1.80			-.012	-.285
Poverty Level			-.093	-2.38*			.087	2.27*
Crime Rate			-.213	-6.28*			.225	6.69*
Constant	2.54		2.32		3.19		2.71	
R-square	.030		.074		.029		.095	

*$p < .05$

Results from Models 4.1 and 4.2 reveal that white and older officers perceive higher levels of citizen respect while those working in poorer neighborhoods or communities with higher crime rates perceive significantly less citizen respect. However, in neither case is police officer perceptions of citizen respect significantly influenced by neighborhood racial composition.

A similar picture emerges from the analysis of police perception of citizen abuse (Models 4.3 and 4.4). Older and more educated officers perceive less abuse from citizens as do officers in supervisory roles. However, the longer an officer has worked in a specific area, the more apt he or she is to perceive a higher likelihood of citizen abuse. Officers working in higher crime and poorer communities are also more likely to regard citizens as potentially abusive, but once these factors are controlled for, the racial composition of the neighborhood has *no effect* on whether police perceive citizens as potentially abusive. Thus, police officers' attitudes regarding citizen abuse and respect do not appear to be influenced by the racial composition of the communities in which they work.

Race and Police Officer Discretion

The previous two sections have identified neighborhoods which may be characterized as areas of mutual disaffection between the police and the public. Neighborhoods with higher crime rates and larger percentages of poor households are areas where residents hold less favorable views of police and where police see themselves as more likely targets of citizen abuse and as receiving less respect from residents. Of course, these are the types of neighborhoods which tend to contain larger proportions of minority residents. Thus, areas with larger minority populations tend to be places where the police and the public hold less favorable views of each other, even though race itself may not be the driving force behind this situation.

But attitudes are one thing and behavior is another, and it is to the behavioral question that we now turn. Specifically, we examine whether police decisions to file official reports of property victimizations and the likelihood of arrest when handling conflicts among citizens are influenced by the race of the citizens involved and/or the racial composition of the communities in which the encounters occur. We have selected these two situations because they lie on opposite ends of the spectrum of discretionary situations. Filing official reports of property victimizations is one of the more routine tasks that police officers are called upon to perform. This does not mean, however, that police file official reports of incidents all of the time, and, in fact, they file reports in only 73.7 percent of cases. Nonetheless, there is little *a priori* reason to suspect that whether police file a report is influenced by the race of the victim or percentage of neighborhood minority population. Indeed, in a previous analysis of these data using a much more diverse set of victimizations, no evidence was uncovered that police decisions to file victimization reports were influenced by the race of the victim (see Smith 1986: 333). However, that analysis did not consider the effect of police officer attitudes or characteristics that are considered in the research presented in this chapter.

Results bearing on this issue are shown in Table 2.5, which reports standardized regression coefficients and t-ratios for three equations. Model 5.1 asks whether police decisions to file reports of property victimizations are influenced by the race and sex of the victim or whether the victim represents a commercial business. While there is evidence that police are somewhat less likely to file victimization reports if the victim is black, the coefficient reflecting this finding is not statistically significant.

Model 5.2 adds officer characteristics and police officer perceptions of citizens to the equation. Once again, police are somewhat less likely to file reports if the victim is black but the difference is not statistically significant. In addition, three officer characteristics have some influence on whether they file reports of victimizations. Specifically, white officers and those in supervisor roles are more likely to file reports while older officers are somewhat less likely to file. Finally, neither officer perceptions of citizen respect or abuse have any influence on whether that officer files a victimization report.

The final equation (Model 5.3) reported in Table 2.5 shows that whether police file reports of victimizations is not directly influenced by the percent of nonwhites living in the area where the victimization occurs. In addition to the results shown in this last equation, additional analysis found no evidence that reporting of property victimizations varied with the crime rate of the neighborhood or its poverty level. Thus, these data show rather clearly that neither the race of the victim nor the racial composition of the neighborhood in which the victimization occurs has a significant influence on whether police file official reports of property victimizations.

At the other end of the spectrum of discretionary situations are cases involving interpersonal conflict between citizens. When these incidents are brought to the attention of police they have a wide range of options available to

Table 2.5

Regression Models of Police Filing an Official Report
of a Property Victimization (N = 556)

Independent Variable	Model 5.1 β	t	Model 5.2 β	t	Model 5.3 β	t
Black Victim	-.075	-1.61	-.068	-1.41	-.052	-.97
Female Victim	.008	.17	.012	.26	.012	.26
Business Victim	-.003	-.08	.014	.30	.012	.25
White Officer			.100	2.11*	.102	2.11*
Length in Area			-.026	-.52		
Officer Education			.022	.48		
Supervisor			.085	1.84	.080	1.76
Officer Age			-.089	-1.72	-.118	-2.53*
Respect			-.047	-.94		
Abuse			.021	.40		
Pct non-white					-.028	-.50
Constant	.726		.838		.900	
R-square	.006		.036		.033	

*p < .05

handle the situation. To some, disputes between citizens provide an ideal setting to evaluate the style of control which police officers exercise (see Black 1980). For example, police may mediate the problem, separate the disputing parties, or take one or more of the disputants into custody. It is this latter case, deciding to take one or both of the parties into custody, that is the focus of our next analysis.

Our primary concern is to discover what, if any, role race plays in how police officers handle conflict situations. The types of disputes we consider involve arguments and fights, some physical, others not, between citizens. Some of these are family disputes, other involve neighbors or strangers. All situations are racially homogeneous.

In the simplest sense, race appears to have little effect on the probability that police will take disputants into custody. Specifically, in disputes involving whites, police make arrests 19 percent of the time, compared to 17.1 percent of the time when the dispute is among nonwhites.

As can be seen in Model 6.1, (Table 2.6), while race may not exert a direct influence on whether police take one or more of the disputants into custody, several other factors do influence this decision. Specifically, police officers who feel they are more likely to be abused by residents in the area are less likely to resolve disputes by making arrests. Alternatively, the chances that an officer will make an arrest increase with the length of time they have worked in the neighborhood and whether they have had previous contact with the disputing parties. Police are also significantly more likely to arrest males than females, and when requested to do so by the complainant. Finally, police are more likely to take one of the disputants into custody when the dispute attracts more bystanders, although this may simply reflect a desire on the part of the police to change the stage of negotiation.

Model 6.2 in Table 2.6 adds the racial composition of the neighborhood to the equation and shows that this factor does not significantly influence police arrest decisions. Thus, neither the race of the disputing parties nor the racial composition of the neighborhood in which the dispute occurs has a significant impact on whether police take at least one of the disputants into custody.

While race does not appear to have a direct effect on whether police use arrest to handle interpersonal conflicts, it should be noted that in another analysis which examined how police handle conflicts involving interpersonal violence between citizens, race did have a strong effect on arrest (Smith 1987). Specifically, when violence is involved police are much less likely to make an arrest if the parties involved are nonwhite. In fact, the model method of handling violent disputes among nonwhites is simply to separate the disputing parties. Thus, the inability to find a race effect in this analysis is probably attributable to the fact that race is not a factor influencing arrest in nonviolent disputes and that most of the

Table 2.6

Regression Models of Whether Police Make an Arrest in Encounters
Involving Conflict Among Citizens (N=229)

Independent Variable	Model 6.1 β	Model 6.1 t	Model 6.2 β	Model 6.2 t	Model 6.3 β	Model 6.3 t
Individual and Situational						
Black	-.017	-.26	.009	.13	-.072	-.90
Male Suspect	.170	2.89*	.173	2.93*	.157	2.66*
Male Victim	.045	.74	.045	.74	.055	.91
Violent Dispute	.087	1.39	.079	1.23	.109	1.68
Family Dispute	-.034	-.53	-.034	-.53	-.026	-.41
Public Place	-.049	-.85	-.053	-.92	-.060	-1.04
No. of Bystanders	.191	3.09*	.195	3.14*	.189	3.06*
Complainant Wants Arrest	.377	6.41*	.376	6.38*	.349	5.86*
Officer						
Officer Age	-.112	-1.75	-.114	-1.79	-.118	-1.86
White Officer	-.114	-1.90	-.122	-2.00*	-.126	-2.08*
Officer Education	-.059	-1.00	-.057	-.96	-.059	-1.01
Length in Area	.164	2.58*	.173	2.68*	.166	2.59*
Prior Knowledge	.140	2.37*	.138	2.32*	-.004	-.06
Supervisor	-.023	-.37	-.024	-.39	-.027	-.44
Abuse	-.130	-2.09*	-.126	-2.02*	-.117	-1.88
Pct non-white			-.054	-.76	-.053	-.74
Black x Prior Knowledge					.212	2.25*
Constant	.472		.479		.535	
R-square	.319		.321		.337	

* p < .05

disputes in this data set do not involve violence. In addition, race may not have
an effect here because all disputes analyzed involved individuals of the same
race. We did not assess whether disputes involving both whites and nonwhites
as either party in a dispute affects police decision making.

The fact that police are more likely to make an arrest in instances of
interpersonal violence involving whites is consistent with Black's (1980) theory
of the behavior of law. Black argues that law varies directly with stratification
and that, on average, disputes involving whites will be subject to more law than
disputes involving nonwhites. An arrest is an instance of law in that it potentially
activates a legal process and subjects the arrested party to possible future legal
control and provides the victim with a modicum of legal protection.

The fact that race appears to matter in whether police make arrests in violent disputes but not in disputes that do not involve violence is an example of an interaction — the situation where one variable's (race) relationship to the outcome measure (arrest) varies with the level of some other variable (violent or nonviolent dispute). Since our focus is on the role of race in how police handle interpersonal conflicts we have tested for the presence of other possible interactions in the data. The results of this test revealed two significant interactions; one with violence and the other with whether police had prior contact with the disputing parties as either complainants or suspects. The latter interaction was the strongest and was added to the equation to produce the results in Model 6.3.

These results show that if police had prior contact with the disputing parties they were significantly more likely to resolve the current dispute by making an arrest. But this effect is only evident for disputes involving nonwhites. For disputes involving whites, police prior knowledge of disputing parties has no bearing on whether they take one or more of the disputants into custody.

Conclusion

In sum, these analyses shed light on several issues. First, nonwhites living in areas of high concentration of nonwhites have *less favorable* views of police than nonwhites living in areas that are racially mixed. Thus, where race does seem to matter is in the attitudes that citizens hold toward police.

Second, police officers' attitudes regarding potential citizen abuse and respect *do not* appear to be influenced by the racial composition of the communities in which the officers work.

Third, whether police file reports of victimization for property offenses *is not* directly influenced by the percentage of nonwhites living in the area where the victimization occurs or the race of the victim. Finally, nonwhites with a prior contact with police are *more likely* to be arrested: while for whites, having prior knowledge of the disputant has no bearing on the arrest decision.

Bias in Formalized
Bail Procedures*

E. Britt Patterson and Michael J. Lynch

A NY ATTEMPT to assess the effect of extra-legal factors (i.e., factors
that are not legally relevant such as age, race, gender, class,
ethnicity, etc.,) upon criminal justice decision making practices is
inherently controversial. The controversy begins with the contrasting assumptions researchers employ to construct and understand how factors
affect decision making. For instance, those who believe in "democratic
ideals" and "justice norms" hold that criminal justice decisions are rendered
in an impartial atmosphere devoid of discriminatory practices. Further, they
tend to be skeptical regarding evidence of race, ethnic, or gender bias.

*We would like to thank Lisa Stolzenberg, Stewart D'Alessio, and Stamatis Spirou for
their research assistance, the Florida Department of Corrections for assistance in
providing the data used in this analysis, and Celeste Albonette, John Hagan, Marjorie
Zatz, Dragan Milovanovic and Brian MacLean for their comments on an earlier draft of
this manuscript.

Extremists in this group have constructed excessively strict definitions of discrimination and bias that minimize the impact and importance of discrimination findings (e.g., Wilbanks 1987a[1]; for criticism see Lynch 1990; Ansari 1990; Georges-Abeyie 1990).

At the opposite extreme are researchers who believe that criminal justice decisions are biased against certain racial, ethnic, class or gender (minority) groups. These researchers are skeptical of studies demonstrating no discrimination, and often question such findings on the grounds that unexamined, informal processes rather than formal process tend to be the culprit (e.g., Georges-Abeyie 1990).

The third group in this controversy takes no pre-defined stand, and attempts to "let the data speak for themselves," or to remain objective when assessing discrimination in criminal justice decision making. This is a difficult position to maintain, given that data must be interpreted within the confines of both a theoretical perspective and the social context in which such decisions are rendered (Lafree 1989; Myrdal 1969; Flakser 1971; Lynch and Nalla 1989).

The fourth and final group is wary of discrimination research and the methodological shortcomings that have plagued such research. These researchers have attended to two primary concerns: (1) addressing methodological deficiencies that plague discrimination research (e.g., Hill et al. 1985), and (2) assessing criminal justice decision making practices within a sociologically relevant context (e.g., LaFree 1989; Myers and Talerico 1987). The sociological context can use historical evidence supporting claims of discrimination (e.g., the vast literature on the history of race, class, ethnic and gender discrimination that has pervaded U.S. development; see Messerschmidt 1986; Schur 1984; Georges-Abeyie 1984 for information related to criminology); or it may focus upon how different forms of law are applied to different class, race and gender groups (Reiman 1990; Milovanovic 1988; Groves and Newman 1987). For this group, the overriding concern is to address discrimination in broad contextual terms, or within a given historical and cultural climate that affects class, race, and gender relationships to describe the social context affecting decision making practices (e.g., Lafree 1989; Zatz 1984, 1985).

Zatz's (1987) review of research on racial/ethnic discrimination in the criminal justice system demonstrates how the concerns noted above have generated distinctive waves of research supporting each view, and the failure of this research to solve the discrimination controversy. As Zatz (1987:69) notes, "this controversy is rooted in ideological, theoretical and methodological conflicts that encompass the meaning and pervasiveness of 'discrimination' and the appropriate methods for assessing its evidence, strength and form."

Zatz outlines four waves of discrimination research. The first wave (1930s-mid 1960s) demonstrated clear, consistent discrimination against nonwhites. Findings from this period must be qualified historically, since they examine discrimination in the pre-civil rights movement era (Zatz 1987:71). It is possible that the civil rights movement succeeded in eliminating racial discrimination in criminal justice decisions during subsequent eras.

The second wave (late 1960s-1970s) emerged following the civil rights movement, and demonstrated no direct race effect on decision making outcomes (Zatz 1987:73; see also Georges-Abeyie 1984:132-136). During this era, researchers began to employ more sophisticated empirical models that controlled for the effect of legally relevant factors. The inclusion of legally relevant factors in decision making models diminished the effects of race (Kleck 1981; Hagan 1974), and gave rise to the conclusion that any race effects were indirect and operated through legally relevant criteria which placed minorities at a disadvantage (Zatz 1987:73).

The third wave (late 1960s-1970s data, conducted in 1970s and 1980s) again demonstrated race effects. Wave three studies captured the insights from wave two and began to examine indirect rather than main or direct effects of race on decision making (Zatz 1987:74). These studies exposed issues such as sample selection bias, specification error, interactive effects, and cumulative race and gender effects (Zatz 1987:75; see discussion below).

During the fourth wave (late 1970s-1980s) researchers began to focus on the effect determinate sentencing policies had upon discrimination. This line of research was based upon the belief that determinate sentencing policies would eliminate various forms of discrimination by establishing rules, standards and sentencing practices applicable to all defendants. Results from this wave are not uniform: some research suggests both direct and indirect discrimination effects (Zatz 1984, 1985; Hagan and Zatz 1985; Zatz and Hagan 1985; Miether and Moore 1985), while other research provides no direct evidence of discrimination (e.g., Kleck 1981). These contrasting findings have yet to resolve the question of whether sentencing guidelines eliminate or institutionalize (hide) discrimination (see Petersilia and Turner 1987).

Despite the inconsistencies and conflicting results pointed out by Zatz's review, several insights into discrimination have emerged from this literature. One insight is that the later the criminal justice decision making stage analyzed, the more methodological and sampling problems researchers encounter, and the more questionable the results. The validity of studies focusing on late stage decision making (e.g., sentencing and incarceration decision), has to do with both sample selection bias and cumulative discrimination effects.

Major Methodological Limitations in Discrimination Research

Sample selection bias is a persistent problem in criminal justice decision making research. Simply put, sample selection bias means that the sample of offenders obtained at any particular stage of the decision making process is biased by the nonrandom decisions made at previous decision making points (Barnow et al. 1980). For example, when incarceration decisions are examined, the sample available is affected by a filtering process that occurs at previous decision stages from arrest, through bail, initial hearing, plea bargaining, etc.[2] As Hill et al. (1985:139) note, "as processing ages, filtering mechanisms have the effect of homogenizing the population and thus reducing the likelihood of bias across stages...[The problem is exacerbated since] it is precisely where bias is least likely to be found that data are most accessible." In other words, data from late stage decision making points— the type of data least likely to provide evidence of bias, and the type of data most likely to incorporate sample selection bias—is the most readily available to researchers.

One method that can be employed to minimize sample selection bias is to examine decisions made at the earliest possible point in the decision making series[3]: the earlier the stage examined, the more sample bias is minimized. Thus, in theory, the best place to begin an analysis of decision making is at the arrest stage. The problem with this strategy is two-fold. First, even decisions brought to the attention of police are nonrandom events (i.e. incorporate sample selection bias). Second, arrest decisions are largely unobservable, except through extraordinary means such as systematic observational studies (e.g., Black and Reiss 1967; Smith and Visher 1982, Smith et al. 1984, Smith, this volume).

Given these qualifications, we choose to concentrate upon the next decision making stage for which data are readily available: jailhouse bail. Jailhouse bail decisions are rendered following arrest, and allow an arrestee to post bail at the stationhouse or jail according to amounts prespecified in a bail schedule (Hall 1984). The bail schedule contains a list of all bailable charges and the dollar amount that corresponds to each offense category.

Bail Research: A Brief Overview

Researchers have demonstrated that bail decisions have a significant impact upon criminal defendants (Nagel 1969; Burk and Turk 1975; Farrell and Swigert 1978; see also Box 1981:188-191; Chambliss 1969; Quinney 1979:309-311; Michalowski 1985:203-208). First, those unable to make bail are punished even though they may be innocent (Reiman 1990:83). Second, defendants unable to make bail are more likely to be found guilty than those who make bail (Morse and Beattie 1932; Foote 1954; Frieland 1965) because they cannot aid in their own defense (e.g., by locating witnesses who may only be known to the defendant by an alias or street name), raise funds for their defense, and enter the courtroom in the company of a bailiff, which may influence the judge's or jury's opinion concerning the defendant's guilt.

Although ability to post bail is important because it affects the "in-out" decision, we instead focus on the relationship between legal, extra-legal factors and bail amount decisions. We do so since we are interested in whether criminal justice decisions (i.e., the bail amount) are biased, not whether defendants' individual situations preclude them from meeting bail requirements. The latter type of study would focus on bias or discrimination that is not solely related to criminal justice decision making practices.

The data for this study come from a North Florida county that employs a bail schedule to make jailhouse bail decisions. In theory, bail schedules, like determinant sentencing guidelines, should minimize discrimination (measured as the statistical association between bail amounts and extra-legal factors controlling for the effect of legally relevant criteria), since they establish rules related to offense seriousness that are equally applicable to all defendants.

In order to assess the extent of discrimination in assigning bail amount, bail amount decisions were divided into the three categories (i.e. below, within schedule, and above schedule) described later in this chapter. Before returning to a discussion and analysis of our data, we turn to a brief examination of the meaning of and evidence for discrimination.

Assessing Discrimination or No-Discrimination Theses

In assessing criminal justice decision making practices we are interested in whether decisions fall into one of two broad outcomes: (1) discriminatory (DT) or (2) non-discriminatory (NDT) (on the DT/NDT debate see: MacLean and Milovanovic 1990; Lynch and Patterson 1990; Lynch 1990; Wilbanks 1990a,b; Headly 1990). In our view, decision making outcomes *can be* classified as discriminatory if they are based in whole or in part upon extra-legal factors such as age, race, gender or class, *and* the association between extralegal factors and outcomes remains significant once legally relevant criteria are considered.

In this view, decision making outcomes *are not* discriminatory if they are based solely upon legally relevant criteria specified by law (assuming that the legally relevant criteria do not amount to a form of institutionalized bias against a particular race, ethnic, age, gender or class group) such as: severity of the offense; the type, quality and amount of evidence; the presence or absence and type of weapon employed in the commission of the crime; prior record; harm done; and even the number of offenders.

The above definitions of DT/NDT are easily subjected to quantitative investigation (Lynch and Patterson 1990). However, we wish to make it clear that empirical investigations of DT/NDT face some serious interpretational problems and fail to address the possibility of discrimination in informal practices (Georges-Abeyie 1990). Thus, there may be specific forms of discrimination that occur relative to jailhouse bail procedures that are not within the purview of our study. It is also possible that certain legally relevant decision making criteria harbor hidden biases against a particular group (Meithe and Moore 1985). Such issues are likewise not amenable to the type of empirical observations we employ here. Since the jailhouse bail decisions for the North Florida county that we analyzed are based primarily upon seriousness of the offense and number of counts (see discussion below), such decisions do not appear to be outwardly biased. In short, we still believe that empirical observations of DT/NDT need to be qualified with qualitative data (Georges-Abeyie 1990) and contextual forms of analysis. As Lafree (1989:49) notes, the problem with many empirical tests of discrimination is that they fail to examine the "social-cultural context" in which these decisions are constructed.

DT Versus NDT Assumptions. DT/NDT perspectives differ on a number of accounts. First, NDT theorists tend to believe in the objectivity of empirical analysis (Wilbanks 1987a; Hindelang 1978; Chiricos and Waldo 1975). This assumption often creates interpretations of results that are detached from the social-cultural context in which decisions are rendered. Second, NDT argues that decision making differentials between groups are explicable with reference to differences in offending across groups (Wilbanks 1987a). This hypothesis is largely untestable given our limited knowledge of the true extent of crime. Third, NDT sometimes argues that where differential treatment occurs, it emerges in the form of increased leniency for a particular group, and hence cannot readily be classified as discrimination (Wilbanks 1987b, 1987a). Such a proposition could, for example, be used to argue that where women receive more lenient treatment than men in the criminal justice system there is no evidence for bias/discrimination (Wilbanks 1987b; Box and Hale 1982a, 1982b). Finally, NDT argues that legally relevant factors rather than extra-legal factors have the greatest, most consistent impact upon decision making.

DT basically holds the reverse assumptions, except in reference to point three. DT does not argue, as is widely assumed, that extra-legal factors must necessarily have a negative impact upon criminal defendants. Neither does it argue that groups subjected to discriminatory practices must be treated more severely than the legal norm. For instance, a group could be discriminated against if it is treated within statutory limits, while comparable groups fall below the stated limits of the code in question, as long as differentials in treatment can be partially or fully explained by extra-legal criteria.

Bail Mechanisms in Florida

Before proceeding with our analysis, we present some background material concerning bail procedures in Florida. The *Florida Rules of Court* (1989, Rule 3.131, p. 224) state that:

> Unless charged with a capital offense or an offense punishable by life imprisonment and the proof of guilt is evident or the presumption is great, every person charged with a crime...shall be entitled to pretrial release on reasonable conditions. If no conditions of release can reasonably protect the community from risk..., assure the presence of the accused at trial, or assure the integrity of judicial process, the accused may be detained.

This statute clearly spells out the criteria to be considered in bail release/retention decisions:

> ...the court may consider the nature of the...offense...the penalty provided by law, the weight of the evidence against the defendant ...defendant's family ties, length of residence in the community, employment history, financial resources, and mental condition; the defendant's past and present conduct, including...convictions, previous flight to avoid prosecution, or failure to appear at court..., the nature and probability of danger which the defendant poses to the community, the source of the funds used to post bail; whether the defendant is already on release pending resolution of another criminal proceeding, or on probation, parole or other release pending completion of sentence, and other facts the court considers relevant (Florida Rules of Court 1989, 3.131, b, 3).

While these rules appear quite specific, the last portion of this rule ("and other factors considered relevant") would appear to destroy the initial intent of the rule.

These rules were adopted in response to a lawsuit arguing that Florida's bail procedures unconstitutionally discriminated against poor defendants (*Pugh v. Rainwater*, 557 F 2nd 1189, 1977). Once adopted, the new bail procedures were again challenged on the grounds that they discriminated against indigent defendants (*Pugh v. Rainwater*, rehearing, 557, F 2nd 1189, 1978). On rehearing, the court held that indigents have no right to non-monetary bail, and that monetary bail does not unconstitutionally discriminate against indigent defendants. According to the court, Florida's bail procedures do not discriminate against the poor. The empirical reality of this finding, as well as the question of whether other forms of bias exist, however, remain open to investigation.

The Present Study: Data and Variables

The data used in this analysis represent a sample of 335 non-narcotics felony arrests made in a northern Florida border county from 1985-1986.[4] In 1986, the county's population was slightly more than 250,000 (living on slightly over 650 square miles). Approximately sixty percent of the population were between the ages of 18 and 64 and an equal percentage were male. Principle forms of employment include trade, service, and government sector jobs, with an unemployment rate slightly over 6 percent. Estimated buying power per household was approximately $23,000. In 1980, median family income for whites was approximately $18,000, and $12,000 for black families. Slightly over 20 percent of the population were black, while about 2 percent were of Hispanic origin. In 1986, the total crime index for the county was over 19,000.

DEPENDENT VARIABLE

The intent of this study is to discern the influence of offender and offense characteristics on decisions to deviate from or to comply with bail schedule amounts. In order to do so, the dependent variable chosen for examination, schedule compliance, was trichotomized: the bail cash amount required is either (1) below schedule amount, (2) above schedule amount, or (3) within schedule amount. A brief example will illustrate the construction of this variable.

For third degree felonies the lowest bond stipulated in the bail guidelines is $1,000, while the upper limit is $5,000 (see Table 3.1). If the arresting officer charges the offender with a third degree felony and this is the only charge, then a bail amount between $1,000 and $5,000 would be within schedule; a bail amount less than $1,000 would be below schedule; a bail amount exceeding $5,000 would be above schedule.

Table 3.1
Bail Schedule

Bail or appearance bonds are hereby fixed for offenses in the following amounts:

Offense	Low Bond	High Bond*
Felony, 3rd degree	$1,000	$5,000
Felony, 2nd degree	$2,500	$10,000
Felony, 1st degree	$10,000	$15,000

---

* Multiply by the number of counts to determine the upper limit of high bond for cases involving multiple counts. For example, for a case involving five (5) counts of a third degree felony, the upper limit of bail amounts to $25,000.

Many suspects, however, were charged with multiple counts and charges.[5] In such cases, the number of counts are taken into consideration by multiplying the number of counts by the upper limit of the bail schedule. Thus, if the most serious offense charged is a third degree felony, *and* there are 10 other counts, the within scheduled bail amount range would be $1000 to $50,000. As is apparent, the within category of this variable is quite liberally defined, and could result in underestimating the extent of discrimination related to extra-legal factors. This categorization was necessary, however, due to the lack of information on additional charges. Using this operationalization, the distribution of cases was as follows: 74% of cases were within the bail schedule; 17% of the cases fell below schedule; and 8% of cases were above guideline limits. The bail amounts for first, second and third degree felonies are presented in Table 3.1.

INDEPENDENT VARIABLES

Offense Characteristics: According to Florida's legal statutes, several offense characteristics that should influence bail schedule compliance (see discussion on bail statute above) were available from these data: statutory degree of the most serious offense charged (first, second or third degree); type of most serious offense (personal or property); and whether a weapon was used in the commission of the offense. These three measures gauge the *seriousness of the offense*. Further, the total number of counts at booking (natural logarithm) as well presence or absence of accomplices are also included as offense related measures.

Offender Characteristics: In addition to the offense characteristics noted above, offender characteristics are included in the analysis to determine whether extra-legal factors influence schedule compliance. Among those

#220 Fri 2003 Feb 21 04:46PM
em(s) checked out to 29006009261490.

LE: RACIAL EQUITY IN SENTENCING.
L #: US7 RC13 R3599
CODE: 1031843832
DATE: 2003 Mar 07

LE: Race and criminal justice / Edite
L #: HV9950.L98
CODE: 36277000010845
DATE: 2003 Mar 07

1 items are subject to Overdue Fines

Table 3.2
Bivariate Associations for Schedule Compliance or Deviation by Offense
and Offender Characteristics

Variable	N	Within	Below	Above
All cases	335	74.3	17.3	8.4
Residence (.24)*				
Local	290	73.4	18.6	7.9
Nonlocal	45	80.0	8.9	11.1
Race (.10)				
White	183	70.5	21.3	8.2
Nonwhite	152	78.9	12.5	8.6
Gender (.14)				
Male	283	76.0	15.5	8.5
Female	52	65.4	26.9	7.7
Arresting Agency (.09)				
Sheriff	217	70.5	19.8	9.7
Local Police	118	81.4	12.7	5.9
Legal Status (.83)				
No restrictions	242	74.4	17.8	7.9
Restrictions	93	74.2	16.1	9.7
Offender role (.02)				
Alone	250	74.0	19.6	6.4
Accomplice	85	75.3	10.6	14.1
Alcohol Use (.26)				
No	269	72.5	18.2	9.3
Yes	66	81.8	13.6	4.5
Weapon Use (.93)				
No	244	73.8	17.6	8.6
Yes	91	75.8	16.5	7.7
Offense Type (.71)				
Personal	120	73.3	16.7	10.0
Property	215	74.9	17.7	7.4
Total Counts (.01)**				
One	193	69.4	22.8	7.8
More than one	142	81.0	9.9	9.2
Prior Arrests (.37)**				
None	109	71.6	21.1	7.3
One to Five	116	71.6	17.2	11.2
Six or more	110	80.0	13.6	6.4
SES (.82)**				
Low	85	75.3	18.8	5.9
Medium	155	74.8	15.5	9.7
High	95	72.6	18.9	8.4
Statutory Degree (.11)				
First	8	62.5	37.5	0.0
Second	106	67.0	21.7	11.3
Third	221	78.3	14.5	7.2

* Probability level for chi-square test of significance
** Variable was recoded to categories for ease of presentation for this table only.

variables considered are: race (white or nonwhite[6]), gender, and social economic status (scale composed of occupation, education, and income; see Nam and Powers 1968 or U.S. Bureau of the Census 1963). These variables can be used to assess race, gender and class related forms of discrimination.

Perceived Dangerousness: We include several additional variables as measures of *perceived dangerousness* to the community and likelihood of appearance at subsequent hearings: the legal status of the suspect at the time of arrest (not restricted or restricted); the suspect's use of alcohol at the time of the offense; the suspect's residence status (local or non-local); and the suspect's number of prior arrests (natural logarithm).

In addition to these variables, the arresting agency was coded as a dummy variable (0 = the sheriff's department; 1 = local police). This information was used to determine whether decision making outcomes were organizationally driven.

Findings: Bivariate

Table 3.2 shows the percentage of cases falling within, above and below schedule bail amounts for different categories of the independent variables. Several examples are given to illustrate the reading of this table. For instance, the findings indicate that *non-local* residents are *more* likely to receive bail amounts *above schedule* and less likely to receive bail amounts below schedule than local residents. Further, while nonwhites and whites are equally likely to be given bail amounts which exceed schedule amounts, *whites* are *more likely* to receive bail amounts *below* schedule than nonwhites. Nonwhite suspects are more likely to be *within* the guidelines, but *less likely* be given a bail amount lower than that specified by the schedule.

Gender also affects schedule compliance. For both males and females, assigned bail amounts are most frequently within schedule limits. However, *females* were almost *twice* as likely as males to be *below* guideline limits.

Several variables have no effect on bail schedule compliance: suspect's restricted status at the time of the arrest, weapon use, whether the offense was a property or personal crime, or the socioeconomic status of the suspect appear unrelated to the allocation of bail amounts within or outside guideline limits.

Findings: Multivariate Analyses

In order to estimate the relative effects of covariates on compliance or deviation from bail guidelines, multinomial logit estimation was employed[7]. This statistical procedure allows the simultaneous influences of independent variables to be examined in a multivariate format that controls

Table 3.3
Estimates from Multinomial Logit Model of Bail Schedule Compliance
or Deviation (N = 335)

Independent Variable	Below	Above
Statutory degree	1.315[a]*	.475
	(3.98)[b]	(1.12)
No. of counts (log)	-1.585*	-.349
	(-3.77)	(-0.97)
Weapon use	-.299	-.672
	(-.605)	(-1.12)
Multiple Offenders	-.726**	.880**
	(-1.66)	(1.94)
Person Offense	-.163	1.157*
	(-.348)	(2.045)
Nonlocal suspect	-1.127**	.350
	(-1.90)	(.603)
Female suspect	.735**	.199
	(1.751)	(.322)
Restricted Status	.174	.324
	(0.438)	(.676)
Alcohol Use	-.415	-1.016
	(-.889)	(-1.49)
Prior Arrests (log)	-.287**	-.078
	(-1.69)	(-.362)
SES	.008	.015
	(.859)	(1.232)
Nonwhite suspect	-1.167*	-.003
	(-3.14)	(-.006)
Local police	-.208	-.697
	(-.534)	(-1.40)
Constant	-.571	-2.982
Likelihood ratio test	68.070	

[a] Maximum likelihood logit coefficient   [b] t-statistic
* significant $p < .05$ ** significant $p < .10$

for the influence of other independent variables. Multinomial logit is an appropriate statistical technique when the dependent variable is a choice between three or more mutually exclusive alternatives. In the present research, police officers had the choice of three mutually exclusive alternatives: assign bail within, below or above guideline boundaries. This statistical method is an extension of logit models in which the dependent variable

Table 3.4
Estimates from Multinomial Logit Model of Bail Schedule Compliance
or Deviation within Categories of Race (N = 335)

Independent Variable	Model 4.1 Whites (N=183)		Model 4.2 Nonwhites(N=152)	
	Below	Above	Below	Above
Statutory degree	1.268 [a]*	.301	1.49*	.642
	(3.03) [b]	(.56)	(2.37)	(.85)
No. of counts (log)	-1.977 *	-.461	-1.001	-.344
	(-3.49)	(-.949)	(-1.41)	(-.56)
Weapon use	.071	-.041	-.962	-1.595
	(0.11)	(-.05)	(-1.07)	(-1.52)
Multiple Offenders	-.346	1.070**	-1.770	.703
	(-.67)	(1.69)	(-1.59)	(.90)
Person Offense	-.201	.645	.011	1.853 *
	(-.33)	(.75)	(.01)	(2.18)
Nonlocal suspect	-1.361 *	-.381	-.210	1.315
	(-1.99)	(-.50)	(-.17)	(1.17)
Female suspect	1.354 *	-.237	-.187	.639
	(2.49)	(-.21)	(-.24)	(.74)
Restricted Status	.245	.544	.045	.252
	(.48)	(.83)	(.06)	(.29)
Alcohol Use	-.450	-1.226	-.267	-.452
	(-.79)	(-1.39)	(-.30)	(-.36)
Prior Arrests (log)	-.088	.240	-.525 **	-.454
	(-.39)	(.85)	(-1.78)	(-1.15)
SES	.011	.022	.007	.005
	(0.94)	(1.45)	(.36)	(.20)
Local police	-.485	.303	.132	-1.471 **
	(-.79)	(.43)	(.23)	(-1.94)
Constant	-1.026		-1.404	
Likelihood ratio test	49.503		34.042	

[a] Maximum likelihood logit coefficient   [b] t-statistic
* significant p < .05   ** significant p < .10

is dichotomous (for discussion see Pindyck and Rubinfeld 1981). Table 3.3 presents the multinomial logit model of direct effects of all independent variables. Table 3.4 examines separately the direct effects of these independent variables for whites (model 4.1) and nonwhites (model 4.2). Finally, Table 3.5 presents the interactive effects of residency and race (model 5.1), and gender and race (model 5.2).

Results reported in Table 3.3 indicate the influence of several factors on noncompliance with bail guidelines. Specifically, *nonwhite* suspects were significantly *less* likely than white suspects to be *below* guideline amounts relative to being within guideline amounts. However, nonwhite suspects are *no more likely* than white suspects to be given bail amounts that exceed the schedule limits. In addition, suspects charged with personal crimes are significantly more likely than those charged with property crimes to have bail set above the guideline amount.

In Table 3.4 a separate model is estimated for nonwhites and whites. Several effects are worth mention. These models indicate that suspect's residency is important for whites but not nonwhites. That is, *non-local whites* are *less likely* than local whites to have bail set below limits relative to being within limits. However, *non-local nonwhites* were *no less* likely than local nonwhites to have bail set below schedule amounts relative to within limits. Further, *white females* are *more likely* to be assigned bail amounts below schedule amounts relative to white males, while black females are treated no differently than black males.

Continuing this inquiry, Table 3.5 examines the interaction between race and residence (model 5.1) and race and gender (model 5.2). These models indicate that both *white non-locals* and *nonwhite locals* are significantly less likely than local whites to have bail set below schedule boundaries relative to within limits[8]. Further, *white females* are significantly *more likely* than others to receive bail amounts below the minimum.

Discussion and Conclusion

Examinations of the influence of extra-legal factors on legal decision making have produced an abundant literature. From arrest (Black and Reiss 1967; Smith et al. 1984) to sentencing (Kleck 1981; LaFree 1980), the effects of illegitimate considerations on discretionary judgments have been strongly debated. Efforts to attenuate the possible influence of such determinants on decision making have led many jurisdictions to implement guidelines in the hope of focusing discretion without eliminating it completely. Findings from the current study of jailhouse bail guideline procedures indicated that extra-legal factors still have a systematic influence on decision making. Thus, in this case at least, guidelines have little impact upon the generation of uniform, non-discriminatory outcomes (i.e., outcomes that are explicable solely with reference to legal criteria).

These data indicate that racial/gender differences among suspects *do not* influence decisions to set bail in *excess* of guideline limits. However, these data do indicate that *white females* are significantly more likely than

Table 3.5
Estimates from Multinomial Logit Models of Bail Schedule Compliance
or Deviation Interactions: Race - Residence, Gender (N = 335)

Independent Variable	Model 5.1 Below	Model 5.1 Above	Model 5.2 Below	Model 5.2 Above
Statutory degree	1.332[a]*	.494	1.342*	.465
	(4.01)[b]	(1.15)	(4.01)	(1.10)
No. of counts (log)	-1.595*	-.355	-1.631*	-.340
	(-3.77)	(-.985)	(-3.81)	(-.94)
Weapon use	-.319	-.748	-.261	-.654
	(-.640)	(-1.23)	(-.53)	(-1.09)
Multiple Offenders	-.721**	.893 *	-.744 **	.872 **
	(-1.65)	(1.97)	(-1.68)	(1.92)
Person Offense	-.142	1.187*	-.199	1.155 *
	(-.302)	(2.082)	(-.42)	(2.04)
Nonlocal suspect			1.145 **	.374
			(-1.92)	(.64)
Female suspect	.774 **	.266		
	(1.832)	(.431)		
Restricted Status	.152	.286	.174	.355
	(.382)	(.588)	(.44)	(.74)
Alcohol Use	-.391	-.947	-.400	-1.011
	(-.831)	(-1.39)	(-.86)	(-1.48)
Prior Arrests (log)	-.266	-.029	-.303 **	-.077
	(-1.55)	(-.132)	(-1.77)	(-.36)
SES	.009	.016	.009	.014
	(.928)	(1.297)	(.96)	(1.18)
Local police	-.204	-.633	-.171	-.734
	(-.522)	(-1.26)	(-.44)	(-1.47)
Black nonlocal	-1.069	1.193		
	(-.92)	(1.20)		
White nonlocal	-1.425*	-.093		
	(-2.11)	(-.13)		
Black locals	-1.271*	-.235		
	(-3.32)	(-.46)		
White male			-1.239 *	.465
			(-2.37)	(.42)
Black female			-2.285 *	.949
			(-2.80)	(.75)
Black male			-2.132*	.332
			(-3.64)	(.29)
Constant	-.593	-2.982	.537	-3.377
Likelihood ratio test	70.454	72.082		

[a] Maximum likelihood logit coefficient   [b] t-statistic
* significant p < .05   ** significant p < .10

others to receive bail amounts *below* schedule guidelines. Further, relative to whites, *nonwhite* suspects are *less likely* to receive bail below schedule amounts.

Thus, similar to research dealing with other stages in the criminalization process (e.g., Plea: Crites 1978; Sentencing: Nagel 1969) there is support for the thesis that there exists a "general protective attitude of man toward women" (Pollack 1950: p. 151). Our research, however, suggests that this explanation applies most fully to white females (i.e., they are more likely to be afforded chivalrous treatment than nonwhite females). While being female is significant when a liberal level of statistical significance is employed (see Table 3.2), further analysis indicates that being white *and* female playes a significant role in decision making (see Table 3.5, model 5.2). Thus, it appears that decision makers do not apply the chivalry thesis equally to whites and nonwhites (see Visher 1983 for similar findings on arrest; Datesman and Scarpitti 1980 in regard to court decisions).

Similarly, a general racial bias exists in these data with regard to guideline compliance—*nonwhites* are significantly *less likely* than whites to receive *low bail*. In addition, when suspect's *residency* is considered, *local nonwhites* and *non-local whites* are *less likely* to be afforded *lower* bail amounts. Thus, even though local residency generally represents a better risk in terms of appearance at subsequent hearings, nonwhite locals are treated similar to non-locals, and are not afforded the privilege associated with being local (and white) residents.

What factors explain the differential treatment afforded nonwhites in the setting of bail when bail amounts are stipulated in predefined guidelines that supposedly reflect the offense committed? Nonwhites do not appear to be subjected to overt attempts by decision makers to set bail above reachable limits, but rather are not afforded the same "benefit of the doubt" as whites in terms of reduced bail. One possible explanation is that white offenders are seen as more dependable and less serious than nonwhites, even when legally relevant criteria (e.g., seriousness of the offense) are taken into account (i.e., a stereotype of blacks is operating, see Lafree 1989; Farrell and Swigert 1978). Thus, preferential treatment is afforded a group due to nothing other than their race.

In short, our research demonstrates several important findings. First, guidelines do not have the intended effect of equalizing treatment across extralegal factors. Second, certain racial (white) and gender (white-females in particular) groups are placed in a *privileged* position relative to other groups, controlling for the effects of legally relevant decision making criteria. As other research notes (Reiman 1990), we often fail to examine the privileges accruing to certain groups based upon extralegal categories, and when this idea is examined, it is often related to the quality of law brought to bear upon groups differentiated by economic criteria (Groves and Newman 1987), not racial disparity in outcomes.

Third, race and gender related discrimination in criminal justice decision making is not a one-sided issue—it does not always result in harsher treatment of specific groups. Rather, groups can be discriminated against where they are not afforded the same alternatives, such as more lenient restrictions, as other groups.

Fourth, our research demonstrates an early stage bias favoring whites and females. This bias works by excluding individuals from more restrictive alternatives that can disadvantage non-excluded groups at later processing phases. For example, given differentials in average black and white family incomes in the county we examined, and given that blacks are more likely than whites to receive higher bail amounts (within the schedule as opposed to below), potentially fewer black defendants possess the ability to post bail, and hence suffer from such restrictions (see literature review above).

In conclusion, discrimination is apparently still "out there," and our ability to locate it, specify its forms, and analyze it depends upon the way we define discrimination, the processing stage examined, and the methodology employed.

NOTES

1. Wilbanks's definition is particularly strict, claiming that evidence of discrimination must show a disadvantage related to extra-legal factors (specifically race) across *both* types of crime *and* jurisdictions.

2. Initial decisions may have a cumulative effect on later stage decisions, biasing outcomes at later phases of decision making. For example, if police arrest blacks more often than whites, and these arrests are not made in proportion to the actual distribution of all crimes by race, then we could conclude that the treatment of blacks by the criminal justice system is biased. This conclusion remains intact *even if* blacks are *as likely* to be tried, convicted and sentenced as whites. Thus, even though later stage decisions appear non-biased empirically, such a conclusion *cannot* be supported unless steps are taken to correct for the initial bias blacks experienced at the arrest stage. In short, the ensuing and apparently equal treatment of the races following arrest *does not erase* the differential treatment of the races incorporated at earlier decision making stages.

3   These biases *should* be corrected by collecting data on earlier decision making points and generating probability based statistical models that correct for sample selection bias (e.g., Achen 1986).

4. The original sample contained 554 cases. Narcotics violations and capital crimes were excluded because they are not bailable offenses.

5. Police can also determine bail amounts by their choice of charges. However, we were not able to examine this decision.

6. We operationalize race as a dichotomous variable, white/nonwhite given race coding procedures employed by criminal justice agencies in Florida. This forced us to include Hispanics within the "white" race category, even though we object to this practice (see Lynch 1990; Ansari 1990). However, Hispanics comprise a small percent of this county's population (2 percent), especially compared to other counties in Florida. Thus, any effect Hispanics have on the difference between white/nonwhite treatment is assumed to be minimal, and would likely act to suppress the appearance of white/nonwhite racial discrimination in these data.

7. A logit model using a dichotomous dependent variable (bail within or outside schedule amounts) was also estimated. Females were not significantly different in their likelihood of being outside the schedule amounts (t-ratio=1.598). However in regard to race, nonwhites were significantly less likely to be outside schedule limits than were whites (t-ratio=2.442). Using these findings we would conclude that no racial or sexual discrimination exists.

8. One unusual finding resulted from this analysis: nonwhite non-locals are no more or less likely than white locals to be within bail guidelines. This finding is most likely the result of sample size for nonwhite nonlocals (N=8). Of these, five were within guideline amounts (63%), 1 below (13%) and 2 above (25%).

Ethnic, Racial, and Minority Disparity in Felony Court Processing*

**Margaret Farnworth, Raymond H.C. Teske, Jr.
and Gina Thurman**

COURT DISCRIMINATION against minority defendants is a familiar theme in criminal justice. For over half a century, researchers have sought to identify suspected disparity against black defendants relative to whites, with more or less successful results.[1] While this is not a new topic for theory and research, what is new is the form that minority disparity is likely to assume in the context of a changing society and sentencing reforms (Zatz 1987).

Demographic changes, for example, direct attention to conventional definitions of minority status. To date, the overwhelming majority of studies have

*The authors thank Charlotte Rhea, Research Analyst with the California Attorney General's Bureau of Criminal Statistics, for providing insights and information about criminal procedure and sentencing in California. The viewpoints expressed here and any errors of interpretation are the sole responsibility of the authors.

focused on sentencing differences between black defendants and their white counterparts. The rationale for equating minority status with race probably stems from the fact that, historically, blacks have constituted the largest single minority group in our society. National statistics, however, indicate that Hispanic populations are now one of the fastest-growing minority groups (Jaffe et al. 1980). Hispanics have in fact replaced blacks in some states as the largest minority group, both demographically and in the c urts. In California, for example, the site for the present study, Hispanics constituted 22 percent of the state's population in 1985 while blacks comprised only about 7.5 percent (State of California 1988). The sheer number of Hispanics in our society and our courts suggests a need for researchers to extend their conceptualization of minority status to consider both ethnic and racial disparity during processing.

Procedural reforms are also an important consideration, since they affect the source and location of disparity by virtue of the limitations they place on judicial discretion. The earliest studies of sentencing disparity tended to focus on differentials in the length of prison terms imposed by judges following conviction, once the final disposition charge was established. The increasingly widespread use of determinate sentencing and negotiated pleas, however, constrains judges' discretion and shifts most of the discretion possible in court processing "behind the scenes" (Zatz 1987:79). Since determinate sentencing mandates specific sentence lengths for specific charges at final sentencing, "the only way to substantially alter the sanction (is) to change the charge" through plea bargaining, with presumed input from prosecuting attorneys (Zatz 1987:79).[2] Even within the constraints of determinate sentencing, however, judges still retain discretionary options concerning probation as an alternative to incarceration.

In jurisdictions subject to determinate sentencing guidelines, therefore, discretionary decisions and disparity are more likely to occur in charge reductions and in the type of sentences imposed, rather than in the length of sentences imposed for the small proportion of felony defendants actually sent to prison.[3] The design of the present study was guided by a consideration of these new forms of expected minority discrimination during court processing. The analyses that follow examine both ethnic and racial disparity in California's felony courts in 1988. Since California court decisions are guided by determinate sentencing, the analysis focuses on those processing decisions involving the greatest discretionary latitude within the limits of determinate sentencing: charge reductions and the use of probation as an alternative to prison or jail. In view of the possible effects of offense type and severity on outcomes, the analysis is limited to one type of felony arrest charge: possession of marijuana with intent to sell.[4]

Background

Most studies of court disparity are guided by one of two theoretical perspectives: conflict or labeling theory. While differing somewhat in their premises and assumptions (Farnworth and Horan 1980), both perspectives posit minority disparity in processing. Minority status in our society is conventionally established on the basis of an individual's racial or ethnic background. Studies of minority disparity, however, particularly those conducted before 1980, have tended to focus exclusively on racial differences in processing. Ethnic differences have been relatively neglected—Hispanic defendants have been excluded, unmentioned, or grouped either explicitly or implicitly with white defendants for comparisons with blacks.

A current-day exclusion of Hispanics in court minority study is a serious oversight in view of their growing number and social impact. A research strategy that groups Hispanics with whites is even more problematic, since it obscures the unique effect of minority status by comparing processing for one minority group (blacks) with processing for a second group which is itself composed partly of minorities (Hispanics). In this way, the separate effects of race, ethnicity, and minority status cannot be compared. Thus, findings of ethnic disparity are impossible since the question of differences for Hispanic defendants is not addressed at all. Findings of racial disparity are handicapped since blacks are compared with Hispanic defendants as well as with whites. In effect, the practice of treating Hispanics as whites (that is, in a black versus nonblack comparison) may lead to a "washing out" effect, indicating no system processing disparity between blacks and nonblacks (Lynch 1990). Treating Hispanics separately would remove the effect of this artifact of measurement, and thereby increase the potential for identifying racial as well as ethnic disparity in system processing.

Relevance for Theory

The labeling perspective (Schur 1971; Bernstein et al. 1977) describes the kinds of "resources" that determine defendants' differential power to resist deviant labeling by criminal justice agencies. Status or personal resources include social and economic position, popular identification of minorities with criminal stereotypes, and skills in negotiation. In this theoretical context, we propose that these aspects of labeling not only direct research attention to both ethnic and racial disparity but, for several reasons, imply a greater likelihood of disparity against Hispanic than black minorities. First, social and economic position in our society tends to correlate negatively with minority position: both Hispanics and blacks are disproportionately overrepresented among the poor, school dropouts, and the unemployed. The social standing of many Hispanic defendants, however, is further attenuated when they are illegal aliens, noncitizens, new citizens, or temporary residents employed sporadically as migrant workers. Second, criminal stereotypes would also operate to the disadvantage of both blacks and Hispanics during processing. It is conceivable, however, that Hispanics in particular are associated by the public with the drug trade, especially the transportation and sale of marijuana. More severe sanctions might therefore be directed at this ethnic group in a symbolic effort at control. Zatz (1987) suggests, therefore, that popular stereotypes of Hispanics as drug traffickers might result in especially severe sanctioning of this ethnic group when they are convicted of drug offenses.

Finally, linguistic and cultural barriers and bias decrease the negotiating skills of foreign-born or foreign language-speaking Hispanics relative to other defendants, minority or not, who enjoy a longer history of acculturation and assimilation in our society. The increasing use of plea bargains under these circumstances has particular implications for Hispanics. Language barriers for Hispanics present a disadvantage in plea negotiation, since the terms "are communicated in subtle ways requiring knowledge of the multiple meanings and intricacies of the English language" (Zatz 1987:80).

In short, we propose that the labeling perspective on court disparity: (1) implies a need to test for ethnic as well as racial disparity; (2) hypothesizes particularly severe sanctions for racial and ethnic minorities relative to whites; and (3) suggests that Hispanic defendants may be even more severely sanctioned than black defendants under certain circumstances. Such circumstances might include the location of courts in states like California, where Hispanics outnumber blacks as the leading minority group, as well as the processing of felony cases involving drugs.

Related Research

The long history of research concerning disparity against black defendants has generated an extensive literature that precludes a comprehensive review here. Moreover, a number of excellent reviews summarize and evaluate the cumulative evidence to date.[5] The overall assessments of that research literature are mixed in their conclusions concerning racial disparity. There is common agreement that the earliest studies were most likely to report black-white differentials in sentencing, but these results are widely discounted because of methodological problems in the design of studies. A failure to control in analyses for such important contingencies to sentencing as defendant's prior record or the severity of offenses, for example, overlooked the possibility that blacks received longer sentences because of their criminal histories or because their offense charges were more serious than those levied against nonminorities (Hagan 1974; Zatz 1987). Thus, evaluative reviews published in the 1980s tended to conclude an absence of "overt" court discrimination against blacks once controls for legal variables were included in the analyses (e.g. Kleck 1981; Wilbanks 1987a).

On the other hand, evidence and arguments have been garnered to argue that blacks are indeed disadvantaged relative to white defendants (e.g., Lynch and Groves 1989; Petersilia 1983; the Southern Regional Council 1969). In an attempt to reconcile these conflicting conclusions, Zatz (1987) has proposed that overt racial discrimination may not be commonplace in current-day court processing; but that more subtle discrimination is revealed when models are properly specified to test for disparity that occurs indirectly, in interactions among variables, and in a cumulative fashion. An earlier review by Hagan (1974) also implicated features of research design that handicapped the identification of disparity of any sort. A major limitation, for example, concerned the tendency of early researchers to analyze differences in final sentencing, using samples and offense charges prescreened in early, informal stages of the sanctioning process. In designs of this type, disparity analyses of important discretionary presentencing decisions (such as charge reduction) are precluded.

The evidence for ethnic disparity parallels that concerning racial disparity in that the findings are also mixed in their implications.[6] Petersilia's (1983) findings from a study of male prison inmates in California, Michigan, and Texas indicated that minority offenders (blacks and Hispanics), once convicted of felonies, were more likely to be sentenced to prison and sentenced for longer terms than whites. Unnever and Hembroff's (1988) study of 313 male drug offenders in Miami provides some evidence that minority disparity is more likely when there are inconsistencies among such case characteristics as the number of charges, the number of prior convictions, the seriousness of the offense, and the defendant's employment status and type of occupation. When these case-related attributes were consistently aligned to justify either probation or incarceration, disparity was not apparent. When there was inconsistency within the set of criteria for disposition, however, blacks and Hispanics were significantly more likely than whites to be incarcerated rather than to receive probation. Unnever's (1982) study with the same sample indicated that Hispanics were sentenced to longer sentences than were whites, but that blacks continued to receive the longest sentences overall.

LaFree's (1985) study of whites, blacks, and Hispanics in El Paso, Texas found that Hispanic defendants "received less favorable pretrial release outcomes than white defendants, were more likely to be convicted in jury trials, and received more severe sentences when found guilty by trial." In the same study, however, LaFree found no evidence of disparate treatment against Hispanics in

Tucson, Arizona. In studies conducted in California with felony arrest data, Zatz (1984, 1985) reported that prior record was differentially invoked to affect sentence lengths, depending on whether the defendant was white, black, or Chicano. But while Zatz (1984) reported that Chicanos with prior records received exceptionally long sentences, there was no evidence of an additive effect of race or ethnicity on sentencing outcomes once legal and procedural variables were controlled in multivariate analyses.

In contrast, Holmes et al. (1987) reported an apparent minority advantage in informal processing. Based on a study of prosecutors' case files for burglary and robbery in Delaware County, Pennsylvania and in Pima County, Arizona, Holmes et al. found that: (1) in Delaware County, black defendants were more likely than whites to receive charge reductions; and (2) in Pima County, Mexican Americans were more likely than whites or blacks to receive charge reductions.

In sum, the findings from various studies that included Hispanic defendants have reported disparity against both racial and ethnic minorities (Petersilia 1983; Unnever and Hembroff 1988); disparity against minorities but greater racial than ethnic disparity (Unnever 1982); disparity against Hispanic defendants (LaFree 1985); and minority advantages in charge reductions, relative to whites (Holmes et al. 1987).[7]

Implications for the Present Study

In these theoretical and empirical contexts, we propose a need for additional study that compares court processing for white defendants versus both ethnic and racial minorities; for Hispanics versus both whites and blacks; and at decision points concerning charge reduction, probation, and the imposition of prison or jail sentences. The first broad question for research concerns the empirical implications of operationalizing minority status in different ways:

Question #1. In the study of minority differentials, what are the empirical ramifications of grouping defendants in different combinations of race and/or ethnicity?

The second question seeks to determine the sanctioning effects that stem from membership in a particular demographic subgroup:

Question #2. When defendants are grouped by race/ethnicity and sex, what defendant groups are systematically advantaged or disadvantaged relative to all others?

In the context of the theoretical framework guiding this analysis, we hypothesize that:

H_1: The greatest disadvantages during processing will be suffered by minorities (Hispanics and blacks) relative to whites; but

H_2: Hispanic defendants will be even more severely sanctioned than blacks.

Description of Data

The data for the analysis are drawn from the California Attorney General's Bureau of Criminal Statistics. The Bureau collects and records statewide information on the final dispositions of each felony-level arrest event, according to the year of disposition. The data include information about individuals arrested and subsequently released by the police, dismissed by the prosecutor, or disposed of by the courts. Classification in the data set is keyed on the most serious original arrest offense. Since the offense charge may change during processing, the data set also includes the disposition offense.

The present study employs data concerning cases disposed in California in 1988, in which the most serious charge was felony marijuana possession for sale. Since the defendant's prior record may affect sanctioning decisions, the analyses focus on convicted defendants with a previous court record.[8] Court data indicated that 774 of the convicted defendants had at least one previous court disposition. Convicted defendants with a prior record were overwhelmingly males (in more than 90 per cent of the cases).

Analysis and Results

The first research question we posed concerns the empirical results of different operationalizations of minority status. To address this question, the population of convicted defendants was divided first into male and female subgroups to allow for the possibility of interactive effects of sex with race and ethnicity. Within the male and female subgroups, defendants were then categorized as white, Hispanic, or black, to estimate the unique effects of race and ethnicity. A fourth grouping combined white and Hispanic defendants to estimate the extent to which this common research strategy obscures the unique effect of race. Finally, blacks and Hispanics were combined for comparison with white defendants to determine the extent to which disparity is associated with minority status, regardless of whether minority status stems from race or ethnicity. In the first step of the analysis, percent distributions of processing outcomes (charge reduction, probation, sentences to jail or prison) were compared within each of the demographic subgroups to determine the effects of different comparison groups for identifying racial, ethnic, or minority disadvantages during processing.

In the population of convicted male defendants with a prior court record (Table 4.1), 26.2 per cent were white (N=203); 49.7 per cent were Hispanic (N=385); and 14.7 per cent were black (N=114). Among the convicted females with a prior record, 4.3 per cent were white (N=33); 2.5 per cent

Hispanic (N=19); and 1.7 per cent were black (N=13). Table 5.1 reports the proportion of each of the subgroups of convicted defendants with prior records who received charge reductions, probation, or prison or jail sentences.

Table 4.1.
Percent distributions of variables across racial/ethnic groups:
convicted defendants with a prior record (N=767)[a]

Part A: MALES (N=702)					
	Whites (N=203)	Hispanics (N=385)	Blacks (N=114)	Wh/Hisp (N=588)	Bl/Hisp (N=499)	All (N=702)
Charges Reduced	30.5	19.0	26.3	23.0	20.6	23.5
Probation	11.8	2.3	8.8	5.6	3.8	6.1
Jail Sentence	78.3	80.8	77.2	80.0	80.0	79.5
Prison Sentence	7.9	16.4	13.2	13.4	15.6	13.4
Jail or Prison	86.2	97.1	90.4	93.4	96.6	92.9

Part B: FEMALES (N=65)					
	Whites (N=33)	Hispanics (N=19)	Blacks (N=13)	Wh/Hisp. (N=52)	Bl/Hisp. (N=32)	All (N=65)
Charges Reduced	39.4	10.5	7.7	28.8	9.4	24.6
Probation	12.1	5.3	23.1	9.6	12.5	12.3
Jail Sentence	78.8	89.5	76.9	82.7	84.4	81.5
Prison Sentence	3.0	5.3	0.0	3.8	3.1	3.1
Jail or Prison	81.8	94.7	76.9	86.5	87.5	84.6

[a] Excludes defendants coded in racial/ethnic groups other than white, black, or Hispanic.

A comparison of males and females undifferentiated by race or ethnicity (the last column in Parts A and B) reveals that females overall are less likely than males to be incarcerated; and, when incarcerated, more likely to receive jail rather than prison sentences. Females are twice as likely as males to receive probation, and slightly more likely than males to have their charges reduced.

Reliability problems in the findings for females because of the small number of convicted female defendants with prior records (Table 4.1) argues against substantive interpretations of the cross-race/ethnicity findings for females. Figure 4.1 therefore focuses on the results concerning charge reductions, probation, and prison terms for males. The percentages on which Figure 4.1 is based are reported in Part A of Table 4.1. Among convicted male defendants with a prior record, charge reductions were most prevalent for whites (31.5 per cent) and least likely for Hispanics (19 per cent). The rate for black males (26 per cent) was intermediate to those for whites and Hispanics. The same pattern occurred in sentences to probation. About twelve per cent of the white male defendants received probation, compared with about nine per cent of the black males and only two per cent of the male Hispanic defendants. Minority males with prior records were more likely than whites to be incarcerated when convicted (97 per cent) than were their white counterparts (86 per cent) and the difference was greatest in the imposition of prison sentences (B/HM in Figure 4.1): minorities were twice as likely as whites to go to prison (16 versus eight per cent). Hispanic males, however, were even more likely than black males to be incarcerated (97 per cent versus 90 per cent) and to receive prison sentences (16 per cent versus 13 per cent).

Figure 4.1

Percent Distributions of Charge Reduction, Probation, and Prison Sentences by Race and Ethnicity: Male Defendants with Prior Record

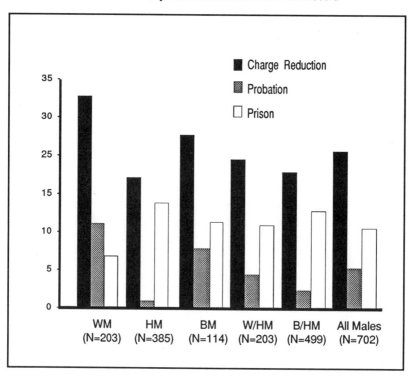

Table 4.2.
Summary of racial, ethnic, or minority disadvantages,[a] for males[b]

Locus	Comparison Groups	Disadvantaged		Advantaged	
Charge Reduction	B vs. W	B	(26%)	Whites	(31%)
	B vs. W/H	W/H	(23%)	Blacks	(26%)
	H vs. W	H	(19%)	Whites	(31%)
	H vs. B	H	(19%)	Blacks	(26%)
Probation	B vs. W	B	(9%)	Whites	(12%)
	B vs. W/H	W/H	(6%)	Blacks	(9%)
	H vs. W	H	(2%)	Whites	(12%)
	H vs. B	H	(2%)	Blacks	(9%)
Prison	B vs. W	B	(13%)	Whites	(8%)
	B vs. W/H	---------------- No Difference (13%) ------------			
	H vs. W	H	(16%)	Whites	(8%)
	H vs. B	H	(16%)	Blacks	(13%)
Jail	B vs. W	W	(78%)	Blacks	(77%)
	B vs. W/H	W/H	(80%)	Blacks	(77%)
	H vs. W	H	(81%)	Whites	(78%)
	H vs. B	H	(81%)	Blacks	(77%)
Jail or Prison	B vs. W	B	(90%)	Whites	(86%)
	B vs. W/H	W/H	(93%)	Blacks	(90%)
	H vs. W	H	(97%)	Whites	(86%)
	H vs. B	H	(97%)	Blacks	(90%)

[a] Disadvantages are operationalized as more severe sanctions: prison or jail; no charge reductions; no probation.
[b] To standardize for the effects of prior record, the analysis is limited to males with a prior court record.
B = Blacks   H = Hispanics   W = Whites   W/H = Whites and Hispanics

Table 4.2 presents the data from Table 4.1 in a format that allows an assessment of the effect on results when male defendants are compared using different racial/ethnic groupings. For each processing decision, results are presented for each of the four possible comparison groups: (1) blacks versus whites excluding Hispanics, to test for the unique effect of race; (2) blacks versus whites and Hispanics treated as a homogeneous group, to identify the extent to which these groupings handicap the identification of minority differences; (3) Hispanics versus whites, to isolate the minority effect of ethnicity; and (4) Hispanics versus blacks, to identify differences in the effects of racial versus ethnic minority status. Disadvantaged outcomes indicating disparity are operationalized as more severe sanctions: prison or jail; no charge reductions; or no probation.

The most striking finding in Table 4.2 is that, regardless of how defendants are grouped, Hispanic male defendants were not granted any sanctioning concessions that represented an advantage relative to either whites or blacks: Hispanic males were disadvantaged in all of the sanctioning decisions. In comparisons with whites (excluding Hispanics), black males are also disadvantaged in plea bargains resulting in charge reductions, in receiving probation, and in sentencing to prison (but not in jail sentences). The results indicate, however, that black male defendants received less severe sanctions than white and Hispanics as a combined group. Blacks were more likely to receive charge reductions and probation, were less likely to be incarcerated, and were equally likely to be sent to prison upon conviction. In all of these instances, the apparent advantages for black males are reversals of the findings when blacks were compared with whites alone.

The analyses to this point have treated the disposition cohort as a population, consistent with statistical principles that reserve statistical tests of significance to generalize findings with random samples to their populations. That is, "differences" between groups were concluded on the basis of patterned effects evident in the distribution of processing decisions across different groups. A more rigorous standard would limit meaningful findings to those that are patterned and systematic, in that they are statistically significant. With this premise, bivariate Chi-square analyses and tests for significance were estimated to address the second question for research: what particular demographic groups, if any, are singled out for preferential or discriminatory treatment relative to all others? Gamma associations were estimated between each processing outcome and each of a set of dichotomous variables that isolated specific demographic groups (white males, Hispanic males, black males, white females, Hispanic females, or black females). As in the earlier analyses, prior record was standardized by focusing on those convicted defendants with a prior court record (see Table 4.3).

Compared with all other defendants, whites of both sexes were advantaged during processing in that their charges were reduced most often and they were significantly less likely to be incarcerated. White males were also more likely

Table 4.3.

Associations (gammas) between processing outcomes and defendant
characteristics: convicted defendants with prior records (N=767[a])

	White Males (N=203)	Hispanic Males (N=385)	Black Males (N=114)	White Females (N=33)	Hispanic Females (N=19)	Black Females (N=13)
Charges Reduced	.24**	-.26**	.09	.37*	-.46	-.58
Probation	.45**	-.68**	.18	.34	-.13	.63*
Jail Sentence	-.06	.07	-.09	-.03	.38	-.08
Prison Sentence	-.32*	.35**	.03	-.65	-.45	-1.00
Jail or Prison	-.45**	.67**	-.14	-.47*	.21	-.57*

[a]Excludes defendants coded in racial/ethnic groups other than white, black, or Hispanic.
* p < or = .05 (Chi-square)   ** p < or = .01 (Chi-square)

than other defendants to receive probation and less likely to go to prison once convicted. The results for Hispanic males are a mirror image of those for white males. The effect of being Hispanic and male was to reduce the likelihood of charge reduction and probation, and to increase the likelihood of imprisonment. Compared to all others, there were no significant differences for black males or for Hispanic females. Black females appeared to enjoy some advantages relative to others: the likelihood of probation was greater, and the likelihood of imprisonment was less. A substantive interpretation of the findings for females, particularly minority females, should be guarded in view of the small number of cases available for the analysis.

Discussion

The first question we posed concerned the effect on results when disparity was examined in comparisons across different groupings by race and/or ethnicity. Since the reliability of findings concerning convicted female defendants with prior records was questionable in view of their small number, findings to address this question derived primarily from analyses of cases with male defendants. The findings for males indicated overall that the most dramatic contrasts in processing occurred in comparisons between Hispanic and white male defendants with a prior record. White males were far more likely than Hispanic males to have their primary charge reduced to a misdemeanor and to receive probation. Hispanic males were more likely than white males to be sentenced to jail, and twice as likely to be sentenced to prison.

The findings indicated further that the strategy of grouping whites and

Hispanics to test for racial differences confounds the identification of racial differences. When Hispanics were excluded from the analyses, the results indicated racial disparity: the sanctioning of white male defendants was less severe than that for black male defendants. Whites were more likely than blacks to have their charges reduced, and to receive probation; blacks were more likely than whites to receive prison sentences. When the comparison group for blacks included Hispanic defendants, the findings suggested no race differences, or preferential treatment of black male defendants. Compared with whites and Hispanics together, blacks were more likely to enjoy charge reductions and probation; and equally likely to be sentenced to prison. The substantive implications of these findings are clear. The findings indicating preferential treatment of blacks are an artifact of measurement. The presence of Hispanics in the comparison group of nonblacks completely obscured the sanctioning advantages of whites relative to blacks.

The second question for research concerned preferential treatment or disparity for particular demographic subgroups. The results relevant to this question underscored the processing advantages for whites and the disadvantages for Hispanics. White males were significantly more likely than all other defendants to have their charges reduced and to receive probation, and significantly less likely to be sentenced to prison. Hispanic males, on the other hand, were significantly more likely than all other defendants to receive prison terms, and less likely to have their charges reduced or to receive probation. A greater likelihood of charge reduction and a lower likelihood of incarceration were apparent for white females compared with all other defendants.

In a theoretical context, we hypothesized that both racial and ethnic minorities would be more severely sanctioned than whites. Clear and consistent support for the hypothesis of ethnic disparity is concluded from comparisons of outcomes for white versus Hispanic male defendants. Comparisons of processing advantages and disadvantages for white versus black males provided evidence that whites are treated with less severity than blacks, but racial differences were smaller than were ethnic differences. Moreover, tests of significance in the second phase of the analysis indicated that, unlike Hispanic males, black males were not disadvantaged relative to all other defendants.

These findings suggest inferential support for our second hypothesis: that Hispanic defendants suffer more severe reprisals than black defendants. Direct support for this hypothesis is provided by comparisons between the two minority groups. In all instances (charge reduction, probation, sentencing to jail or prison), the sanctions were greater for Hispanic male defendants compared with black male defendants.

Summary and Conclusions

Within a theoretical framework drawn from labeling theory, we hypothesized that both ethnic and racial minorities would suffer disadvantages during the court processing of felony drug offenders. In view of the constraints of determinate sentencing in California, we expected that disparity against minorities would be evident in decisions concerning incarceration or probation, and in the reduction of felony charges to the misdemeanor level. The results for male defendants indicated consistent support for this hypothesis. In every comparison but one, white males enjoyed processing advantages compared with either black or Hispanic males. The single exception was in the black-white comparison concerning sentencing to jail, which indicated virtually no difference in the proportion of white or black males receiving a jail term. Since all of the cases involved felonies at arrest, however, it is debatable that a sentence to jail (rather than prison) represents a truly "severe" sanction.

We extended conventional interpretations of labeling theory that posit court disparity against minorities to hypothesize that Hispanics were even more likely than blacks to be singled out for relatively severe sanctions. This hypothesis was proposed with the premise that the social and personal resources needed to resist the "deviant label" represented by court sanctions are even more deficient among Hispanics than among American blacks. Three aspects of labeling were argued as especially pertinent for Hispanic defendants: their standing in the larger society, popular stereotypes as drug dealers, and linguistic difficulties that would handicap their negotiation skills. The findings were consistent with theoretical expectations. The most dramatic differences were apparent in the disadvantages Hispanic males suffer in charge reductions, probation and imprisonment, compared with the advantages of white male defendants in all of these court decisions. While white males also fared somewhat better than black male defendants, the racial contrasts were not as striking as were the ethnic differences. Direct comparisons between the two minority groups provided further support that Hispanic males were more severely sanctioned than were black males.

Overall, then, the findings were consistent with expectations derived from the tenets of labeling that guided this analysis. As in most court studies of this type, however, the support we conclude for labeling theory is somewhat suggestive in that we did not have direct measures of ethnic stereotypes, differential language fluency, or social standing. The findings here, it might be argued, fit as well within the premises of a conflict perspective that posits repressive social control against a fast-growing minority group that threatens the established power structure in our society.[9] In this theoretical context, further research might extend the analyses reported here to compare ethnic and racial disparity in court processing across jurisdictions that differ in minority composition, and therefore differ in the "threat" that growing minorities represent to established power structures.

Further research is also needed to explore more thoroughly the extent to which the findings reported here generalize to the court treatment of minority females. Sex differences in our cross-race and cross-ethnicity analyses were handicapped because of the diminished numbers of minority female defendants once the arrest cohort was screened to focus on convicted offenders with a prior record. Comparing females to males overall, however, the evidence suggested a tendency toward less severe sanctioning of females, particularly in the decision to incarcerate; and white females appeared to be treated with particular deference.

In closing, we believe the most important findings from this analysis are those that provide a few more clues to explain why empirical studies have provided so little evidence of minority discrimination in a criminal justice system widely and popularly viewed as less than perfect in its assurance of equal justice. Court disparity is premised on the possibility of discretionary decision making. Court studies that continue to focus on those stages of processing where discretion is most constrained or even impossible (such as the length of prison sentences in jurisdictions guided by determinate sentencing and mandatory sentences) will continue to report an absence of disparity. The findings here illustrate the value of refocusing attention to examine less frequently studied decisions, such as those involved in charge reduction. By the same token, disparity studies that continue to focus exclusively on racial differences in court processing negate by design the very possibility of identifying disadvantages that stem from membership in a minority ethnic group. The findings from this study suggest that, in some contexts, ethnicity may be an even greater impediment than race to the assurance of equal justice in our courts.

NOTES

1. As of 1985, LaFree reported an estimate of over 500 research articles dealing with the legal treatment of black defendants.

2. See similar observations by Holmes et al. (1987) and Spohn et al. (1987).

3. In the present study, 2,003 of the 4,081 arrests resulted in conviction, and 220 convictions resulted in prison sentences. Thus only about five per cent of the original arrests and eleven per cent of the convictions resulted in sentences to prison.

4. The decision to focus selectively on one type of felony was based on a desire to simplify the analysis while at the same time avoiding the confounding effects of variation in the severity of the offense charge. This particular type of felony was selected because (1) the relative lack of consensus about the sanctioning of drug offenders is likely to increase the possibility of discretionary processing; (2) the absence of a personal victim avoids a need to control for that effect; (3) arrests for this type of drug offense were distributed across all three racial/ethnic groups; (4) criminal justice responses to drug offenses are of particular current-day interest; and (5) we expected that the theory guiding the analysis would have particular relevance for drug offenders.

5. Summary reviews of the literature on racial disparity are provided by Kleck (1981), Hagan (1974), Hagan and Bumiller (1983), and Zatz (1987).

6. Two features of the research literature on ethnic disparity also limit the conclusions that can be drawn empirically. First, relatively few empirical studies have focused on the court treatment of Hispanics. As LaFree (1985) noted, a review of this literature by Carter in 1986 located only seven relevant studies. In reviewing the literature for this study, we located eight additional studies of disparity published since 1986 in which Hispanic defendants were included either as a separate group or grouped with blacks as minorities (Holmes and Daudistel 1984; Holmes et al. 1987; Spohn et al. 1987; Unnever and Hembroff 1988). The second limiting feature concerns the noncomparibility of various research designs and, in some cases, methodological problems in the research conducted (see LaFree 1985).

7. One of the more provocative findings in past studies suggests that whites are disadvantaged relative to minorities (both blacks and Hispanics) in the earliest dispositional stage: police or prosecutorial dismissal before trial (see, e.g., Petersilia 1983). Zatz (1987), LaFree (1985), and Holmes et al. (1987), however, suggest interpretations of this finding as a reflection of "selective arrest," which questions its unambiguous interpretation as preferential treatment for minorities.

8. A more conventional approach to disparity study employs multivariate analyses and controls for the effect of prior record by comparing those with or without a prior criminal history (e.g., Farnworth and Horan 1980). In the present study, there was a substantial proportion of missing information about prior criminal records: prior record data were available for 72 per cent of the cases at arrest, and for 71 per cent of the convicted defendants. On balance, we placed more confidence in those cases

in which a prior record was indicated than those in which there was no indication of a prior record. While we cannot assess the substantive effect of prior record on outcomes, the strategy used here serves to "control" in a sense for prior record, in that all of the convicted defendants in the study had a prior court record.

9. For expositions of conflict or radical perspectives on court processing, see Chambliss and Seidman (1982); Greenberg and Humphries (1980); Chapter 8 in Lynch and Groves (1989); Michalowski (1985); and Quinney (1974).

Race and the Death Penalty
in the United States

Robert Bohm

A COMPREHENSIVE understanding of the death penalty in the United States requires an awareness of the influence of race. Whether interest is in public opinion or in the administration of capital punishment statutes, race is an integral factor. This chapter examines five aspects of the death penalty in the United States where race plays a major role: (1) capital offenders, (2) capital statutes or definitions of capital crimes, (3) the victims of capital crimes, (4) the prosecutorial decision to charge a defendant with a capital crime, and (5) opinions about the death penalty.

In the 1972 landmark case of *Furman v. Georgia* (408 U.S. 238) the Supreme Court held that the death penalty, as administered in the United States, was unconstitutional because it violated the Eighth Amendment prohibition against cruel and unusual punishment. The decision invalidated the death penalty statutes of thirty-nine states and the District of Columbia. The case was

71

unusual because all nine justices wrote separate opinions either concurring with or dissenting from the Court's decision. Though their analyses differed, all five of the justices in the majority were concerned that the death penalty had been administered in an arbitrary and discriminatory way. Two of the justices, Marshall (at 364-5) and Douglas (at 256-7), concluded that the death penalty had been imposed in a racially discriminatory fashion.[1]

With the *Furman* decision, many abolitionists believed that the issue of the death penalty in the United States finally had been laid to rest. They were wrong. After the Court's decision in *Furman* thirty-five states adopted new death penalty statutes designed to meet the Court's objections. On July 2, 1976, in the cases of *Gregg v. Georgia* (428 U.S. 153), *Jurek v. Texas* (428 U.S. 262), and *Proffitt v. Florida* (428 U.S. 242), the Court held that the new "guided discretion statutes" employed in those three states were constitutional.[2] Shortly thereafter, executions in the United States resumed.

The Court accepted the new guided discretion statutes "on their face." That is, the Court assumed that the new statutes would eliminate the kinds of arbitrariness and discrimination that were found problematical in *Furman*. However, there is considerable evidence, some of which is presented in this chapter,[3] that the Court was wrong. Arbitrariness and discrimination apparently continue to be a problem under post-*Furman* statutes. The Court, moreover, appears to be aware of the situation. Following the *Gregg* decision and the resumption of executions in the United States, the Court, in several cases (e.g., *Zant v. Stephens,* 103 S. Ct. 2733, 1983, and *Baldwin v. Alabama*, 105 S. Ct. 2727, 1985), has continued to find it necessary to emphasize that discrimination based on the race of the defendant in death sentencing is impermissible and a violation of the equal protection clause of the Fourteenth Amendment. More recently, in the 1987 case of *McCleskey v. Kemp* (107 S. Ct. 1756), the Court acknowledged explicitly that race continues to be implicated in death sentencing in the United States but, for a variety of reasons, has decided to do nothing about it (Gross and Mauro 1989:xiii).

Before turning to the subject of race and capital offenders, a few definitional matters need to be addressed. First, throughout this chapter reference is made to racial disparities. Racial disparities refer to numerical differences based on race. Thus, for example, there has been a historical pattern of racial disparities in the imposition of the death penalty in the United States, since the penalty has been imposed on blacks disproportionately to their numbers in the population. As long as racial disparities can be justified by reference to relevant legal factors (e.g., that blacks commit a disproportionate number of capital crimes), there is nothing inherently problematical with racial disparities in the administration of capital punishment.

Racial discrimination, however, is another matter. In the context of capital punishment, racial discrimination is always objectionable and a violation of the equal protection clause of the Fourteenth Amendment and of special restrictions on the use of capital punishment under the Eighth Amendment. Racial discrimination occurs when the death penalty is intentionally or purposefully imposed on certain persons because of their race and not because of, or in addition to, legitimate sentencing considerations. Proving intentional discrimination in specific cases is an extremely difficult, if not impossible task. However, in some cases (cf. *Village of Arlington Heights v. Metropolitan Hous. Dev. Corp.,* 429 U.S. 252, 266, 1977), but, interestingly, not in capital cases (*McCleskey v. Kemp,* 107 S. Ct. 1756, 1987), the Supreme Court has allowed discriminatory intent to be inferred from "a clear pattern, unexplainable on grounds other than race."

A purpose of this chapter is to identify and distinguish between past and present conditions of racial disparity and racial discrimination in the administration of the death penalty in the United States. For purposes of this analysis, the concept of race is limited to whites and blacks, although occasionally reference is made to other minorities where appropriate.

Capital Offenders

Between 1608, the date of the first confirmed lawful execution in the American colonies, and the present, there has been substantial variation by region and offense in the race of persons executed in the United States under state and local authority (Schneider and Smykla 1991). Nevertheless, without question the death penalty has been and continues to be imposed on blacks disproportionately to their numbers in the population. This is especially true in the South. Thus, for the crime of murder in the North and the West, from the 1600s to the present, about 69 percent of those executed were white (N=2316), 19 percent were black (N=634), and 12 percent were other minorities (N=415; Schneider and Smykla 1991:13). In the South, on the other hand, over the same time period, about 68 percent of those executed were black (N=2703), 28 percent were white (N=1125), and 4 percent were other minorities (N=161; Schneider and Smykla,1991:11-13).[4]

The percentage of whites executed for murder in the North and the West since the 1600s has been between about 56 percent in the 1600s (N=20) and 77 percent between 1866 and 1879 (N=160). For blacks the range in executions for murder in the North and the West has been between about 9 percent between 1866 and 1879 (N=18) and 31 percent in the 1940s (N=70). For other minorities the range in executions for murder has been between about 7 percent in the 1950s (N=9) and 25 percent in the 1600s (N=9; Schneider and Smykla 1991:11-13). In the South the range for murder since the 1600s has been between about 18 percent in the 1900s (N=79) and 67 percent in the 1600s (N=6) for whites; approximately 22 percent in the 1600s (N=2) and about 80 percent in the 1900s (N=354) for blacks; and between about one-half percent in the 1950s (N = 1) and about 11 percent in the 1600s (N=1) for other minorities (Schneider and Smykla 1991:11-13). Data for the twentieth century show that the percentage of whites executed for murder in the South has steadily increased from about 18 percent in 1900 to around 55 percent in the 1960s and later, while the percentage of blacks executed for murder in the South has declined from about 80 percent in 1900 to about 40 percent in the 1960s and later (Schneider and Smykla 1991:11-13). Schneider and Smykla (1991:13) suggest that these trends may be attributable to changes in population migration, criminal procedure, and attitudes toward punishment. Whatever the reasons, the fact remains that a greater number of blacks have been executed in the United States for murder, especially in the South, than would be expected given their numbers in the population (see Zahn 1989 for homicide trends during the twentieth century).

Racial disparities in executions for rape are even greater. Rape was a capital crime in the United States until 1977, when in *Coker v. Georgia* (433 U.S. 584), the Supreme Court held that the death penalty for the rape of an adult woman who is not killed violated the Eighth Amendment. According to Schneider and Smykla (1991:11-13), from the 1600s to 1977, a third of the people executed for rape in the North and the West were white (N=19), about 63 percent were black (N=36), and 3.5 percent were other minorities (N=2). During the same time period in the South, about 9 percent of those executed for rape were white (N=65), a little over 90 percent were black (N=678), and about 2 percent were other minorities (N=8). Regarding rape in the South, Schneider and Smykla (1991:13) observe that "nine out of ten executions were imposed on blacks in each decade throughout the history of capital punishment until the 1940s and later, when the figure drops a few points below the 90 percent mark." Examining a more truncated period (1930-1977) but finding essentially the same pattern, Bedau (1982:58-61) reports that four hundred fifty-five persons were executed for the crime of rape in the United States: 11% were white, 89% were black, and 97% were executed in the South. In the South, moreover, the death penalty for rape was imposed almost exclusively on black men who raped white women (Wolfgang and Riedel 1975; 1973). Between 1930 and 1980, sixty percent of all executions in the United States occurred in the South. Of those executed, 28 percent were white and 72 percent were black (cf. Bedau 1982:58-59). Thus, the statistics on executions for the crime of rape, and to a lesser extent for the crime of murder, indicate that a *prima facie* case for racial discrimination in the imposition of the death penalty is strongest for the South (cf. Hagan 1974; Kleck 1981).

While the aforementioned figures clearly demonstrate a historic pattern of racial disparity in the imposition of capital punishment in the United States, especially in the South, they do not necessarily indicate racial discrimination, even in the South, if blacks committed a disproportionately greater number of death-eligible murders or rapes. Available evidence for the twentieth century shows that blacks have been arrested or prosecuted for committing a disproportionate number of murders and rapes[5], but not in sufficient numbers to justify the disparities in executions (for racial trends in homicides during the twentieth century, see Zahn 1989). Bowers' (1984:221-222) examination of murder trends in three southern states from 1973 through 1977, found that 617 persons were arrested or suspected by police of death-eligible murder in Florida, 535 in Georgia, and 702 in Texas. In Florida, 49 percent of the death-eligible murderers were black; in Georgia, 63 percent were black; and in Texas, 42 percent were black (Bowers 1984:230). Racial distributions for rape were similar. While these figures show that blacks committed a disproportionate number of death-eligible murders and rapes between 1973 and 1977 (42-63% of death-eligible murders), they also raise the interesting question of why 89 percent of the death-eligible rapists and 72 percent of the death-eligible murderers executed in the South were black? Given the social history of the South, racial discrimination is a probable answer.

More recent experience seems to belie the charge of continued racial discrimination in the imposition of the death penalty. For example, between January 17, 1977 (date of the first post-*Furman* execution) and September 21, 1990, 140 persons were executed in the United States: 56 percent were white, 39 percent were black, and 5 percent were Hispanic (*Death Row, U.S.A.*, 1990). Of the 2,393 death row inmates on September 21, 1990, 50 percent were white, 40 percent were black, 7 percent were Hispanic, and the remainder were of other or unknown race (*Death Row, U.S.A.*, 1990). Thus, under post-*Furman* statutes, a greater proportion of those persons sentenced to death and executed in the United States have been white. Yet, this alone neither confirms nor refutes charges of racial discrimination against blacks.

Regarding the greater percentage of whites executed under post-*Furman* statutes, the number of persons executed so far probably is too small to draw any definitive conclusions about racial discrimination (against blacks or whites). Nevertheless, it appears that states, especially southern states, may have made a concerted effort at first to execute a greater number of white persons, perhaps to give the impression that racial discrimination against blacks in the area of the death penalty is no longer a problem (Jolly and Sagarin 1984; White 1987:116; Zeisel 1981:465-66). When the first 120 post-*Furman* executions in the South (88% of post-*Furman* executions have occurred in the South, N=123) are divided into deciles and cumulative percentages by race are compared, the percentage of whites executed decreases from 75 percent in the first decile to 51 percent in the tenth decile. For blacks, the percentage executed increases from 25 percent in the first decile to 49 percent in the tenth decile (calculated from data reported in *Death Row, U.S.A.,* 1990). Looked at somewhat differently, when the 123 post-*Furman* executions in the South are divided in half, one finds that of the first 61 executions, 57 percent of those executed were white and 43 percent were black or Hispanic (2 Hispanics). The percentages are nearly reversed for the second 62 executions: 45 percent of those executed were white and 55 percent were black or Hispanic (4 Hispanics; calculated from data reported in *Death Row, U.S.A.,* 1990). These data clearly show a declining trend in the execution of whites and an increasing trend in the execution of minorities, especially blacks.

Georgia is one state that apparently has not attempted to execute a greater number of whites to belie charges of continued racial discrimination in the imposition of its death penalty. Of the fourteen persons executed in Georgia under its post-*Furman* statute (through September 21,1990), ten (71%) have been black (*Death Row, U.S.A.,* 1990). Interestingly, in studies that represent the "state-of-the-art" in research on racial discrimination in the imposition of the death penalty, Baldus et al. (1983; 1985) discovered no statewide discrimination in Georgia against black defendants because of their race. However, when these data were disaggregated, Baldus et al. found that discrimination based on the race of the defendant did exist. The reason that discrimination did not appear statewide in Georgia is because discrimination against black defendants in rural areas was offset by discrimination against white defendants in urban areas. This finding underscores the need to exercise caution when interpreting results from aggregate data.

In sum, as more people are executed in the United States, especially in the South, it is possible that the racial distribution of those executed will duplicate, if it has not already, the racial distribution of executions under pre-*Furman* statutes. Though it is too early to determine with any certainty whether post-*Furman* statutes have eliminated racial discrimination in the imposition of the death penalty against black persons, recent evidence suggests they have not.

Capital Statutes and Definitions of Capital Crimes

One factor that contributes to some of the racial disparity noted above is the way in which capital crimes, especially death-eligible murders, are defined. Historically, legal interpretations of death-eligible murder have been restricted to the kinds of actions more typically committed by members of the lower socioeconomic strata in which blacks are disproportionately represented. As

Justice Douglas wrote in his *Furman* decision, "One searches our chronicles in vain for the execution of any member of the affluent strata of this society" (at 251-2). Defined in such a way, many potentially capital crimes, especially those committed by members of the affluent strata of society, are simply ignored altogether or treated as less serious offenses.

For example, conservative estimates indicate that each year in the United States at least 10,000 lives are lost because of unnecessary surgeries, 20,000 to errors in prescribing drugs, 20,000 to doctors spreading diseases in hospitals, 100,000 to industrial disease, 200,000 to environmentally caused cancer, and an unknown number to lethal industrial products (Pepinsky and Jesilow 1984; Reiman 1979; Simon and Eitzen 1982). While the proximate decision makers and perpetrators in most of these deaths are not death-eligible (because their actions or inactions are neither intentional nor criminally negligent), a small but significant fraction are. Yet, few are defined legally as murderers, especially death-eligible murderers. One reason that few upper class offenders are readily identifiable is because their decisions are hidden by the complexities of the work place environment or corporate chains of command. Another more cynical reason is that, by virtue of their class position, the perpetrators of these "white-collar crimes," no matter how malicious and heinous their actions, simply are not considered appropriate candidates for capital punishment in the United States. The point, however, is not to argue for the death penalty for such offenses and offenders, but to show that an unacceptable form of discrimination is created by the way death-eligible murders are defined (cf. Reiman 1985; Tifft 1982). If death-eligible murder also included those actions and inactions listed above that are particularly reprehensible, then the distribution of persons convicted of death-eligible murder would be more evenly divided among social classes and, as a consequence, racial disparities would be reduced.

The Victims of Capital Crimes

The race of victims of capital crimes generally has paralleled the racial distribution of capital offenders. In other words, capital crimes are usually intraracial (cf. Zahn 1989 for homicide trends during the twentieth century). In 1967, for example, ninety percent of all murders, in which the race of the offender and the victim was known, were intraracial (Zahn 1989:224-25). From 1976 through 1980, 63.5 percent of homicide victims in Georgia, 58.6 percent in Illinois, and 43.3 percent in Florida were black (Gross and Mauro 1989). Note, however, that probably less than twenty percent of legally defined murders are death-eligible (Bowers 1984:229), and that the percentage of interracial murders is likely somewhat greater for capital murders than it is for noncapital murders. Nevertheless, what is astonishing and requires explanation is the huge disparity in the race of the victims of capital offenders who are executed.

As indicated above, between January 17, 1977 (the first post-*Furman* execution) and September 21, 1990, one hundred forty persons have been executed in the United States; 56 percent were white, 39 percent were black, and 5 percent were Hispanic (*Death Row, U.S.A.*, 1990). Of the one hundred forty-two victims, 85 percent were white, 11 percent were black, 3 percent were Hispanic, and about 1 percent were Asian (*Death Row, U.S.A.*, 1990). Disaggregating the percentages, one finds that all seventy-eight whites executed victimized whites. Under post-*Furman* statutes a white person has yet to be executed for the killing of a minority, any minority, and whites do kill minorities. On the other hand, of the fifty-five black persons executed, about 71 percent were executed for the killing of a white victim and 29 percent for the killing of a black (see *Death Row, U.S.A.*, 1990). Yet, as noted above, murder, including capital murder, generally is an intraracial crime.

An examination of Table 5.1 reveals that, as of September 21, 1990, sixteen states had executed at least one person under post-*Furman* statutes. Nine of the sixteen states (56%) have executed a minority, while only seven states (44%) have executed a person for the killing of a minority (see Table 5.1). Even in Georgia, Virginia, Alabama, and Mississippi, the only states where a majority of those executed under post-*Furman* statutes have been black, the majority of the victims of those executed have been white (see Table 5.1). These data, together with those described previously, suggest that the killing of a white, regardless of the race of the offender, has become a de facto aggravating circumstance that often makes what ordinarily might be a noncapital murder into a capital one.

The offender-victim racial disparities described above have drawn considerable recent attention to a probable second, less obvious form of racial discrimination in the imposition of the death penalty: "victim-based" racial discrimination. A growing body of research at the state-level has discovered that whether the death penalty is imposed in potentially capital cases depends to a large degree on the race of the victim. For example, in an early study of capital cases under Florida's post-*Furman* statute from 1973 to 1977, the probability of a black receiving the death penalty for the aggravated murder of a white was 32 percent (143 offenders; 46 persons sentenced to death), while the probability of a white receiving the death penalty for aggravated murder of a white was 21.5 percent (303 offenders; 65 persons sentenced to death).

In addition, consider that the probability of receiving the death penalty for a black who killed a black was 4 percent (160 offenders; 7 persons sentenced to death), and the probability of receiving the death penalty for a white who killed

Table 5.1
Post-*Furman* Executions by State, Race of Offender,
and Race of Victim.

State	Total	Race of Offender					Race of Victim				
		W	B	H	NA	A	W	B	H	NA	A
Texas	37	19	11	7			29	3	4		1
Florida	24	15	9				21	4			
Louisiana	19	11	8				17	2			
Georgia	14	4	10				13	1			
Virginia	9	3	6				7	2			
Alabama	8	2	6				6	3			
Nevada	5	5					5				
Missouri	5	4	1				5				
Mississippi	4	1	3				2	1			1
N. Carolina	3	3					3				
Utah	3	2	1				3				
S. Carolina	3	3					3				
Indiana	2	2					2				
Arkansas	2	2					2				
Oklahoma	1	1					1				
Illinois	1	1					1				
Totals	140	78	55	7	0	0	120	16	4	0	2

Adapted from *Death Row, U.S.A.*, September 21, 1990.

a black was 0 percent (11 offenders; no persons sentenced to death; see: Bowers 1984:230; cf. Arkin 1980; Baldus et al. 1986; Gross and Mauro 1989; Radelet 1981; Zeisel 1981). In other words, a black person convicted of an aggravated murder of a white in Florida between 1973 and 1977 was more than seven times more likely to receive a death sentence than was a black who killed a black, while a white person convicted of an aggravated murder of a white was almost five times more likely to receive a death sentence than was a black who killed a black. A person convicted of aggravated murder of a white, in short, whether a black or a white, was more likely to receive the death penalty than was a person of either race convicted of aggravated murder of a black. Moreover, a white person convicted of aggravated murder of a black almost never received a death sentence (the total of such cases for Florida, Georgia, and Texas was 54; in three (5.5%) there was a death sentence; Bowers 1984:230). A similar pattern was found for Georgia (Baldus et al. 1986; 1983; Bowers 1984:230; Gross and Mauro 1989), Texas (Baldus et al. 1986; 1983; Bowers 1984:230), South Carolina (Paternoster 1991; 1984; 1983), North Carolina (Gross and Mauro 1989; Nakell and Hardy 1987; but see Paternoster 1991), Louisiana (Smith 1987), Alabama (Baldus et al. 1986), Mississippi (Baldus et al. 1986; Gross and Mauro 1989), Tennessee (Baldus et al. 1986), Kentucky (Keil and Vito 1990), California (Baldus et al. 1986), Illinois (Baldus et al. 1986; Gross and Mauro 1989), Missouri (Baldus et al. 1986), Oklahoma (Gross and Mauro 1989), Maryland (Baldus et al. 1986), Virginia (Baldus et al. 1986), and New Jersey (Bienen et al. 1988). At least in the aforementioned states, these findings suggest that the life of a black victim is valued less than the life of a white victim regardless of the race of the offender.

An extensive body of case law holds that the equal protection clause of the Fourteenth Amendment prohibits racial discrimination in the sentencing of criminal defendants. Before *McCleskey*, no cases specifically addressed the implications of the equal protection clause as it affected discrimination by race of the victim (Gross and Mauro 1989:119).[6] However, it seems clear from the language of the Fourteenth Amendment that the protection of black victims is one of its goals. Indeed, one of the primary purposes of the equal protection clause was to defeat the Black Codes that were enacted to preserve white supremacy in the South after the Civil War. These codes not only established differential punishments for white and black defendants but, in some cases, also provided more severe punishments when victims were white and less severe punishments or no punishment at all if victims were black (Gross and Mauro 1989:119).

Thus, there is little question that the equal protection clause of the Fourteenth Amendment is applicable to claims of victim-based racial discrimination in the imposition of the death penalty. The problem, as noted above, is demonstrating that the discrimination in a particular case is "intentional" or "purposeful" as required. Aside from the difficulty of proving intent or purpose,[7] Gross and Mauro (1989:113-14) surmise that jurors and other actors in the legal system generally are not racially prejudiced or conscious that they are influenced by the race of the victim in capital cases. Nevertheless, through the psychological process of victim identification, victim-based racial discrimination occurs:

> We are more...horrified by a death if we empathize or identify with the victim,...than if the victim appears to us as a stranger. In a society that remains segregated socially if not legally, and in which the great majority of jurors are white, jurors are not likely to identify with black victims....Thus jurors are more likely to be horrified by the killing of a white than of a black, and more likely to act against the killer of a white than the killer of a black. This reaction is not an expression of racial hostility but a natural product of the patterns of interracial relations in our society (Gross and Mauro 1989:113).

The Prosecutorial Decision to
Charge a Defendant with a Capital Crime

More important than jurors, or even judges, in capital cases are prosecutors who ultimately determine whether a particular crime will be prosecuted as a capital case. Prosecutors probably are not immune to the process of victim identification described above. Prosecutors, however, are affected by other factors as well. Given scarce resources, an important factor in deciding whether to pursue a death sentence in a potentially capital case is the likelihood that a conviction can be obtained. Prosecutors may believe that white-victim cases, which are more visible and disturbing to the majority of the community, are more "winnable" than black-victim cases (Gross and Mauro 1989:114-15). Additionally, since prosecutors in many jurisdictions are elected officials, some of them may believe that white-victim cases are the ones that the majority of their constituents are most interested in seeing prosecuted.

Regardless of the reason, a potential and hidden source of continued racial discrimination in the imposition of the death penalty is prosecutorial discretion. Under post-*Furman* statutes, certain "aggravating" circumstances must be proven before a murder is death-eligible (see Bowers 1984). In Florida, under a post-*Furman* statute, prosecutors were found to "upgrade" and "downgrade" capital cases by alleging aggravating circumstances, charging defendants with an accompanying felony, ignoring evidence in police reports, and withholding an accompanying charge *depending on the race of the offender and the victim* (Bowers 1984:340-1; Radelet 1981; Radelet and Pierce 1985). In Georgia, Baldus et al. (1983) discovered that racial disparity was in part the result of the rate by which Georgia prosecutors advanced cases to a capital sentencing hearing, where a death penalty was a possible outcome, rather than permitting an automatic life sentence. Georgia prosecutors advanced black defendants, whose victims were white, to a capital sentencing hearing at a rate nearly five times that of black defendants whose victims were black, and more than three times the rate of white defendants whose victims were black. Prosecutors engaged in similar actions in South Carolina (Jacoby and Paternoster 1982; Paternoster 1991; 1984), Kentucky (Vito and Keil 1988), New Jersey (Bienen et al. 1988) and other states (Baldus et al. 1986; Gross and Mauro 1989). These findings are truly ironic in light of the majority's response in *Gregg* that:

> Petitioner's argument that...prosecutor's decisions in plea bargaining or in declining to charge capital murder are standardless and...result in the wanton or freakish imposition of the death penalty condemned in *Furman*, is without merit,...the assumption cannot be made that prosecutors will be motivated...by factors other than the strength of their case and the likelihood that a jury would impose the death penalty... (at 157).

Death Penalty and Public Opinion

For over fifty years, with few exceptions, race has been the demographic characteristic that has best distinguished the death penalty opinions of proponents from opponents; more so than gender, age, politics, education, income or SES, etc., (Bohm 1991). In the 22 Gallup polls conducted between 1936 and 1988 that asked questions about the death penalty for murder, the percentage of whites who favored the death penalty has always exceeded the percentage of blacks, while the percentage of blacks opposed and undecided has always been greater than the percentage of whites (see Bohm 1991). On average, 61 percent of whites favored the death penalty for murder compared to 41 percent of blacks, while 48 percent of blacks opposed the death penalty for murder compared to 31 percent of whites (see Bohm 1991). In every polling year except 1953 and 1965, the percentage of blacks undecided about the death penalty surpassed the percentage of whites by about four percent (Bohm 1991).

Racial differences in support/opposition to the death penalty, however, vary greatly over the fifty-plus year period. As indicated, the mean difference is about 20 percent. The largest differential in support, 32 percent, occurred in both 1976 and 1985, while the smallest difference, 6 percent, was recorded in 1953. The largest racial differential in opposition, 28 percent, occurred in 1985, while the smallest, 5 percent, was registered in both 1937 and 1957 (Bohm 1991).

For whites, the highpoint in support and lowpoint in opposition was recorded in the 1988 poll, where 82 percent indicated support and only 14 percent registered opposition. The lowpoint in support and highpoint in opposition for whites was 1966, when 44 percent supported the death penalty and 46 percent opposed it. In only 1965 and 1966 has less than 50 percent of whites supported the death penalty. As for blacks, the highpoint in support was 1953, when 65 percent expressed support; the lowpoint was in 1966 when only 22 percent did so. The highpoint in opposition for blacks came in 1972, when 64 percent opposed the death penalty; the lowpoint was in both 1953 and 1985, when 35 percent were opposed. In only 4 of the 22 polling years, 1953, 1982, 1985, and 1988, have a majority of blacks favored the death penalty. However, in 13 of the 22 poll years, a majority of blacks did not oppose the death penalty either, which is attributable to the large percentages of blacks who have been undecided about the death penalty. The percentage of blacks undecided has varied between 0 percent in 1953 and 20 percent in 1957 and 1966, while the percentage of whites undecided has varied between 1 percent in 1953 and 18 percent in 1957 (See Bohm 1991; Gallup Report 1989).

Smith (1975:269) suggests that racial differences in support/opposition to the death penalty can be attributed to "the disproportionate application of the death penalty to blacks" and to "the civil rights movement, which increased black sensitivity to such inequalities." That may be true for the 1953-1966 and 1960-1966 periods where a 16 and 5 percent greater decrease in support and a 7 and 3 percent greater increase in opposition were recorded for blacks compared to whites, but it does not seem to apply as neatly to the other periods (see Bohm 1991). Between 1966 and 1985, for example, black support of the death penalty increased by 24 percent, just 10 percent less than the increase by whites. White opposition, on the other hand, declined 31 percent between 1966 and 1985, while black opposition declined only 16 percent. In the 1966-1967 period, during the heart of the civil rights movement, black support of the death penalty increased 6 percent more than white support (Bohm 1991).

While it seems logical to attribute racial disparities in death penalty support/opposition to an awareness on the part of blacks of the apparent discriminatory application of capital punishment described above, available evidence suggests that most people are not well informed about the death penalty and its effects (Bohm et al. 1991; Ellsworth and Ross 1983; Sarat and Vidmar 1976; Vidmar and Dittenhoffer 1981). Thus, a more plausible explanation is that black opposition to the death penalty is a function of experience with discrimination in general which has been characteristic of the social history of race relations in the United States.

Conclusion

Although race has been and continues to be an integral part of the administration of capital punishment in the United States, the irony is that blacks (and other minorities) are only significantly related to the process in one capacity: as defendants in capital cases. Despite a lack of quantitative data, anecdotal evidence suggests that nearly all judges, prosecutors, and defense attorneys and the vast majority of jurors in capital cases are white. Moreover, 85 percent of the victims of capital offenders who are executed are white. All of this is true under post-*Furman* statutes that were supposed to rid the administration of the death penalty from objectionable forms of racial discrimination. However, the Supreme Court has not and likely cannot rid the imposition of the death penalty from repugnant forms of racial discrimination. Even under post-*Furman* statutes:

> race is truly a pervasive influence on the criminal justice processing of
> potentially capital cases, one that is evident at every stage of the
> process...it is an influence that persists despite separate sentencing hear-
> ings, explicitly articulated sentencing guidelines, and automatic appellate
> review of all death sentences (Bowers and Pierce 1982:220; also cf. Gross
> and Mauro 1989).

The continuing practice of racial discrimination in the administration of the death penalty suggests that capital punishment in the United States serves other latent purposes: as an instrument of minority group oppression ("to keep blacks in the South in a position of subjugation and subservience"), of majority group protection ("to secure the integrity of the white community in the face of threats or perceived challenges from blacks"), and as a repressive response ("to conditions of social dislocation and turmoil in...time of economic hardship;" Bowers 1984:131-2; also see Douglas in *Furman v. Georgia* 1972; Rusche and Kirchheimer 1968). The death penalty, as administered, devalues the lives of blacks—particularly in the South—as they are used as tools in a social (racial) and economic power struggle. The death penalty in the United States is, at least in part, a race relations mechanism that controls blacks by extermination or, perhaps even more importantly, by threat of extermination.

NOTES

1. Discrimination was not the only nor even the most important grounds on which the death penalty was held to be unconstitutional by the five justices in the majority (Nakell and Hardy 1987:68). Furthermore, not all of the justices were persuaded by evidence of racial discrimination (e.g., see Burger at 389-90, fn. 12; Stewart at 310). Nevertheless, both Burger (at 389-90, fn. 12) and Powell (at 448-50), in their dissents, conceded that, historically, there had been discrimination against blacks in the South, particularly with regard to the crime of rape.

2. At the same time, in *Woodson v. North Carolina* (428 U.S. 280) and *Roberts v. Louisiana* (428 U.S. 325), the Court rejected mandatory death penalty statutes that automatically imposed the death penalty on people convicted of certain crimes.

3. Space limitations preclude an exhaustive summary of pre and post-*Furman* studies of racial discrimination in the imposition of the death penalty. In this chapter, only selected studies are cited. The most thorough summaries of this research can be found in Bowers 1984, and Bienan et al. 1988.

4. These figures refer to legally authorized executions, and not illegal executions by lynching, mostly of blacks, which, according to Bedau (1982:3) have "claimed about half as many victims as have judicially authorized executions."

5. These figures are misleading to the extent that racial discrimination may also play a part in who is charged with death-eligible murder (e.g. blacks may be more likely to be charged with such crimes). Thus these figures do not necessarily represent the actual occurrence of such crimes by blacks and whites.

6. A claim of victim-based racial discrimination also could be made under the Eighth Amendment's cruel and unusual punishment clause which prohibits arbitrary sentencing in capital cases. However, a stronger case is made under the equal protection clause of the Fourteenth Amendment (see Gross and Mauro 1989).

7. In capital cases statistical evidence is not considered sufficient to prove intentional discrimination "unless the evidence of disparate impact is so strong that the only permissible inference is one of intentional discrimination" (Gross and Mauro 1989:136). This extremely rigorous standard has not been required in other types of cases (e.g., jury-selection, employment discrimination cases). In *McCleskey*, the Court claimed that the statistical evidence presented was less than compelling, and that a capital case is unlike jury-selection and employment discrimination cases because "death sentencing involves extremely wide discretion, which is exercised by many independent decisionmakers on the basis of numerous possible legitimate considerations" (Gross and Mauro 1989:173). Since discretion is constitutionally required in capital sentencing and occurs at several different decision points, the kind of evidence of racial discrimination required by the Supreme Court in *McCleskey* ultimately may be impossible to produce.

The Over-representation of Blacks in Florida's Juvenile Justice System

Ted Tollett and Billy R. Close

THERE IS GREAT concern at the state and federal level about the extent of over-representation of minority youth in the juvenile justice system. There is no question that the proportion of minority youth of color in the system, particularly African-Americans, far exceeds their representation in the population at risk. This over-representation is of significance because of: 1) the lasting effects extensive involvement in the juvenile justice system can have on youths; and 2) the difficulties this can create for them in completing their educations, getting good jobs and developing into successful, law-abiding citizens. Given the paucity of opportunities already faced by many minority youth due to social, economic and political circumstances, they can ill afford the additional stigma associated with criminal justice intervention.

Critical analysis of the historical use and abuse of power, violence, and subsequently the law as mechanisms of oppression raise questions concerning the validity of existing institutions of social control such as the juvenile justice system. Admittedly, mechanisms of social control are needed to establish and maintain order in society. The necessity of a system designed specifically for juveniles is equally recognized. Thus, the problem, as we see it, is not social control itself, but the disproportionate application of social control measures.

Historically, American minorities have been on the receiving end of abusive measures camouflaged as mechanisms of social control (see Bailey, this volume). Historically, discrimination has manifested itself in overt ways, leading, in the contemporary era, to institutionalized and hidden discriminatory practices (i.e., through repressive social policies such as current drug laws). The extent of cultural genocide which many minority groups have encountered is exemplary of the oppressive nature of such policies. Robbed of many of their cultural values through legitimate violence that is justified by an imbalance of power within American society, many minority groups have suffered the dubious experience of having their 'forced objectivated reality' defined in such a manner that the behavior on their part which enhances their survival and well-being is often defined as `criminal' (see Curtis 1975; Berger 1967). The gates of juvenile justice are no exception.

The legitimation and perpetuation of social policies that ascribe positions of superiority and inferiority based upon power (and ethnicity and race) seem to be the "theory in use" by courts, police, corrections and other agencies of social control such as the Florida Juvenile Justice System, even while the "espoused theory" is one based upon freedom, justice and equality for all.

It is not our intent to suggest that Florida's juvenile justice system has been used *only* as an oppressive instrument, but rather to question its application as a mechanism of social control by policy-making and law enforcing institutions (e.g., courts, police and correctional agencies) with respect to blacks youth.

This reasoning is supported by Petersilia's (1983) study on racial disparities in the adult criminal justice system, which argued that minor differences (statistically insignificant) among criminality by race were not large enough to explain the over-representation of minorities in the criminal justice system. That is, other social factors must be responsible for the disproportionate incarceration of minorities. Other observers have reached similar conclusions (e.g., Moss 1989).

For example, a recent study by Bishop and Frazier (1988), examined the effects of defendant's race on juvenile justice processing in the State of Florida. The authors suggest that race has a far more pervasive influence than previous research has indicated. They found that blacks were more likely to be recommended for formal processing, referred to court, adjudicated delinquent, and given harsher dispositions than comparable white offenders. The cumulative effect of differential treatment translates into sizable incremental differences that place black youth at a substantial disadvantage relative to white youth (Bishop and Frazier 1988).

Studies such as those mentioned above have profound implications for future research and social policy. Social policies which fail to take into consideration the different cultural and historical experiences of minority groups are inherently biased and result in misleading conclusions (see Zatz 1984; Kuhn 1970). Thus, additional research that takes history and culture into account is needed to identify and rediagnose the problem. Only then can effective social policies be developed which deal with ethnic minorities through social control mechanisms such as the juvenile justice system.

A recent study conducted under the sponsorship of the Florida Supreme Court Racial and Ethnic Bias Study Commission documents the over-representation of black youth in Florida's juvenile justice system. The study utilized aggregate level data on juvenile arrests, case processing and dispositions to: (1) assess the extent of black over-representation at various stages in the juvenile process; (2) analyze the impact of race on programmatic dispositions; and (3) present policy recommendations that would address this problem. In order to gain additional information, a series of interviews were performed with experienced and knowledgeable professionals who provided recommendations concerning solutions to increasing over-representation of minorities in the juvenile justice system. Moreover, county level data were examined to determine if over-representation of black youth in the system varied geographically.

As noted above, this study was designed to deal exclusively with aggregate level data, and focused upon differences between race and gender groupings for offense categories, specific major felonies and misdemeanor charges at various points in the system. There are obviously numerous other variables which affect decisions made in the processing and disposition of individual delinquency cases. An examination of such factors was beyond the scope of this short study. An ongoing study is dealing with some of these individual level variables. This chapter presents a summary of the findings from the study described above.

Data

Information on juvenile arrests by age (those under age 18) and race (black/white) was obtained from Uniform Crime Report data compiled by the Florida Department of Law Enforcement. The racial categories utilized in official reports included "white," "black" and "other." The category "other" was excluded from the analysis because the number of arrests reported was less than one half of one percent. However, in Florida, as in other states, the categorization of individuals into "black" and "white" is imprecise and ultimately problematic (see Farnworth et al., and Patterson and Lynch, this volume). This division groups Hispanics with whites, thus increasing the likelihood that statistical studies of criminal justice bias may underestimate or minimize disparity (see Lynch 1990).

Impact of Race on Programmatic Decisions: Significant Findings

In this section we briefly review some of the major findings from the study performed for the Florida Supreme Court Racial and Ethnic Bias Study Commission. We present this data in relation to various decision making stages. The population at risk of delinquency used for comparisons includes all youth between the ages of ten and seventeen. Official state population estimates break down figures for race into categories labeled as non-white and white. This information, which indicates a slight increase (1 percent) in the non-white population in Florida between 1982 and 1990, is used below to compare trends in juvenile justice outcomes to population at risk probabilities.

Arrest. The arrest rate for black youth in 1989 was two and one-half times higher than the rate for white youth. The 1989 arrest rate for black youth was 128 per 1,000 while the arrest rate for white males was 49 per 1,000. Blacks accounted for 42 percent of all juvenile arrests during 1989 while comprising only 21.75 percent of the at risk population.

Delinquency Referrals. From 1982 to 1990, delinquency cases received increased 113 percent for blacks and only 36 percent for whites. For the same time period, felony drug cases (excluding marijuana) involving black males increased from 15 to 86 percent of all male cases received. Over 90 percent of such cases were for cocaine. Between 1982 and 1990, black male violent felony cases increased by 144 percent, while white male cases grew by 70 percent. These increases do not compare favorably to the 1 percent increase in Florida's non-white juvenile at risk population.

Detention Admissions. For 1989-90, black males accounted for 57 percent of all male cases detained while black females accounted for 42 percent of all female cases detained. For 1989-90 black females accounted for 71 percent of all female violent felony cases and 73 percent of the female cases detained. In 1982-83 black males accounted for 54 percent of the male cases detained for carrying a concealed firearm. By 1989-90 this figure had increased to 80 percent. The highest increase in cases involving black males detained was for felony drug cases (excluding marijuana). From 1982 to 1990, black males detained for drug offenses increased from 21 percent to 91 percent of total male cases detained.

Non-judicial Handling. Of all cases disposed of in 1989-90, 28 percent of cases involving black males were handled non-judicially compared to 40 percent for white males. For the same time period, 45 percent of all black females and 55 percent of all white females were handled non-judicially. These data point to clear differences in the use of non-judicial alternatives by race.

Judicial Handling. Of all cases disposed of in 1989-90, 72 percent of the black males were handled judicially, compared to 60 percent of the white males. During the same time period, 55 percent of all black females were handled judicially, compared to 45 percent of all white females. During the study period, Health and Rehabilitative Services (HRS) staff (who make many of the initial contacts in cases involving juveniles in the state of Florida), recommended judicial handling at a much higher rate for black juveniles, especially males.

Diversion to Juvenile Alternative Services Programs (JASP). JASP referrals involve minor offenses or individuals with little or no previous record. In 1989-90, 18 percent of all juvenile alternative diversions were referred to JASP. Race and gender specific JASP referrals break down as follows: 13 percent of all black males; 20 percent of all white males; 24 percent of all black females; and 27 percent of all white females. These data indicate that both race and gender are associated with whether a referral to JASP will be made.

Delinquency Commitment Programs. From 1982 to 1990 the number of black males committed to delinquency programs increased from 45 to 60 percent of the total male cases reported committed. During the same time period, the black proportion of female cases committed increased from 45 to 52 percent. Thus, for both male and female cases, the percent of white cases committed to delinquency programs decreased.

Juvenile Transfers to Adult Court. From 1982 to 1990 the percent of black males transferred to adult court increased from 47 to 55 percent of all male cases direct filed, waived or indicted. During the same time period, black females transferred to adult court increased from 42 to 48 percent of all females cases transferred. Once again, both figures indicate a decrease in the proportion of cases involving whites transferred to adult court. During this period, State attorneys filed cases, and sought waivers and indictments in far more cases than recommended by HRS.

Juvenile Admissions to Adult Prison. In 1989, black juveniles were incarcerated in adult prisons at a rate *eight and one-half times greater* than that of white juveniles. In addition, blacks were sent to adult facilities at an earlier age.

Summary of Findings Across Dispositional Stages

From 1982 to 1990 the number of intake cases for black males increased 122 percent compared to a 37 percent increase for white males. The number of cases for black females rose by 79 percent, from 4,751 to 8,511. Cases for white females increased by 32 percent, from 9,533 to 12,679.

For 1989-90 the HRS was two-and-one-half times more likely to recommend that petitions for delinquency be filed for black males compared to white males, and twice as likely to recommend that petitions for delinquency be filed for black females compared to white females. State attorneys filed fewer delinquency proceedings for black males (compared to HRS recommendations), but were still *more likely* to direct file or seek a waiver to adult court for black male juveniles than for white males. Similar action was taken by state attorneys for black females. For cases which were eventually disposed of non-judicially during 1989-90, HRS staff had recommended not filing petitions at a much higher rate for white males and females. For cases which ended up being handled judicially during 1989-90, HRS intake also recommended not filing petitions on a higher proportion of white juvenile cases than black juvenile cases.

For cases transferred to adult court during 1989-90, HRS staff recommended that more cases involving black cases be direct filed than cases involving white males. Recommendations for direct file transfers to adult court were about the same for white and black females.

Using the change in felony drug cases (excluding marijuana) from 1982 to 1990 as an example of findings across dispositions, we discovered that the percent of black males increased form 15 to 86. The proportion of cases involving black females increased from 13 to 67 percent. Referrals and detentions for felony drug cases by race and sex are reviewed below.

Delinquency Referrals. From 1982 through 1989 the number of felony drug cases received increased by 103 percent for white males (from N=299 to N=606), *while the comparable number for black male juveniles increased an astounding 6,706 percent* (from N=54 to N=3675). Non-marijuana felony drug cases for white females increased in number from 118 to 123, while the number of cases involving black females increased from 18 to 201.

Intake Cases Detained. From 1982 through 1990 the percent of felony drug cases handled non-judicially rose from 13 to 77 percent for black males and from 10 to 54 percent for black females. During the same time period, felony drug cases handled judicially rose from 17 to 87 percent for black males and from 15 to 72 percent for black females. The percent of cases diverted to JASP alternative sentencing also increased for black males (from 7 to 55 percent) and black females (from 8 to 57 percent). There was also an increase in the percent of black males (13 to 85 percent) and females (17 to 75 percent) placed in community control for this time period. Similarly, there was an increase in the percent of black males (from 33 to 94 percent) and females (from 0 to 81 percent) placed in delinquency programs. In addition, from 1982 through 1990 black male felony drug cases transferred to adult court increased from 27 to 91 percent. Black female cases transferred to the adult court increased from 11 percent to 68 percent.

In each and every case noted above, the increase for black males and females exceeded the increase in commitments, intake decisions or referrals for white males and females. In fact, in most cases, increases in commitments, intakes, etc., for blacks signalled that the percent of cases involving whites decreased.

Geographical Analysis of Black Over-Representation

An effort was undertaken to determine whether black over-representation was a statewide phenomenon or whether it varied by jurisdiction. To accomplish this, data were obtained on the 1990 black proportion of the juvenile population age ten to seventeen in each of Florida's 67 counties. The number of delinquency cases received, detained and referred to HRS delinquency programs in 1989 were examined relative to county juvenile at-risk populations. These data indicated widespread differences between a county's black at risk population and the percentage of black cases received.[1]

These same data were used to examine the relationship between the non-white population at risk and the black proportion of delinquency cases received. Data for the twelve counties with over 30,000 population at risk revealed that the proportion of black juveniles committed exceeded the non-white proportion of the population at risk in each of these counties by over 30 percent. In seven of these counties the differential is over 40 percent (Orange, Palm Beach, Hillsborough, Escambia, Pinellas, Seminole and Broward). For the fourteen next most populous counties (10,000 to 29,000 population at risk), six counties show that the differential between black population at risk and black commitment proportions exceeded 30 percent, with two surpassing 40 percent (Leon and St. Lucie). Similar trends were noted in the remaining counties.[2]

The data were also examined to determine, statewide, which counties exhibited the largest discrepancies on each of three variables as compared with the black proportion of their population at risk. Counties were chosen if the differential for black delinquency cases *received* exceeded 25 percent, the differential for black cases reported *detained* exceeded 40 percent, and the differential for black cases reported *committed* exceeded 45 percent. Five Florida counties (Leon, St. Lucie, Taylor, Jefferson and Flagler) met these criteria during 1989. Broward, Putnam and Bradford counties met two of the criteria. These data indicate increased racial disparity at later processing stages, and show statewide, though varied, bias against black juveniles.

Interview Results: Sources of Bias and Policy Recommendations

As part of the juvenile justice study prepared for the Racial and Ethnic Bias Study Commission, interviews[3] were conducted with key actors in the Florida system. Table 6.1 presents a summary of the characteristics of those interviewed.

Table 6.1
Summary of Interviewee Background

Agency or Group Represented	Total Interviewed	Total Minorities Interviewed	Total Non-Minorities Interviewed
Legal	4	3	1
Child Advocacy	3	1	2
Law Enforcement	3	2	1
Judicial	2	1	1
Academia	2	1	1
Juvenile Justice Worker	2	1	1
Totals	16	9	7

The rationale behind these interviews was two-fold. First, each interviewee was asked about his or her opinions concerning the treatment of minorities within the juvenile justice system. Specifically, each interviewee was asked whether (1) he or she believed that disparity exists between the treatment of minorities and non-minorities; (2) if yes, is this disparity based upon racial or ethnic bias; (3) at what levels of the juvenile justice system does this bias appear most prevalent; and (4) what are the causes of such disparity. Second, regardless of whether or not the interviewees believed differential treatment exists, it was explained to them that minorities do enter the juvenile justice system at a rate which is twice as high per population at risk than the rate for non-minorities. Each interviewee was then asked if he or she could offer any solutions as to how to change this trend. The following discussion offers a summary of responses to these two sets of questions.

Findings

An overwhelming majority of those interviewed believed that a disparity exists between the treatment of minority and non-minority juvenile offenders.

Only one interviewee did not believe that a disparity exists in his city. Most interviewees believed that the differential treatment begins at the arrest level.

Surprisingly, law enforcement officials concurred with this conclusion. There was a belief that even before a situation escalates into an arrest, the way an officer perceives a minority juvenile is different from the perception of a non-minority juvenile.[4]

Interviewees differed on whether or not officer race or ethnicity makes a difference in the handling of juveniles. Some believed that differential percep-tions are systematically ingrained in police officers regardless of officer's race or ethnicity. Others believed that the officer's race/ethnicity does have an affect on the handling of juveniles and that minority officers may be more sensitive to the needs of minority juveniles.

All those interviewed (excluding the one exception mentioned earlier) believed that differential treatment continues on through the juvenile justice system. And though personal biases do appear to play a role, it is the justice system itself which perpetuates differential treatment throughout arrest, deten-tion, conviction and commitment. Specifically, there was a belief that the juvenile justice system operates with bias against those of lower socioeconomic status. Therefore, since a high proportion of low income families are also minorities, they are stuck in what was often referred to as a "self-fulfilling prophecy" of poverty and crime. Overall, the system as it now functions perpetuates the problem instead of helping juveniles.

It is important to note that many interviewees thought that the Florida educational system perpetuates a differential treatment bias which inevitably flows into the criminal justice system. Reasons for this type of systematic differential treatment were given as follows:

1. Socialization: At an early age, minorities come to view police officers as the bad guys, and the entire juvenile justice system as a means to manipulate and control minorities. Non-minorities, however, often view police as "protectors." Also, police are socialized to believe that minority juveniles, living in low income areas, are more likely to be guilty of committing a crime or are automatically going to lie or "shuck and jive" to an officer as compared to a non-minority juvenile.

2. Environmental: There is a connection between environment and crime: low income areas are high crime areas, these areas are patrolled more often, and since minorities are more likely to reside in such neighborhoods, the probability of being caught committing a crime and arrested are influenced merely by where the individual resides. In addition, residence affects the attitude of the police toward that juvenile.

3. Physical Appearance: Certain types of dress, hair style or the "wearing of colors" by a juvenile affects the perception of juvenile justice system actors. Consciously or subconsciously, a delinquent profile is developed based upon the appearance of the juvenile.

4. Educational: Some interviewees believed that there is a lack of sensitivity toward the educational needs of minorities and low income level juveniles. However, the blame should not be place on teachers because large classroom sizes inhibit the ability of teachers to devote special attention to problem children. Without identification and help at an early age these children become discarded by the educational system. There also appears to be a lack of good minority role models within the educational system.

5. Breakdown of the Family Unit: Florida's system is currently not designed to deal with the special needs and problems of the single parent household. Interviewees believed that a lack of supervision and authority figures, which could be provided by schools and community centers, perpetuates the involvement of juveniles in illegal and disruptive behavior.

6. Lack of Job Opportunities (Economic): For many minorities, the lack of adequate job training and employment may lead to greater involvement in the juvenile justice system.

Each interviewee was asked to suggest ways to reduce the extent of minority over-representation in the juvenile justice system. Table 6.2 provides a brief overview of some of their recommendations.

The policy recommendations contained in Table 6.2 are instructive in two senses. First, they point to the need to divert minorities from the criminal justice system or to address the problem of minority over-representation by expanding non-justice services. Second, the recommendations offered by minority and non-minority interviewees are quite different. Minority members were more likely to make non-criminal justice policy recommendations than non-minority members. Clearly, these interview data point to the need to have more minorities involved in making decisions concerning how to affect minority over-representation in the criminal justice system.

Considering these data on minority over-representation in the Florida juvenile justice system and the interviewee policy recommendations outlined above, we present our own policy recommendations below.

First, there is a need to collect more detailed information on race and ethnicity of individuals at every stage of the system. Race cannot be treated as an ethnic monolith. Second, law enforcement agencies need to employ more minority law enforcement officers, establish cultural/minority sensitivity training with annual follow-up training, and utilize community policing to increase cooperation and understanding between law enforcement and the community it patrols, while placing less emphasis on arrests. In addition, law enforcement

Table 6.2
Interviewee Recommendations by Interviewer Minority Membership

---

Minority Interviewees: emphasized drug rehabilitation and prevention; need for more black judges and minorities in decision making and policy making positions; educate teachers to deal with the special problems of minority and low SES children; provide alternatives to traditional educational tracts; decentralize police departments; bring back foot patrols; stop pumping more money into a bad system; develop "Officer Friendly" programs in the schools; increase the utilization of community centers in all areas of the city and provide competent supervision at such facilities; after school, utilize local schools in a community center capacity; provide employment development in the middle and high schools; place more funding into the "Head Start" projects; provide teenage birth control education; establish stronger screening of law enforcement officer applicants for potential cultural and racial biases; improve the employability of minority juveniles.

Non-Minority Interviewees: invest more funds in school resource officers; remove repeat offenders from the streets and place in secure facilities with a strong emphasis on education; place more emphasis on the need for quality day care for lower SES families; change the kindergarten through 5th grade structure into a more social institution; establish school breakfast and lunch programs; ensure children have clean clothes and a bath; bring social services into the schools; sponsor more research to analyze how juveniles, especially minority juveniles, are handled by law enforcement; redistribution and equalization of wealth in terms of school funding; at the high school, and perhaps middle school level, require a multi-cultural sensitivity class; offer after school programs to eliminate boredom, provide positive role models and authority figures and supply necessary after school supervision; fund more in-school counseling.

---

officials must provide minority law enforcement officers with the opportunity to obtain advanced education and training through programs which grant administrative leave and paid tuition, including opportunities for undergraduate and graduate degrees that will enhance the ability of minority law enforcement officers to achieve promotions.

Third, state attorneys must eliminate the transfer of juveniles to the adult system by direct file for misdemeanor charges, and establish strict, specific guidelines and criteria to limit the direct filing of juveniles to the adult system. Public defenders' funding and resources must be increased to ensure proper representation of minorities at each stage of the system. Fourth, since many juvenile who come into contact with Florida's juvenile justice system do so through HRS, this agency, too, must emphasize cultural/minority sensitivity training for HRS delinquency staff. In addition, HRS should examine all instruments used to aid decision making in delinquency cases to assure objectivity with regard to racial and ethnic influence on resulting decisions, employ additional minority professionals, increase funding for agencies and organizations which provide non-judicial diversion services for HRS, place increased emphasis on delinquency prevention and front end services for at-risk juveniles, and establish strict and specific guidelines and criteria for recommending transfer of juveniles to the adult system.

Fifth, there is a need to restructure the educational system. Specifically, school resources should be utilized to a greater degree (e.g., supervised after school and weekend programs utilizing school playgrounds, classrooms and equipment; use the school setting as a focus of social services programs; and have school personnel work closely with the community control counselors assigned to their specific schools). Equity in school funding, which would affect student/teacher ratios in minority school districts, is also desirable. Further, schools should provide alternatives to traditional educational tracts, (e.g., magnet schools) and multi-cultural sensitivity classes.

Sixth, judges and judicial personnel should also be exposed to cultural/minority sensitivity training. There is a dire need to increase the number of minority judges.

Finally, in order for any of these recommendations to be successful, the legislature must provide appropriate levels of funding and pay continuing attention to the problem of minority over-representation in any future legislative initiatives.

Conclusions

Data from Florida indicated that black juveniles are substantially over-represented at every stage of the juvenile justice system when compared to the size of the population at risk. This over-representation was far more pronounced for black males. The extent of over-representation varies greatly across Florida's counties, but is evident in all of them. The offenses for which black males are most over-represented are violent felonies, carrying concealed firearms and, most dramatically, serious felony drug offense charges.

Over the last three years the number of black males reported detained has increased, while the number of white males has decreased to the extent that blacks now constitute a majority of those juveniles who are detained. Non-judicial handling for black youths was lower than that for white youths, regardless of gender. Although the system did provide for a much greater increase in non-judicial handling and diversion for minority youth, the overall increase in delinquency cases was so large that the number and proportion of blacks handled non-judicially did increase. Conversely, judicial handling rates were higher for black youth.

Diversion was more likely for white youth, especially for males. The proportion of cases reported committed involving blacks continues to increase, as does their proportion of transfers to adult court and admissions to state prison.

While our data are suggestive of over-representation, our study does not control for a variety of other factors in a multivariate format. However, we believe that these data demonstrate undeniably that a bias against blacks exists that would not "wash out" with more sophisticated models. In fact, more sophisticated models also suffer from certain methodological constraints that may mask biases, such as the inclusion of *too* many control variables, and the inability to include or assess the effects of culture and history or other qualitative variables on bias. To assess many of these qualitative effects, alternative methodologies, such as interviews, must be used. The examination of racial biases in criminal justice systems is an area ripe for new direction, and we urge researchers to consider this before embarking on future research. In order to locate causality, it is not enough for researchers and policy makers to carefully inspect the historical blueprints (rationale) used to create the system (or institution); in addition, they must undertake an internal audit which focuses on the subsequent developmental policies and procedures. A combination of these methodologies will provide valuable insight about the inner design and purpose of the system, thereby providing an adequate diagnosis of social control mechanisms such as the juvenile justice system. A proper diagnosis is essential to an adequate response since the response is inherent in the diagnosis (Jones 1991).

NOTES

1. Data for thirteen counties with less than 2,000 population at risk contain too few cases to make an analysis feasible. Findings for the remaining counties are as follows (population figures refer to size of the black at-risk population): (1) population greater than 30,000: Duval, Dade and Escambia had the highest proportion of black population at risk and percentages of cases received who were black, followed by Orange, Broward, and Palm Beach counties. In Duval, Broward, Orange, Escambia and Dade counties, over 63 percent of cases admitted to detention involved blacks; (2) population 10,000 to 30,000; Leon and St. Lucie counties stand out in regard to black over-representation, followed by Alachua county; (3) population 5,000 to 10,000; Gadsden, Putnam and Nassua stand out; (4) population 2,000 to 4,000; Taylor, Madison and Bradford show the highest rates.

2. Seven of the fourteen counties in the next category (from 5,000 to 10,000 population at risk) showed discrepancies between the proportion of non-white population at risk and the black proportion of committed cases that exceeded 30 percent. In several counties,

the difference exceeded 40 percent (Putnam, Santa Rosa and Nassau; Martin county exceeded 50 percent; St. Johns county exceeded 67 percent). Seven of the fourteen counties in the next category (2,000 to 4,000 population at risk) also had rate differentials in excess of 30 percent, with the highest in Levy (84%), Bradford (57%) and Taylor (50%) counties. Of the remaining thirteen counties (those with less than 2,000 population at risk), seven (Lafayette, Glades, Dixie, Flagler, Jefferson, Franklin and Gilchrist counties) had disparities of more than 30 percent between the proportion of black population 10-17 and the proportion of cases reported committed who were black.

3. Time and expense limited the number of interviews conducted. Interviewees were chosen based upon their background and knowledge. The opinions and recommendations noted above should not be assumed to be those of the larger population since as these interviews were not conducted randomly, and should be viewed as "windows" into the attitudes of persons who are currently working within Florida's juvenile justice system. Special thanks goes to Kimberly Budnick, Woodrow Harper, and Bob Barrios for their work on collection of these data.

4. A common example given by many interviewees was the situation of the juvenile caught joy-riding in their parent's or friend's car. The interviewees believed the officers assume that minority youth stole the car, so he or she is taken into custody. However, the non-minority juveniles were not assumed to have stolen the car, and would likely be returned to the home without any official action being taken.

American Indians and Criminal Justice: Some Conceptual and Methodological Considerations

**Marjorie S. Zatz, Carol Chiago Lujan
and Zoann K. Snyder-Joy**

THE QUESTION of whether or not criminal justice processing and sanctioning decisions are racially biased has divided the criminological community for several decades. While several comprehensive reviews of this literature have been published (e.g., Hagan 1974; Kleck 1981; Garber et al. 1983; Hagan and Bumiller 1983; Klepper et al. 1983; Zatz 1987), this question is still the focus of considerable debate within the discipline and in the courts (e.g., Wilbanks 1987a; MacLean and Milovanovic 1990; see also the 1987 Supreme Court opinion in *McClesky v. Kemp* (1987) concerning race discrimination in the application of the death penalty).

The vast majority of criminological studies of racial discrimination have focused on black-white differentials. During the 1980s, a small but increasing number of studies included latinos (e.g., Gruhl et al. 1984; Zatz 1984, 1985; Hagan and Zatz 1985; LaFree 1985). However, few studies have examined the involvement of American Indians in the criminal justice system. We suggest that this is a serious omission in the literature, and that this omission cannot be solved simply by adding American Indians as yet another category in a regression analysis. We assert this because of the unique status of American Indians and due to their relationship with the federal government. This chapter delineates some jurisdictional issues, summarizes certain differences between dominant and Indian views of crime and sanctioning, reviews the extant literature on the involvement of American Indians in the U.S. criminal justice system, and seeks to explicate some of the conceptual and methodological issues relevant to the study of American Indians as criminal defendants in the U.S. criminal justice system.

Jurisdictional Considerations

Legally, the status of American Indian tribes in the U.S. is that of domestic dependent nations within a nation.[1] This status is also known as limited tribal sovereignty. Consequently, American Indian law is one of the most complicated areas of legal study. The jurisdictional problems alone are confusing. In criminal cases, tribal members are subject to at least three levels of government—the tribe, the state, and the federal government. Jurisdiction depends on several factors, including (1) the type of crime; (2) whether it occurred on or off a reservation; and (3) whether Indians or non-Indians were involved, both as the victim and the accused (Deloria and Lytle 1983; Ragsdale 1985).

In the late 1800s, the Department of Interior established *Courts of Indian Offenses*, also known as *Code of Federal Regulation Courts* because they operate under the written guidelines of the Code of Federal Regulation (CFR). These courts were created to handle cases involving both whites and Indians, and as a means of assimilating Indians into white society. The CFR must also be viewed as instruments of cultural oppression, since some important parts of Indian religious ceremonies were defined as criminal offenses under the CFR (Kerr 1969; Deloria and Lytle 1983). During the peak of their activity, in the early 1900s, CFR Courts existed on two-thirds of Indian reservations.

In 1934, the Indian Reorganization Act, designed to give some authority back to the Indians by allowing tribes to establish their own courts to enforce tribal codes, was passed. Tribal courts and codes were not subject directly to regulation by the Department of the Interior, but they were monitored by the Bureau of Indian Affairs, which is a part of the Department of the Interior (Kerr 1969). Thus, some federal oversight was retained. In addition, because native religions and other mechanisms for integrating and upholding traditional legal systems had already been seriously disrupted by assimilation pressures, the traditional legal institutions were not reinstituted. Rather, a new form of tribal courts emerged.

Today, limited sovereignty for Indian tribes means that the federal government maintains the greatest scope of jurisdiction in criminal cases.[2] The government restricts the length of sentence and the amount of fines tribes can impose in their courts to one year in jail and/or a $5,000 fine. Furthermore, concurrent with the tribe, the federal government handles all major crimes by Indians that occur on the reservation. Generally, if a non-Indian is involved in a crime on the reservation, either as victim or perpetrator, jurisdiction falls to the state or federal court, depending on the type of crime.

Moreover, many tribes have limited budgets for their courts and are unable to provide basic services such as probation or innovative alternatives to incarceration. Thus, as Weber has noted, American Indians "are forced to try to exist under two conflicting systems of rules, one being their own, informal living-law and the other being the formal bureaucratic legal machine" (1982:47).

The multiple jurisdictions under which Indian peoples live frequently result in inconsistent processing and sanctioning of persons accused of committing crimes. This inconsistency is often a function of how heavy the federal caseload is at the time that the crime occurred. If it is very heavy, tribal police may conduct the criminal investigation and then pass their findings on to the federal prosecutor, or charges may be reduced so that the case can be handled by the tribal court. The latter situation may increase perceptions of injustice when the charge of one person is reduced to fit the tribal jurisdiction, and another person who commits the same or a lesser crime is tried by the federal or state system and receives a lengthy prison sentence (Weber 1982).

To add to this complex jurisdictional structure, tribal court processing and sentencing differs among the more than 300 federally recognized American Indian tribes and Alaskan Natives. The overall structure of American Indian tribes varies along a traditional to modern continuum. This continuum is reflected in the tribal court systems. Traditionally, Indian courts were not always a body of appointed or elected "judges." Rather, offenses were typically handled by tribal officials, clan members, or family elders (Deloria and Lytle 1983).

The Navajo have elaborate court systems that mirror the U.S. judicial system, complete with court houses and jail facilities. Yet even within the Navajo tribe there are differences. In isolated areas of the Navajo reservation traditional "grass roots" methods of handling disputes are also used. According to Van Valkenburgh (1937), these traditional methods dealt with crime and other forms of deviant behavior on a person-to-person or clan-to-clan basis, rather than on a tribal level. The extended family was instrumental in seeing that some form of justice prevailed. Where mediators were needed to assist in settling disputes, they were respected members of the family or clan, or neutral third parties (Van Valkenburgh 1937; Shepardson and Blodwen 1970; Zion 1983:94). Usually, restitution in the form of payment of goods and livestock was the accepted method of dealing with the crime amongst the Navajo (Van Valkenburgh 1937).

Other tribes, such as the Pueblos, defer to tribal leaders to act as tribal court judges. In these instances, cases are usually handled with a traditional, holistic family and/or community approach. The emphasis of the Keresan Pueblos is that "all persons are obligated to the maintenance of the whole" (Hoebel 1969:100). Thus, unlike the Navajo, for the Keresan Pueblo justice was centered on the community. Individuals, families, or clans could not settle conflicts amongst themselves. All legal power was centralized within the religious leadership of the Pueblo (Hoebel 1969).

Despite these differences, there are also important similarities that tie tribes together. One, as discussed above, is the intervention of state and federal government into Indian affairs. A second concerns the general orientation of Indian legal institutions. While legal systems influenced by Western European jurisprudential concepts are largely based along formal rational lines, Indian legal institutions are strongly influenced by a religious orientation which includes important cultural features (Weber 1982).

Similarly, definitions of crime and deviance and perceptions of how best to treat people who deviate are likely to vary greatly between Indians and non-Indians. For Indian peoples, all members of the community (whether defined as the extended family, clan, or tribe) are affected by the deviant acts of an offender, and the community has a responsibility to help restore harmony. The primary goal of traditional Indian courts is to mediate the case to the satisfaction of all involved so that harmonious relations can be restored, not to ascertain guilt or punish offenders (Deloria and Lytle 1983:111). In the past and today for those closer to the traditional end of the traditional-modern continuum, social control is enforced through restitution, compensation, and social and religious sanctions including ostracism, gossip, and ridicule (Kerr 1969). Thus, for traditional Indians, locking someone up in a penal institution is far from an ideal solution (Weber 1982).

Perceptions of Justice

American Indians are knowledgeable about the different levels of judicial systems to which they are subject. Surveys of American Indian attitudes toward the legal structure indicate that a majority of Indian respondents hold negative views toward the judicial system. As Deloria and Lytle (1983:xiii) note:

> The efficacy of law ultimately depends on society's perception of its ability to provide justice...Indian people, from the establishment of the reservations, were forced into a situation where they could not always perceive the justness of federal laws. And the federal laws were not always just, nor were they suited to the needs of many tribes.

Lujan (1990a) asked Navajo and Pueblo respondents to compare and assess the three levels of legal systems to which they are subject—tribal, state and local—and the Supreme Court. While the majority of respondents held favorable views of the Supreme Court, they were most critical of the state and local police and courts. These negative views of local, non-Indian, judicial institutions and actors appear to be reinforced by perceived discriminatory treatment of Indians who have been processed through the local system. Additionally, American Indians perceive themselves as lacking input into the non-Indian legal structure and feel excluded from the process of law making and law reform (Lujan 1986; 1990a). Thus, while other studies have found that relative to whites, blacks perceive the criminal justice system to be more unjust and feel alienated from it (cf. Hagan and Albonetti 1982), Lujan's study suggests that Indians regard the local system as *foreign*. That difference, we argue, is an important one.

It is not uncommon for an Indian defendant to plead guilty to a charge without adequate legal representation. Some of the reasons are common to other poor defendants or defendants of color. However, other reasons appear unique to Indians and include: (1) unfamiliarity and uncomfortableness with the court and its ambiance, including its physical structure and the formality of its rituals; (2) lack of confidence in receiving a fair trial, particularly given the extreme unlikelihood of a jury of one's peers (i.e., other Indians); (3) uncertainty of their ability to communicate what they see as the relevant aspects of their case, even to non-Indian defense attorneys; and (4) desire to get the process over with as soon as possible. In contrast, tribal courts operate within a well integrated community in which everyone knows everyone else or has knowledge of the family. Thus, there is no need to speak about things that are already known. In the U.S. system, mitigating factors must be spelled out in open court, and this may be exceedingly awkward for persons in what is essentially unfamiliar physical and cultural territory.

Processing and Sanctioning of Indians through the U.S. Criminal Justice System

The number of American Indians in the U.S. criminal justice system is climbing. Based on data from the Bureau of Justice Statistics, Feimer et al. (1990) report that nationwide the American Indian prison population climbed by 102 percent between 1978 and 1984, double the rate for whites during the same period. In South Dakota alone, Indians made up over 24 percent of the state prison inmate population between 1980 and 1989, although Indians comprised only 8.2 percent of the state's population. Since the state criminal justice system only has jurisdiction over crimes committed by Indians off the reservations, this figure is particularly alarming (Feimer et al. 1990:86-87).

There are very few empirical studies of the processing and sanctioning of Indians by police, prosecutors, judges, and parole boards. This extreme paucity of data makes any discussion of patterns very tentative. Nevertheless, a review of existing literature suggests that American Indians are treated more harshly in some stages of criminal justice decision making compared to non-Indians. The bias against Indians is particularly apparent in arrest decisions, type of sentence, and parole decisions.

Peak and Spencer (1987) examined FBI Uniform Crime Reports (UCR) for the period 1976 through 1985, comparing Indian arrest rates with rates for whites, blacks, and Asians. They also compared their findings to those reported by Stewart (1964). Peak and Spencer report that while Indians represented about 0.6 percent of the U.S. population in 1985, they accounted for 1.1 percent of all arrests for the same year. Indians ranked the lowest of the four ethnic groups in percentage of arrests for violent and serious property crimes. However, they had the highest arrest rate for alcohol-related offenses—47 percent in 1985—compared to a national average of 33 percent. Peak and Spencer noted further that although most Indians live in rural areas, they are most likely to experience legal difficulties in cities, with 75.1 percent of all Indian arrests from 1976 to 1985 occurring in urban areas.

A comparison of UCR data and records maintained by 207 reservation and Bureau of Indian Affairs (BIA) enforcement and investigation agencies provides some interesting results (Peak and Spencer 1987). In 1982, 69.3 percent of the offenses investigated by the BIA were alcohol-related, 42 percent of all arrests were for disorderly conduct, and 22.2 percent of arrests were for drunkenness or public intoxication. Similarly, Stratton (1973) found that alcohol-related offenses accounted for 85-90 percent of all arrests of Indians in Gallup, New Mexico, in 1969.

Peak and Spencer (1987) found that homicide rates on reservations are as much as nine times higher than the rate among non-Indians, although off-reservation arrests of Indians for violent crimes are lower than the national average. Levy et al. (1969) linked concern about alcohol with concern about homicide. They used Navajo police files for the period 1956 through 1965 to assess the veracity of the perception that the homicide rate within the Navajo nation was growing, and that it was linked to increased alcoholism. It was further thought that this perceived increase was a consequence of a 1953 law allowing Indians to purchase alcohol off-reservation. Levy et al. found that alcohol-related arrests were indeed increasing, but there was no relationship between alcohol and the homicide rate, which remained stable.

One finding in Levy et al.'s study was counter-intuitive. Although the Navajos accord women a great deal of status and are matrilineal, Levy et al.

found that Navajo women were more likely to be the victims of homicide than were black or white women (1969:135). They suggest that blacks and whites are more likely than Navajos to murder friends and acquaintances, while Navajo men are more likely to murder close relatives, with their wives being their primary targets (1969:137).

Turning next to sentencing data, Hall and Simkus (1975) examined the type of sentence handed down to Indians and non-Indians in a state with a large Indian population. They found that American Indians were substantially more likely to receive a sentence of incarceration than were non-Indians, for the same offenses. That is, non-Indians were more apt to receive deferred sentences that did not involve incarceration, while Indians received split sentences or sentences of full imprisonment more often.

Whether Indians sentenced to incarceration receive *longer* sentences than non-Indians is not so clear, however. In part, the inconsistencies within the literature may be due to differences between studies of the federal system and studies of state systems. They may also be due to variation in use of control variables. Within the federal system, Swift and Bickel (1974) found that Indians received longer sentences than whites. In contrast, Bynum (1981; Bynum and Paternoster 1984) found that in an upper plains state with a large Indian population, amongst those persons sentenced to incarceration, non-Indians received longer sentences than did Indians. Similarly, Pommersheim and Wise (1989) and Feimer et al. (1990) found that in the South Dakota state system between 1981 and 1985, Indian offenders did not receive significantly more severe sentences than non-Indians. Indeed, by some measures non-Indians received statistically more severe punishments.

Importantly, however, stepwise regression models conducted separately for Indians and non-Indians indicated a difference in the factors that influenced punishment severity. Feimer et al. (1990) found that four factors—age, number of convictions, number of priors, and weapon used—affected the sentence length for whites, while for Indians only the number of priors had a significant effect on sentence length. Yet the number of prior felonies did not differ significantly between Indians and whites; only its relative importance differed. The importance of prior record is also suggested by Bynum and Paternoster (1984) who found an interaction effect of being Indian and having prior felony convictions on likelihood of parole. This interaction was marginally significant for all inmates, and much stronger for persons serving time for burglaries.

Parole decisions may be a particularly important stage in criminal justice processing for Indians. Perhaps because of the pattern they found for Indians to receive longer sentences, Swift and Bickel (1974) also found that American Indians served a longer time in prison prior to release on parole than did non-

Indians. While Swift and Bickel's study suffers from a lack of controls for factors that may legitimately influence the parole decision (e.g., major infractions while in prison, criminal history), Bynum (1981; see also Bynum and Paternoster 1984) did control for such factors. Bynum found that non-Indians sentenced to prison received longer sentences than did Indians. But, if whites are granted probation while Indians are incarcerated for similar offenses, then the short(er) term of incarceration for Indians would actually reflect harsher treatment of Indians. In addition, Indians were less likely to be paroled than non-Indians. This may reflect compensation by parole boards for the prior (judicial) decision to give longer sentences to those whites who were sentenced to prison. Whatever the reason, whites were released when they had served shorter parts of their sentences than Indians.

In sum, most of the researchers cited in this review conclude by posing the possibility of a funnelling effect whereby Indians may be more likely than non-Indians to be funnelled through the system as a consequence of police officers' decisions about whom to arrest; prosecutors' decisions on whether to bring a case to court and what charges to file; judges' decisions to sentence an offender to probation or prison; and parole officials' decisions to release or retain a prisoner. Bynum and Paternoster (1984) further suggest that the differences in what they call "frontstage" (sentencing) and "backstage" (parole) decisions could be indicative of discrimination.

Explanations for the Harsh Treatment of Indians

Various explanations for the harsh treatment of Indians have been suggested. They center around racist labeling and stereotyping of Indian defendants; paternalism; and cultural differences such as language, dress, and demeanor. As a whole, these explanations suggest the importance of how non-Indian actors in the criminal justice system perceive the attitude of Indian defendants towards the court and legal officials.

Racist Stereotyping and Labelling. Racist, negative stereotyping and labeling have contributed to the unequal treatment of American Indians in the judicial system. The image of the "drunken Indian" who lives on government handouts is most common (e.g., Stratton 1973; Levy et al. 1969). Some negative stereotyping may be male-oriented. For instance, the racist image of the uncivilized "savage" is male-oriented. Indian women may fare better in the non-Indian criminal justice system than their male counterparts as a consequence.

Stratton (1973) explains the high arrest rate of Indians for alcohol-related offenses in New Mexico as resulting, at least in part, from a combination of blatant discrimination against Indians, a perception of Indians as "outsiders," and paternalism on the part of the police. Thus, Indians were seen as outsiders from the community, coming off their reservations only to get alcohol. While whites in the community who got drunk could call on the police for a ride home, Indians who got drunk were arrested. Furthermore, the police force was composed mostly of Spanish-speaking and Anglo males, resulting in language as well as cultural differences between the Indian "outsiders" and those policing the community.

Bynum (1981) and Bynum and Paternoster (1984) suggest that the inmate's appearance, demeanor, and perceived attitude may be determining factors in parole decisions. If Indians are perceived by members of their parole boards as having inadequate community support *as defined by non-Indians* (e.g., poor prospects for employment or unstable living arrangements), this may account for the harsher treatment of Indians.

Paternalism. Indians have been given longer sentences because the court considered jails preferable to what they saw as negative conditions on the reservation. Stratton (1973) notes a paternalistic attitude on the part of the police. The police in that study felt that locking up drunken Indians was the best thing they could do for them, viewing the opportunity to sober them up and give them a meal as rehabilitative.

Language and Cultural Factors. Language and cultural differences are also critical factors in court proceedings. A number of courts in areas with large Indian populations are beginning to utilize interpreters to assist in the court proceedings. Yet even when interpreters are provided, it may be very difficult for Indian defendants to understand the proceedings if the native language does not have words for the legal concepts invoked by the court (Weber 1982). Because of their religious beliefs and traditions, many Indian men continue to wear their hair long. This could create negative perceptions by non-Indian officials both in the educational system and the criminal justice system.

The literature is replete with references to the impact of defendants' demeanors and attitudes before justice system officials (Bynum and Paternoster 1984; Feimer et al. 1990; Pommersheim and Wise 1989; Hall and Simkus 1975; Weber 1982). Indian cultures are characterized by behaviors and attitudes which are different from those found in the dominant culture. For example, maintaining eye contact with someone while engaged in conversation is a sign of respect and honesty in the dominant culture. Indian defendants who do not look directly at the judge may be presumed to be guilty or disrespectful, thus evidencing a "bad attitude" (Hall and Simkus 1975). This may be a very incorrect reading of the Indian defendant, however, since in some Indian cultures eye contact is seen as disrespectful. Thus, legal officials may come to the opposite conclusion from that which is true if they use one cultural code (i.e., the dominant code which says avoidance of eye contact indicates deceit or lack of respect) to interpret a different cultural code (i.e., avoidance of eye contact as a sign of respect).

Cultural variation among Indian tribes and differing relations with non-Indians in the larger community are also likely to create differences in court officials' perceptions of Indians. In the example above, only some tribes avoid eye contact as an indicator of respect. Depending on the individual's tribal background, she or he could either appear too aggressive or too quiet. Plains tribes (e.g., Sioux) tend to be more aggressive and assertive in demeanor, in contrast to members of some Southwestern tribes (e.g., Pueblos, Navajos, Hopi, Pima), who are typically more reserved. Consequently, a Plains Indian may be viewed by police and court officials as a threat to the community, while a Southwestern Indian may be viewed as sullen and unrepentant.

Furthermore, on-reservation crimes are likely to be between Indians while off-reservation crimes, in contrast, may involve non-Indian victims. As a consequence of devaluation of Indian victims, on-reservation crimes may be viewed as less serious than off-reservation crimes. Also, crimes that cross racial boundaries may be perceived as more threatening to mainstream society, resulting in the incarceration of the Indian offender (Hall and Simkus 1975; Bynum and Paternoster 1984).

Finally, Peak and Spencer (1987) emphasize the need for increased attention to on-reservation problems of poverty, unemployment, alcoholism, and drug abuse. The over-representation of Indians among alcohol-related arrests and the incidence of violence between Indians are issues requiring more research.

Problems in Studying the Involvement of Indians in the U.S. and Tribal Legal Systems

A serious problem in studies of Indians and the U.S. criminal justice system is the identification of who is and who is not an Indian. As Zatz (1987:82) has noted, the coding of race or ethnicity in court data is often unclear and inconsistent. Sometimes defendants are asked to self-define their ethnicity; other times the determination is made by police, court, or prison officials based on language, surname, or physical appearance. It is difficult to separate American Indians from members of other ethnic groups by surname since many Indians have Spanish or English surnames. Moreover, in the Southwest, there may be little difference in physical appearance between American Indians and persons of Mexican (or perhaps more appropriately, Mexican-Indian) ancestry.

In addition, people who claim to be American Indian may not have any tribal affiliation. This is one of the problems the census bureau is confronted with in their attempt to get an accurate count of the population by race. According to the U.S. Bureau of the Census (1991), since 1960 the American Indian population has tripled. It is exceedingly unlikely that this marked increase can be attributed to new births of Indians. Alternative explanations center on prior census undercounts, improved data collection efforts by the Census Bureau (e.g., hiring Indians as census-enumerators within their communities), and an increased number of people defining themselves as Indians (Passel and Berman 1986; Lujan 1990b). For centuries it was unpopular to be identified as an American Indian. However, beginning in the 1960s and continuing through the 1990 census, it has become trendy, and economically beneficial, to claim Indian ancestry.

Access to Indian communities is another obstacle to studying Indians and the criminal justice system. Tribes have been hesitant to allow community-wide surveys on the reservation due to the insensitive and exploitive manner of many early social scientists. Recently, this suspicion toward social scientists conducting research on reservations has decreased. This can probably be attributed to the necessity and appreciation by tribes for good research to document their needs and by the fact that social scientists are becoming more responsive and sensitive to tribal culture and to tribal needs (Lujan 1986).

Language and cultural barriers are also serious considerations for obtaining accurate data. To bridge linguistic and cultural gaps, it is important that researchers be culturally sensitive, and even that they speak the language of the tribe. It is common for bilingual respondents to answer a question based on what they feel the interviewer wants to hear rather than on factual information. This may be done out of respect for the person asking the question or politeness, but nevertheless this acquiescence bias will result in inaccurate data.

The literature on American Indians and the criminal justice system suggests an additional problem. That is, operational definitions of theoretical concepts that are based on the dominant society's norms often have little applicability in the Indian cultures. For example, Robbins (1984) attempted to test Hirschi's control theory on a sample of Seminole youths in Florida, finding that the measures of attachment used by Hirschi were culturally incompatible with Seminole norms. As she noted,

> The existence and relevance of these constructs in both Anglo and Indian
> cultures are not in question. Rather, it is the way in which these are
> expressed and the functional significance which they hold for each culture
> that may vary markedly (1984:240).

Conclusions and Implications for Future Research

As this analysis demonstrates, there is a tremendous paucity of research on American Indians and their involvement in the criminal justice system. Moreover, the research that does exist is inconsistent in important ways. This is particularly evident in studies of sentencing decisions. If these voids are to be filled, social science and legal researchers will need to know more about the population under study, including traditional customs, language, the tribal organization; the relationship between the tribe and the federal and state governments; and the tribal legal system.

More accurate coding of Indian identification is also needed. Indian scholars suggest that only those persons who are enrolled in tribes or who can otherwise document tribal affiliation should be coded as Indian. As the discussion above suggests, coding decisions are often made by legal officials on the basis of surname or appearance, resulting in inconsistent categorizations.

It must also be recognized that the paternalism on the part of the federal government towards the American Indian population has led to a loss of cultural identity, including religion, lifestyle, and governance. This loss of cultural identity has been an important factor in creating a wide range of historically persistent social problems including unemployment, substandard housing, lack of education, alcoholism, very high rates of violent death, infant mortality, and death from diseases such as diabetes, influenza, pneumonia, and tuberculosis (Stewart 1964; Kerr 1969; Peak and Spencer 1987). As almost all scholars studying Indians and crime acknowledge, poverty and its correlates are closely related to crime and to the use of incarceration as a means of sanctioning and/or paternalistic efforts to rehabilitate Indian offenders.

At the same time, the portion of the federal budget allocated to Indian affairs is very small. Peak and Spencer (1987:486) estimate that it would buy just one aircraft carrier. As a result, tribes are turning to anything profitable for potential sources of revenue, including gambling. While Indians have received payment for the lands taken from them, they have never been allowed to manage their own affairs and to determine for themselves how to spend that money (Stewart 1964; Peak and Spencer 1987). Future research must specifically address the impact that the loss of material and non-material cultures has had for American Indian populations in the United States.

Finally, we stress the fact that there are important differences amongst Indian peoples, and between the tribal, state, and federal systems. Research on a specific Indian population cannot be generalized to members of other tribes. As has already been discussed, behavior and attitudes vary by cultural groups. Specification of which tribes are examined in a particular piece of research is thus a crucial element in discussions of research methodology.

NOTES

1. This chapter focuses solely on American Indians within the United States. Native peoples
    of Canada and other parts of the Americas are excluded from the analysis due to the
    differing legal and jurisdictional arrangements between tribes in other countries and the
    federal governments of those countries.

2. The Supreme Court held in *Duro v. Reina*, 100 S. Ct. 2053 (1990), that tribal courts did
    not have jurisdiction over Indians who were not members of their particular tribe.
    However, realizing the severe jurisdictional limitations that the Duro decision places on
    tribes, a moratorium was issued on this ruling until September 30, 1991. At the time of
    this writing (April, 1991), American Indian tribes across the nation are lobbying their
    U.S. representatives and senators to make the Duro moratorium permanent.

Ethnic Bias in a Correctional Setting: The Mariel Cubans*

David D. Clark

IN LATE November 1987, Cuban prisoners took over the Federal Detention Center in Oakdale, Louisiana and the Federal Penitentiary in Atlanta, Georgia. These riots resulted in the near complete destruction of the Oakdale facility and severely damaged the Atlanta facility (*Corrections Today* 1988).

Extensive media coverage of these riots focused national attention on the "Cuban Detention Problem." The Cuban prisoners, numbering over two-thousand, were immigrants who had arrived in the United States during the 1980 "Freedom Flotilla." They had been incarcerated in federal facilities since their arrival because it had been determined that they had a history of criminal

*I would like to thank David W. Aziz for his comments on this manuscript.

113

activities and mental health problems in Cuba and were, therefore, excludable aliens under U.S. Immigration Law and subject to deportation (Federal Bureau of Prisons 1988).

Typically, such detention is short term preventive detention designed to insure control over aliens until they can be deported. However, in the case of the Cubans, deportation did not occur quickly. At the time of the riots, most of the detainees had been incarcerated for seven years (Bosarge 1987). This long term detention was the direct result of the inability of United States Government officials to work out and execute a repatriation agreement with the government of Cuba. Consequently, the detainees found themselves in a state of limbo in which they could be detained until deported, but since deportation arrangements were at best uncertain, the length of their detention was indefinite (Klimko 1986; Federal Bureau of Prisons 1988).

This situation has been described by one U.S. Representative as a mockery of American Justice (Washington Crime News Service 1988b). Private social assistance groups involved with the Cuban detainee problem were also highly critical of the American Government's handling of the Cuban problem (DiMarzio 1988). Given such negative appraisals of the treatment of the Cuban detainees, the question of biased governmental treatment of the Cubans has been raised (Washington Crime News Service 1988b). The purpose of the present chapter is to examine the Cuban detention problem in relation to the issue of ethnic bias in a correctional setting.

Bias, Mariel Cubans and Social Control

For purposes of this discussion, the term "bias" is defined as the unequal treatment of one social group relative to the treatment of other social groups by a government or agents of a government. This definition implies that biased treatment of a social group is the direct result of official action.

In 1980, the largest Cuban migration to the United States took place between the months of April and October. These Cuban immigrants have come to be known as the "Mariel" Cubans. As an ethnic group, they can be described as Hispanic and relatively homogeneous; sharing a common homeland, language, and cultural heritage, as well as similar social, economic, and political histories unique to post-revolutionary Cuba (Fernandez 1982).

Cuban migration to the United States is a relatively recent phenomenon, beginning essentially with Fidel Castro's rise to power in 1959 (Portes and Bach 1985). Immediately following the Revolution, supporters of the former government sought and were granted political asylum in America. They viewed their presence in America as a temporary exile while they developed support for a retaking of Cuba. After the ill-fated Bay of Pigs invasion in 1962, Cuban presence in America took on a permanent nature (Clark 1975).

Since 1959, Cuban migration to the United States has taken place in several waves. The United States government welcomed these new immigrants and established a Cuban refugee center in Miami, Florida to assist the new arrivals with the formalities of immigration processing and provide financial as well as other support services. Although these Cuban immigrants were not formally defined as such, they were generally viewed as political refugees thereby justifying the development of special processing and financial support structures (Pedraza-Bailey 1985; Boswell and Curtis 1984).

As a result of government policies at the federal, state, and local levels, a fairly cohesive Cuban-American community emerged that served as a support group for newly arriving Cuban immigrants. Moreover, in each of the migration waves preceding the Mariel Exodus, the American Government assumed a proactive role in the development of orderly transportation and processing procedures with the Cuban Government. In sum, prior to the Mariel Exodus, Cuban migration to the United States was supported by a formal policy of the American Government that provided both financial and resettlement assistance (Pedraza-Bailey 1985).

The resettlement experiences of Mariel Cubans, however, was not as positive as were the experiences of previous Cuban immigrants. Problems of sponsorship, employment, and an unstable political relationship between the Cuban and American governments plagued the Mariels from the beginning (DiMarzio 1988; Portes et al. 1985). The financial and resettlement assistance that had been a long standing policy of the American Government was simply not as strong as it was for earlier Cuban immigrants (Portes and Stepick 1985). Therefore, in general, the treatment of the Mariels as a group was biased relative to the treatment of other Cuban immigrants.

This lack of public policy support was partially the result of an economic recession which had two effects. First, it decreased public support for allowing large numbers of immigrants into the country (Bach 1980). Second, the faltering economy served to link economic support for Cuban immigrants with the need to provide support for other immigrant groups. The amount of financial resources required for such an effort was considered to be prohibitive (Clark et al. 1981).

Another problem unique to the Mariel migration was that a small proportion of the Mariel group consisted of persons with histories of criminal convictions and mental illness. It was this subgroup of Mariels that received a considerable amount of attention in the popular media and presented a social control dilemma for the United States (Hunt 1980; *Time* 1981).

The social control problem created by the criminal and mentally ill Mariels concerned balancing individual liberty interests with the government's duty to protect the community. This problem arose because government options were limited by circumstances over which it either had no control or had lost control (Boswell and Curtis 1984).

Under normal conditions, the problem could have been avoided in two ways. First, under U.S. Immigration Law, criminals and the mentally ill are defined as excludable aliens, and would not be granted visas allowing them to enter the United States legally. They would have been screened in Cuba and most likely denied permission to come to the United States (Carliner 1977). In the Mariel Exodus, however, the American Government was unable to screen the immigrants prior to their departure from Cuba. Second, had criminals and the mentally ill illegally entered the United States, they probably would have been deported back to Cuba upon apprehension by the U.S. Immigration and Naturalization Service following an administrative review (Carliner 1977). This was not an option during the Mariel Exodus because there was no repatriation agreement with Cuba that would allow for the return of the criminals and mentally ill. Therefore, the criminals and mentally ill who entered during the Mariel migration would remain in America until a repatriation agreement could be signed with Cuba. Given that relations between the United States and Cuba were unstable, it was unlikely that a repatriation agreement would be signed anytime soon.

Consequently, the American Government had to decide what to do with a potentially dangerous group of individuals. Incarceration was chosen because it would effectively neutralize their threat to society, and protect the safety interests of the community (Federal Bureau of Prisons 1988). Because these individuals had not been convicted of a crime in the United States, their incarceration was civil in nature, and amounted to preventive detention. Moreover, because repatriation was an unlikely option for the foreseeable future, the duration of incarceration of these Mariels was indefinite (Klimko 1986; DiMarzio 1988).

The Development of Political and Economic Constraints

To better understand the problem facing the American Government, it is useful to examine both the origins and number of Mariel refugees involved in the flotilla. The political nature of the migration coupled with its size and composition placed constraints on the ability of the American Government to control the situation and strained social control mechanisms designed to deal with immigration matters.

The Origin of the Mariel Migration. The Mariel Exodus began simply enough when a small group of Cubans seeking political asylum drove a bus through the main gate of the Peruvian Embassy in Havana, Cuba on March 28,

1980 (Nichols 1982). During the forced entry through the Embassy gate, Cuban guards stationed outside of the Embassy opened fire on the bus. One of the bullets ricocheted off of the bus and killed a soldier. The Cuban government asked the Peruvian Embassy to extradite the gate crashing Cubans so they could be prosecuted. Instead, the Peruvians granted the refugees political asylum, thereby infuriating the Castro regime (Clark et al. 1981).

In response, suspecting that as many as a few hundred additional dissidents would also seek political asylum at the Peruvian Embassy if given the chance, the Cuban Government publicly announced the withdrawal of its military guard from the front of the Embassy. This action was designed to overcrowd the Embassy compound thereby creating severe logistical problems for the Embassy (e.g., food, water, sanitation, etc.) while publicly embarrassing the Peruvians (Fernandez and Narvaez 1987).

However, the Castro government grossly underestimated the number of people that would take advantage of the situation at the Peruvian Embassy. Within twenty-four hours, approximately 11,000 Cubans had entered the compound and requested asylum. Consequently, rather than placing the Peruvian government in an embarrassing position, Castro unwittingly placed himself in the unenviable position of exposing to the world the extent of the political and economic dissatisfaction that existed in Cuba (Clark et al. 1981). Castro's immediate reaction was to label the would-be exiles taking refuge in the Peruvian Embassy as social scum that Cuba would be happy to get rid of (Azicri 1981-1982). Despite initial stalling by the Cuban Government, international pressure forced Castro to allow the departure of the 11,000 asylees. Contrary to Castro's assertions, most of the asylees were actually working class people, not socioeconomic marginals (Bach et al. 1981-1982). This presented another potentially embarrassing situation for Castro. When these asylees arrived in other Latin American countries, it would become apparent that they were not social misfits at all. Rather, they were precisely the people that the Cuban Revolution was supposed to help. Therefore, in an effort to redirect world attention, Castro offered Cuban-Americans an opportunity to come to Cuba and pick up their relatives (Boswell and Curtis 1984).

The point of departure for Cubans wishing to leave for the United States was a small port about 20 miles west of Havana called Mariel. It is from this port that the Mariel Exodus derived its name. Unlike prior waves of Cuban migration to the United States, the Mariel Exodus was not coordinated between the Cuban and American governments (Pedraza-Bailey 1985). Rather, large numbers of Cuban-Americans bought, rented, and hired boats to make the trip to Mariel to pick up their relatives. This was not done with the approval or support of the American Government, thus the Cuban-Americans were risking criminal prosecution by bringing illegal aliens into the United States (Hunt 1980).

Therefore, contrary to formal diplomatic procedure, the individuals leaving Cuba had not been interviewed by U.S. State Department personnel prior to their departure, nor were they granted entry visas that would allow them to legally enter the United States (Bach 1980; Bach et al. 1981-1982). Normally, the investigations conducted as part of the visa granting process are an initial step in determining whether potential immigrants and refugees are admissible under the U.S. Immigration Law. The departure from standard procedure meant that persons who might normally be denied permission to enter the United States could not be investigated until they arrived (U.S. Immigration and Naturalization Service 1987; Steel 1985).

Castro used this opportunity to rid Cuba of its anti-social elements and social burdens. He included in the boatlift individuals who had served or were serving prison terms (for either political or criminal offenses), individuals who had histories of mental illness, and, according to some reports, even lepers (Boswell and Curtis 1984; Pedraza-Bailey 1985). Consequently, it was not uncommon for Cuban-Americans to be forced to take prisoners, or the mentally or physically ill in their boats as a condition for being allowed to take the relatives they initially came to retrieve (Clark et al. 1981).

It is clear that the political maneuvers of the Cuban Government precluded any United States involvement in screening potential immigrants and resulted in the inclusion of individuals who would likely have been excluded under normal processing conditions. In addition, events proceeded so rapidly that the American Government was unaware of the size or composition of the flotilla. Therefore, the need for alternate screening and processing strategies was not known until the Mariels began to arrive in southern Florida (Bach 1980).

The Size and Composition of the Migration. Between the months of April and October 1980, an estimated 124,779 Cubans entered the United States as part of the Mariel Exodus. Official Department of State statistics indicate that the number of monthly arrivals were as follows: April, 7,655; May, 86,488; June, 20,800; July, 2,629; August, 3,939; September, 3,258; and October, 10 (Clark et al. 1981).

To put these figures in perspective, it has been estimated that approximately one percent of the total Cuban population fled Cuba via the Mariel boatlift (Boswell and Curtis 1984). Moreover, the largest Cuban migration prior to the Mariel Exodus occurred in 1962, when the annual migration was estimated to have been 73,632 people (Clark et al. 1981). Therefore, during the month of May, 1980, more Cuban immigrants entered the United States than in any preceding year (Portes et al. 1985).

The size of this migration had serious economic implications for the United

States Government. For example, one of the first policy dilemma's facing the Carter administration at the early stages of the boatlift concerned the immigration status of the immigrants. Since they had not been preinspected by the U.S. State Department and no visas had been granted, the Cubans could not legally enter the United States. If they did enter the United States under these conditions, their legal status would be that of illegal alien and they would be subject to deportation (Steel 1985; Fragomen et al. 1989).

The legal status of the Cuban immigrants, therefore, spawned a difficult political question. One option was to avoid the problem altogether and turn them away upon arrival; not permitting them to enter the United States. In fact, this was the intended effect of the naval blockade ordered by President Carter. However, since they could not return to Cuba, and no other country offered to accept them, turning them away in their overcrowded boats was a potential death sentence. For this reason, and because the United States Coast Guard was informally assisting flotilla boats in distress, the blockade option was dropped (Clark et al. 1981).

On the other hand, if President Carter chose to classify the Cubans as refugees under the 1980 Refugee Act (i.e., immigrants seeking political asylum as opposed to economic opportunity), then the Cubans would be entitled to financial refugee assistance from the federal government (Peterson 1984). Unfortunately, the American Government felt that assigning the refugee classification would be a dangerous precedent to set given the size of the migration. Simply stated, the federal government did not want to encourage large scale migrations from other countries (Bach 1980).

The refugee classification was also a dangerous precedent to set for another reason. The United States was still suffering the effects of a recession and public support for the provision of economic assistance to immigrants was weak at best (Bach et al. 1981-1982). In addition, boatloads of Haitian immigrants had also been arriving in southern Florida around this time (*Time* 1981; Portes and Stepick 1985). Granting refugee status to one group and not the other would be difficult to justify. Moreover, the federal government appeared to be unwilling to commit itself to the economic responsibility that would result from proclaiming either or both of the groups as refugees. Therefore, economic constraints influenced the political decision to classify the Mariels as parolees as opposed to refugees (Bach 1980; Violet 1990).

Under U.S. immigration law, parole status is a temporary admission status granted to aliens who appear to be otherwise inadmissible (U.S. Immigration and Naturalization Service 1987). This was not, however, the first time that parole status was applied to Cuban immigrants. Between 1959 and 1974 approximately two-thirds of the 640,237 Cuban immigrants who entered the United States did so under parole status (Clark 1975). Therefore, given this precedent and the successful adjustment of previous Cuban immigrants, the assignment of parole status by itself did not involve biased treatment of the Mariels (Bach 1980). However, the parole status decision was a product of a crisis management approach. The effect of the decision was economic, and it was the failure of the federal government to accept economic responsibility as it did for previous Cuban immigrants that represented biased treatment of the Mariels relative to those earlier immigrants (Pedraza-Bailey 1981-1982).

Also, before the size of the flotilla was known, existing support organizations assumed responsibility for assisting in the processing and settling of the immigrants. For example, the initial group of Cuban exiles arriving in southern Florida from the port of Mariel were assisted by local government agencies (Dade County and the cities of Miami and Hialeah), volunteers from the Cuban-American community, the Federal Cuban Refugee Center, and other volunteer agencies (Clark et al. 1981). The Cuban Refugee Emergency Center in Coral Gables, Florida registered approximately 2,000 of the first Mariel Cubans to reach the United States. Many of the 2,000 refugees had been involved in the incident at the Peruvian Embassy (Bach 1980; Bach et al. 1981-1982). Had the size of the flotilla been in the thousands rather than exceeding one hundred thousand, these processing procedures would have probably sufficed.

However, in May 1980, as the magnitude of the boatlift was becoming apparent, the Federal government took over the operation of refugee reception. The agency given the task of directing the flow of incoming refugees was the Federal Emergency Management Agency (FEMA). Under FEMA's direction, arriving Mariels were detained in newly established processing centers. The purpose of this administrative detention was to screen, interview, register and place the Cubans with willing sponsors in the community (Clark et al. 1981).

Most of the refugees were admitted into the United States following a brief detention and initial screening in government processing camps. However, there was a group of hard-to-sponsor Mariels whose detention was long-term (Fernandez 1984). In addition, the U.S. Immigration and Naturalization Service (INS) refused to admit approximately two-thousand Mariels, deeming them unfit due to mental illness or criminal records (Washington Crime News Services 1988a). This number was probably an underestimate for two reasons. First, the screening questions posed by INS relied upon self-report data, and the veracity of the responses of criminals and the mentally ill is questionable (Nichols 1982). Second, serious crimes were reportedly committed by Mariels already released into American communities. On the basis of these reports a contrasting estimate offered by some placed the number of criminals at 5,000 (Boswell and Curtis 1984).

Further support for the allegation that the number of criminals involved in the Mariel Exodus was underestimated by federal officials comes from estimates of the number of Mariels under custody in state prison facilities. For example, in February 1983, the state of Florida reported that 281 Mariel Cubans incarcerated in the Florida Department of Corrections and 1,079 Mariels were under state probation supervision in Dade and Broward counties (Florida Department of Corrections 1983). By federal fiscal year 1990, there were 710 Mariel Cubans incarcerated in Florida's State Department of Corrections (Bureau of Justice Assistance 1990).

In addition, on a national level, recent figures indicate that for federal fiscal year 1988-1989 there were 2,358 INS verified Mariel Cubans in state correctional facilities across the United States. In federal fiscal year 1989-1990, the number had risen to 2,483 (Bureau of Justice Assistance 1990). While it must be noted that the state and federal figures regarding criminal Mariels do not cover the exact same time periods, the sum of these two numbers is more than twice the number of Mariels originally denied admission to the United States.

The actual number of criminals included in the Mariel migration, therefore, ranged between one-and-a-half and four percent of all Mariels entering the United States (Fernandez 1981-1982; recent account put the figure at ten to twelve percent; see: Hallum and Lynn 1990:26). While this percentage is relatively small, it must be remembered that this population sub-group required a greater amount of processing resources than non-criminals because of the potential threat its members posed to the community (Washington Crime News Services 1988c). Furthermore, if one focuses on the raw numbers, it would take three to four large (e.g., 1,500 bed) prison facilities to incarcerate 5,000 criminals without overcrowding each facility. Consequently, a strategy for dealing with this unique sub-group had to be developed.

Political and Economic Pressures and the
Rise of Crisis Management

The discussion to this point has shown that the inability of the United States Government to control the size and composition of the Mariel migration led to the collapse of established processing procedures. The magnitude of the flotilla gave rise to the decision to use short-term administrative (preventive) detention to facilitate the screening, interviewing, registering, and community placement of the Mariels. In addition, approximately 2,000 Mariels were identified as either criminals or mentally ill and were to remain in federal custody indefinitely.

Normally, immigrants subject to preventive detention are placed in INS detention centers. However, INS detention centers are not typically designed to handle either large numbers of detainees, or high security risk detainees. Since both of these attributes were characteristics of deportable Mariels, the use of federal correctional facilities was necessary. Thus, even though the Mariel detention was civil in nature, the Cubans were incarcerated in prison facilities (Federal Bureau of Prisons 1988).

Given the extensive publicity of the types of crimes that Mariels released into the community had committed (e.g., murder, rape, robbery), the decision to further detain identified criminals was certainly consistent with the social control goals of the INS (Nowicki 1987). However, the investigation, charging, and administrative review process associated with ordering an alien to be deported was less than expeditious in the case of the Mariels (Klimko 1986).

In 1981, the Federal Bureau of Prisons (FBOP) consolidated most of the detainees at the maximum security Federal Penitentiary in Atlanta, Georgia. This consolidation move was done for two reasons. First, it was the American Government's intention to deport the detainees as soon as possible, and consolidating them would facilitate the organization of a large scale deportation effort. Second, it was a tacit admission that the detention of the Mariels might be anything but short term (Federal Bureau of Prisons 1988).

The consolidation decision also indicated that, given the dangerousness of some of the detainees, government officials felt it wise to assume a prison management perspective with regard to the Mariel incarceration. Consolidation, from a prison management perspective, was based on the theory that more effective management of the "Marielitos" could be achieved by dealing with them as a homogeneous group as opposed to intermingling them among the Federal criminal population (Washington Crime News Services 1988a). At first glance, the rationale for consolidation appears reasonable. However, by the mid-1980s the Atlanta prison was overcrowded. In addition to the Cubans awaiting INS decisions regarding their immigration status, Marielito's who had been convicted of criminal offenses in states and localities were being sent to the Atlanta Penitentiary (see Florida Department of Corrections 1983). Moreover, the deteriorating physical condition of the aging penitentiary raised questions concerning the conditions under which the Mariels were being confined (Klimko 1986).

In response to overcrowding problems in Atlanta, FBOP and INS decided to use the Federal Alien Detention Center in Oakdale, Louisiana exclusively for Cubans. In 1986, FBOP transferred 987 low security level Cuban inmates from the prison in Atlanta to the detention center in Oakdale. This left approximately 1,400 Cuban detainees in the Atlanta Penitentiary. In addition to the Cubans, a small cadre of American prisoners were also assigned to both facilities to perform maintenance and administrative work (Federal Bureau of Prisons 1988).

In the meantime, administrative review processes that determined immigration status for individual Mariels was slow moving (Klimko 1986). The Mariels were, in essence, caught in a legal limbo. As parolees, they could be administratively detained for up to a year at a time. However, many had already been incarcerated for at least six years (Smaka et al. 1983).

Moreover, the United States had repeatedly tried to work out a repatriation agreement with the Cuban Government with varying degrees of success. Thus, even if a Mariel was ordered deported by an administrative judge, they were likely to be incarcerated until a repatriation agreement could be agreed upon. Consequently, Mariels with deportation orders still faced indefinite incarceration (Washington Crime News Services 1988c).

In addition to an uncertain length of confinement, conditions of confinement were an important issue at the Atlanta Penitentiary. Overcrowding led to a small disturbance in November 1984, when 50 Cuban prisoners took over a cell block and started a fire. The siege ended without injury following six hours of negotiations. However, after order was restored, the inmates were locked down for twenty-four hours a day for the next eighteen months (Klimko 1986; Federal Bureau of Prisons 1988).

It is important to note that the Atlanta Penitentiary was an aging structure and slated to close prior to the advent of the Mariel problem (Klimko 1986). The prison was overcrowded even after the transfer of almost 1,000 detainees to the Federal Detention Center at Oakdale, Louisiana because portions of the Atlanta facility were unusable due to construction (Washington Crime News Services 1988a).

The situation reached a critical stage when a repatriation agreement was established with the Cuban Government in November 1987, and the American Government made another questionable decision. The U.S. Attorney General publicly announced the agreement only a few hours after informing the FBOP that repatriation would soon begin. This gave the wardens at Oakdale Federal Detention Center and the Atlanta Prison little time to inform their detainees and to respond to a possible negative reaction (Bosarge 1987).

Moreover, the Federal Government made no special efforts to communicate the terms or implication of the repatriation agreement to the Mariel detainees. This failure to consider the reactions of the Mariels proved to be a major policy blunder on the part of the American Government because the Mariels already perceived their treatment as unfair. Their perception was based upon the indeterminate nature of their confinement as well as the lack of progress with the review of their immigration status (Washington Crime News Services 1988b).

Not only did wardens at Oakdale and Atlanta have little time to develop strategies for dealing with the Mariels' reaction to possible repatriation, they were also constrained by the characteristics of their respective facilities when choosing a response strategy. For example, a typical strategy for dealing with a potential mass disturbance in a prison setting is a lock-down until tensions have subsided (as Atlanta had done in 1984). A lockdown of the entire facility was not a viable strategy in Oakdale, however, because it was a low-medium security facility which housed the inmates in dormitories, not cells. A lockdown under those conditions would have placed detention center staff in jeopardy. Nor was this a viable strategy in Atlanta due to ongoing construction and the fact that locking mechanisms did not function on a number of cells (Federal Bureau of Prisons 1988). Consequently, when inmates at Oakdale and Atlanta were informed of the repatriation agreement (November 21, 1987), tensions rose and more than 1,000 Cubans took control of the Federal Detention Center at Oakdale. Efforts to negotiate with the detainees (November 22) failed to produce any results. On November 23, approximately 1,400 Cubans took over the Federal Penitentiary in Atlanta (*Corrections Today* 1988).

After several days of negotiations with the detainees at both facilities, the crisis was resolved without any deaths. On November 29, the Oakdale detainees ended their siege, while the Atlanta detainees held out until December 3. The product of the negotiations was an eight point agreement that promised to delay deportation and immigration hearings. In essence, the extreme reaction of the detainees not only bought some time, it secured a more thorough and expeditious review of their cases (*Corrections Today* 1988).

Conclusion

The story of the Mariels is both complex and intriguing, involving international politics and several levels of government. It is a story that illustrates the multifaceted nature of social control and the intersection of American civil and criminal legal systems.

The question of whether the detained Mariels were the victims of biased treatment, however, is not a simple one to answer. The sheer magnitude of the flotilla overwhelmed the existing immigration processing mechanisms. Since any immigrant must be inspected by the INS at the port of their arrival, the size of the migration made short term detention unavoidable and would likely have been applied to any immigrant group regardless of their country of origin. In fact, because INS processing relied upon self-report data, it is likely that a number of individuals with criminal histories were released into the community before INS decided to deny release to the 2,000 excludables.

According to the material reviewed above, the detention of "dangerous" Mariels does not seem to constitute bias in itself. Preventive detention is a common INS practice, and foreign nationals other than Cubans have been detained pending deportation. The indeterminate nature of the confinement was due to the unstable political relationship between the United States and Cuba. Therefore, the Mariels were not singled out for detention. While the indeterminate nature of the Mariel confinement appears to be biased treatment on its face, it was simply a by-product of the existing international political atmosphere. The Mariel detention does, however, illustrate the difficulty in balancing individual liberty interests with concerns for protecting the community.

The overcrowded conditions in which Mariels were held is a problem that has plagued American correctional systems at all levels of government throughout the 1980s (Baro 1988). Therefore, the conditions of confinement did not constitute a biased treatment of Cubans, since other groups had been subjected to the same conditions. That is not to say that poor conditions of imprisonment cannot be a form of biased treatment; it simply means that the Cubans as an ethnic group were not singled out in terms of that treatment.

In sum, while the experiences of incarcerated Mariels is a situation that the American Government should seek to avoid in the future, it does not appear to be classifiable as ethnic bias. It is more appropriate to describe the Mariel experience as a classic example of how ineffective bureaucracies can be when dealing with problems that are relatively rare events. But one has to wonder whether a similar scenario would have occurred if the immigrants were white-anglos.

The consequences of poor management do not mitigate the very real harm that the Mariels perceived to be thrust upon them, nor does it justify the overcrowded conditions that they actually experienced. Though a product of several factors, this ethnic group was exposed to and experienced unequal treatment. However, using the definition of bias presented above, it does not appear that the Mariels were the victims of overt ethnic bias.

It may be, however, that detention of immigrants, and even imprisonment itself is a biased form of social control; that is, imprisonment as a form of social control is most likely to be used on certain racial, ethnic or class groups. Future research should address this question further by examining the treatment of Mariels relative to other ethnic and racial immigrant groups. In addition, it is possible that bias exists in the differential treatment of sub-populations (either racial or ethnic sub-divisions) within the Mariel population. Thus, while this general analysis of the treatment of the Mariels reveals little in the way of bias, more specific and probing investigations may uncover more subtle forms of bias.

Racial Codes in Prison Culture: Snapshots in Black and White*

Jim Thomas

CULTURALLY IMPOSED categories contain political meanings and codes that shape access to power and privilege. Prison culture reflects the symbols, myths, values and control systems (i.e. the political meanings and codes) found in free society. However, within prison culture certain cultural categories and meanings, especially those tied to race, are more important. Given the context of prison life, the consequences of misunderstanding the role and meaning of race are severe, reward and power systems are more unbalanced, and interpreting race is more complex.

As a cultural category, race provides cues (coded text) that define culturally preferred definitions of social reality and reflect broader forms of social

*I am indebted to Sharon Boehlefeld, Shubie Moore, Ra Rabb Chaka, Alex Neal, Milo Cross, and many others who helped shape the ideas and provided data for this paper.

oppression. The cultural symbols and meaning embedded in race are used in interpretive processes that "make sense" of power relationships. Prison culture is shaped by a priori racial symbols and images that guide behavior, allocate scarce resources, and elevate some groups (whites) to privileged status while relegating others (non-whites) to subordination[1]. It is no secret that racial polarization and tension are facts of prison life (Jacobs 1977, 1983; Carroll 1988). The consequences of this polarization include an asymmetrical system of punishment in which non-whites do harder time than whites. In short, racial codes not only segregate, label and divide and make the prison a racial experience: Racial codes add an additional layer of hardship to the prison sentence by increasing unnecessary suffering.

This chapter describes how race provides cues that shape how prison is experienced. First, I examine race as a code that provides cultural meanings that format prison experiences for both whites and non-whites. Second, the impact of these codes on selected aspects of prison life is used to illustrate how prison metes out greater punishment for non-whites. Finally, I discuss two forms of resistance to racial disparity, gangs and prisoner litigation, and suggest how prisoners can attempt to at least partially alter the power imbalance. My purpose is to describe what prisoner culture signifies for its primary cultural workers—prisoners—and to fill descriptive gaps in current research on images of race in prisons.

The data used in this chapter were drawn from an on-going (1980-1991) study of prison culture employing participant observation, prison visitations, documents, news articles and interviews with prisoners and ex-offenders in Illinois. This study focuses on four Illinois maximum security institutions, which currently house 27 percent of the state's adult inmate population of 28,056. These prisons range in size from 1,300 to 2,600 inmates. Non-whites currently constitute about 71 percent of the state's total prison population. Two of the prisons studied (Pontiac and Stateville), however, are 85 percent non-white while the remaining two are about 70 percent non-white. In the context of this demographic imbalance, the prison experience becomes one laden with racial meanings.

The Semiotics of Race

Cultural cues code complex rules, roles, power relations, language games, control and resistance strategies and coping techniques. Semiotics produces a way to understand the complexity behind racially embedded meanings:

> Semiotics provides a set of assumptions and concepts that permit the systematic analysis of symbolic systems. A sign is something that represents or stands for something else in the mind of someone. A sign is

composed of an expression and a content. The connections made between expressions and content and among signs are mental. For example, a rose is conventionally linked with romance as a content. Smoke is linked to fire, and the American flag to courage. The nature of the link can be indexical, semantic, or iconic (Manning 1989).

Even within the limited ambience of prisons, inmates may not share cultural meanings. Take race for example. One's racial identity is a sign system which "sends off" cues that allocate power and privilege, establish social, political, and other boundaries, shape interactions and serve as an account-generating mechanism to "explain" behavior. Racial differences contribute to differing goals, agendas, orientations toward the past and future, peer-group affiliations, and personal attitudes that guide how prisoners define and participate in the racial environment. In short, culturally proscribed behaviors embedded in the racial identity assigned to people are important because they define ways non-whites and whites compete for power, status and resources in an environment filled with racial tension.

Race as a Metaphor

All knowledge and concepts are metaphoric: they provide clues and mapping techniques for interpreting the social terrain (Brown 1977; Lakoff and Johnson 1980). As part of our social map, metaphors allow us to examine and discuss objects/concepts from several vantage points, employing various images that expand knowledge and understanding. Metaphors provide a focus and a frame that suggest interpretive rules for assigning meaning to the discursive tropes by which we name and pull together meaning (M. Black 1962; Brown 1977; Lakoff and Johnson 1980; Lodge 1988; Manning 1979; Pepper 1948; White 1978).

Prison metaphors convey various images: "warehouses of violence" (Fleisher 1989), bureaucratic "human management systems" (DiIulio 1987; Jacobs 1977), houses of pain and deprivation (Sykes 1958; Johnson and Toch 1988). These metaphors are based on principles of selection and substitution which allow disparate features of an object to be reduced to factors the observer considers salient. Some dissimilar, yet encompassing, image is selected for its similarity to the remaining features of the initial object as a part of this "language game" that provides a way of speaking of the object to be described (e.g., Lodge 1988: 74-77; Manning 1979).

Racially imbued metaphoric images take on the character of social myths by creating accounts, normative judgments and actions directed toward a subordinate culture. In so doing, they reproduce power relations by creating and consolidating icons that reinforce stigma, define societal responses and establish the boundaries between the sacred dominant groups and profane subordinate ones.

Metaphoric images of race are a form of symbolic violence (Bourdieu and Passeron 1977:4) because they arbitrarily impose symbols onto a framework in ways that grotesquely distort the "reality" of what is seen and what is signified. The distortions reflect oppressive power relations that promote the interests of the more powerful "both by its mode of imposition and by its delimitation of what and on whom, it imposes" (Bourdieu and Passeron 1977: 6).

Racial codes that make up prison culture connote and denote status, identity and also allocate various structurally-induced rewards and translate broader social meanings into codes appropriate to prison culture and action. In prisons, for example, the label "nigger" is more than a hostile epithet. It carries connotative conceptual baggage and implications for social interpretation and policy. Race becomes a metaphor that conveys pictures about how prisoners should act in dealing with "the niggers" to whom the images pertain.

When groups coexist in a clearly-defined hierarchy, the culture that emerges entails forms of expression and communication, as well as resistance and accommodation, that are at once complex and primitive. At first glance, race-related behaviors, speech, and other communicative devices may seem dysfunctional, arbitrary or valueless. However, those familiar with these signs can read their meaning and integrate that meaning into an intelligible cognitive map that makes navigating the murky sea of a debilitating culture less difficult.

The Racial Experience: Whites

The cues embedded in race and ethnicity shape the prison experience for whites by providing an identity, behavioral codes, and affective responses that include suspicion, fear or hostility toward non-whites. Whites, especially those isolated from other ethnic cultures, may interpret another's race as a cue that symbolizes the terror of prisons because, in maximum security prisons, whites are likely to be in the minority.

Interactional Experiences of Race. The following narrative of a white prisoner's encounter with a non-white staff member is more than a story of culture shock experienced on the first day in an institution; when reformatted as a metaphor that stands for prison racial culture, the story reveals much about the relationship between race, communication, social control, socialization, fear and ambiguity.

> The young prisoner's introduction to his new culture began poorly. He had been led, alone...to take his first shower in the presence of a correctional officer. He removed his clothes and stepped into the shower....His guard spoke: "Milk down your penis!" Standing naked and cold, the youth

stared at the guard, uncomprehending. Short, muscular, and menacing, the guard continued to watch the...inmate shower, then repeated: "I said milk down your penis!" The youth shuddered, recalling stories...about forced sex in prison. Was this burly Spic...going to "rip him off" [rape] on his first day in this miserable Texas institution?... What should he do? He was Anglo, 17, too cocky for his own good, and very, very frightened. He...assumed that his rep as an armed robber...would provide some status and...respect among the prisoners. He had not considered that staff might consider it a challenge to break a northern "hot-shot." The closest he had ever come to a Hispanic was watching reruns of the "Cisco Kid"....."Milk down my penis?" he thought. "I'm sure as shit not going to beat off for this son of a bitch!" The guard was staring at the prisoner's genitals; the youth stared back. The guard advanced. In the argot of contemporary social theorists, there were dysfunctional gaps in the information feedback loops...."This," he thought, "is bad karma." He decided to bluff it out and forced a weak laugh: "Milk down my penis? What do you mean?" (Narrator's diary, undated, non-Illinois).

The multiple messages created by the two authors in this text are compounded by racial suspicion. Racial identity distorts the "meaning of the message" that either person intends to convey and illustrates how formatting racial cues and inferring corresponding meanings occurs. It begins with a series of communicative acts shaped by "objective" structural influences (e.g., institutional rules) over which the participants have little or no control, but are carried out by reciprocal misunderstandings that generate a game of compliance or resistance.

As a constitutive format, the participants recreate themselves and each other by cultural frames of reference, in this case, those of ethnicity. The guard "sent" messages interpreted as sexually threatening; to avoid an unpleasant denouement, the prisoner made a quick reading, influenced by ethnic stereotypes, and selected from a repertoire of appropriate actions. The youth faced an uneasy choice between two antithetical problems: Assuming racial meaning where none existed, or ignoring it if present.

The narrative reveals distrust and suspicion between members of two seemingly alien cultures. Would, for example, the youth be as suspicious of the intentions of another Anglo? (He claimed not). Would the officer be as forward with another Hispanic or non-white prisoner? The latent racist undertones of an "all spics are fags" ideology creeps in and becomes reinforced, regardless of the outcome of the situation. Here, race becomes a symbol for a set of images connoting sexual aggression, suspicion, potential danger, fear and uncertainty. In the absence of alternative cues, race becomes the primary organizing metaphor for meaning and action that intensified the new inmate's initial experience of this threatening new culture. His story illustrates how racial dynamics shape the prison experience.

In every encounter between members of different racial groups, whether prisoners or staff, the encounter is recoded: new layers are added which consist of cues and additional possible meanings that must be correctly "read-off" if the prison experience is to proceed with minimal problems. Each encounter also intensifies the otherness that separates various groups. For whites, racial identity promotes white unity by conferring a set of hostile meanings upon non-whites. These meanings provide a code which devalues the stigmatized group through a hostile discourse that separates "decent criminals" from presumably indecent ones, as the following excerpt demonstrates:

> Generally, blacks create the biggest problem. As a group they are uneducated, and they have no respect for the rights of others. They are the predators...and they are cowards. The only way they exist is by the gang. Alone, all they have is a big mouth, and no common sense. In many cases the Puerto Ricans are worse than the blacks. They are noise makers from morning to night. The ideal solution would be for all the Latinos in this country to swim south with a nigger under each arm...then shoot them like sharks.

The racial identity expressed in such views polarizes prisoners by creating a series of stigmatizing metaphors (e.g., "animalistic, "social misfits," "targets of violence") and by providing a rhetorical strategy that justifies continued hostility and degradation rituals of harassment, stigma, and exclusion. These metaphors translate symbols into "literals" that provide myths about both prison life and other prisoners. These may influence how new white inmates respond to their initial immersion in the culture. For example, on arriving at a maximum security institution, many whites attempt to move into protective custody—not because they are more vulnerable, but because of their self-perceived inability to move smoothly within the "alien" culture. For example, one small white prisoner, fearing for his safety but unwilling to be locked-up in protective custody, began his second day in Stateville by assaulting a black prisoner with a chair:

> ...I had already made up my mind that if I got a chance to hit somebody, either with a weapon, or with something, this was what I was going to do....I'd made my mind up that the only way I was going to send out an effective message was to act like a "crazy white boy" which I had been instructed to act like in the county jails, by...two black guys who had been in Stateville before....[T]hey told me this is the effective way to deal with pressure for sex....[T]here was a guy...sitting...at a table, just minding his own business. I'd never talked to the guy before, never saw him before,

didn't know who he was. He was just sitting there....And there was a chair there,...and I just picked up the chair and hit him in the head. The officer was surprised, he ran over — and I didn't hurt him. I knocked him off the chair, and he's on the floor...looking up, and he said, "God damn, what the fuck," and the officer grabbed me and said, "what's wrong with you?" I didn't say anything, just stood there.

Another white explained how he successfully avoided being caught up in victimization or polarizing behavior when he was placed in a large cell with eleven black inmates. He was older than his cell-mates, which gave him a limited amount of respect, and maintained tranquility either by avoiding taking sides or by pitting the gang members against each other.

However damaging these individual reactions are, the most devastating consequence of racial polarization lies in the potential for violence that occurs when individual hostilities are translated into group combat with race providing the code that demarcates the combatants. One white prisoner explained how an attack on his brother became generalized into a potentially violent racial incident when he was caught with a homemade bomb that he intended to use in an attack:

> JT: What were you going to do with [the bomb]?
> MA: Well, it's a long story...There was a bunch of black guys on the tier that were trying to fuck [my brother].... [T]hey ran into his room, and threw him on the bed.... He fought them off, but I was really mad, you know? And they all used to hang around by the phone over there, so I just put together a little thing, and I was going to toss it over there, and when they all started scrambling, I was going to start knocking them out, you know what I mean? I was going to go for it. That was it. Bang. I ain't about to take that shit, you know? Well, they caught me before this happened....they knew there was some tension on the floor, because a couple of black guys were starting to make knives,...carry knives around...and stuff like that... And they knew that I was mad and gonna do something....

Staff can further exacerbate volatile situations with racial slurs or verbal harassment. In one prison, for example, death row inmates filed numerous complaints with a prison monitoring agency complaining of racial taunting; staff assigned to the general population commonly refer to the "niggers" and made little effort to hide their animosity. Three prison monitors barely averted a brawl when it became known they were prison reformers[2]. A crowd of about 15 guards began insulting them, complaining of "outside nigger lovers," and threatening violence.

Although whites do not bear the brunt of racial oppression, it is clear from the discussion above that it is distorted racial meanings which feed suspicion, violence and other forms of polarization. These meanings, which keep inmates from recognizing mutual interests, are as debilitating for whites as for non-whites. Non-whites, by contrast, are doubly victimized. Not only are they subject to cultural discrimination, but more subtly, they are also victims of structural consequences that occur along racial lines.

The Racial Experience: Non-Whites

The racial experience of non-whites has been documented well enough (Carroll 1988, 1977a, 1977b; Colvin 1981, 1982; Jackson 1970; Jacobs 1977, 1978) so that only a few examples suffice to illustrate their subordinate status.

Interactional Experiences. Despite the fact that non-whites may be the majority, racial abuse permeates their prison experience in both dramatic and subtle ways. For example, one black activist inmate complained that someone with access to keys, presumably guards, entered his locked cell and painted racial epithets and Ku Klux Klan messages on the walls in what he interpreted as a "message" intended to intimate him into compliance with institutional white "norms." The message, he said, was clear: "White was right," and staff would be among those to remind him. Another inmate described the "culture shock" he experienced upon entering the institution:

> [When] I first arrived...we were told...to keep all eyes forward, no talking,
> no "reckless eyeballing," and...to stay behind the man...in front of you. It
> was then that I noticed that the white boys...all of 'em over six-foot or
> better,... set up [beat] a guy...about 5-9 or 5-11, being jacked up off the
> ground and literally whupped, with blackjacks....[He] still had on a set
> of...dogcuffs, them cuffs that you put on your wrists and they hold you
> between your legs with a chain. The chains is directly up under the
> nutsack, and one yank of this heavy chain, man, and you just look at this
> and say, "Hey, man, these some cooool folks, man," and it's really a heavy
> experience. It was right then and there I made up my mind...hey, there's
> "no win" under these conditions, refusing, going against the administration
> by brute force. You couldn't win. When you walked into the building you
> sense it, these big ol' hillbillies standing here, all around, all you see is
> white folks, and you hardly ever see black.

Another inmate noted the connection between race and violence in relating the following incident: "One of the guards kept calling him 'nigger this, nigger that' and finally the fellow 'jumped off' and they locked him up in seg. But before they did, they really whupped him."

These continuing racial divisions block recognition of shared problems by prisoners, and perpetuate the tension between a white administrative power structure and a non-white prisoner social order. As prison incidents or public revelations draw increasing attention to racism in prisons, there occurs a growing awareness among the public and policy makers that the gap between state power (the formal rules and resources) and state apparatus (the functionaries and organizations who implement it)—at least in prison operations—is widening (e.g., Unger 1980). The prevalence of prison gangs (Camp and Camp 1985; Jacobs 1974), racially-motivated sexual assaults (Carroll 1977a), and retaliatory racially-motivated beatings of ethnic prisoners by white guards (e.g., Possley 1981), are examples of how racial tensions reflect the contradiction between state power and apparatus. These contradictions generate prisoner resistance and intensify the current "crisis in corrections." As a consequence, even if one could push a magic button to eliminate racist behavior, other factors that make "doing time" more difficult for non-whites would still exist. The most understudied consequences include those that occur in the structural realm. These occur because race affects prison existence in ways that simply changing existing attitudes or behaviors cannot touch. Two examples characterize structural factors that make non-whites' prison experience more difficult.

Structural Example of Race

A prison's organizational structure and social networks are embedded in and subject to external pressures from the larger society (Jacobs 1977; Thomas et. al. 1980, 1981). Just as in the "free world" of street society, prisons are subject to fiscal and control factors that shape the formal apparatus of prison organization and control, and the social organization of staff and inmates. Each of these constraints has roots in the larger society and dramatically shape prison existence in ways that make it different for non-whites.

Fiscal Experiences. Fiscal restraints affect both the general prison structure (e.g., quality and quantity of security personnel, facilities, etc.) and the conditions of existence within prison. In Illinois, fiscal problems have delayed the opening of three new prisons, while Department of Corrections officials anticipate that at least 26 new penitentiaries, costing $1.4 billion, will be needed to house the projected 1999 prison population of 55,000. This has generated calls to modify sentencing statutes and find alternatives to prison ("State Urged to Revamp Sentencing," 1991:2).

Fiscal constraints generate de facto discriminatory policy-generated repression that more severely restrict or eliminate basic requisites for dignified human existence among non-whites. Food, shelter, clothing, health care, vocational and educational training, access to reading materials, leisure-time diversions, and basic amenities (e.g., writing paper, telephone money) are a few features of prison existence affected by fiscal limitations. Prison budgets continually reflect fiscal crises, economic fluctuations and public and political cost-saving pressures. Work-release furloughs, quality of food, etc., can be affected by budgetary constraints. Residents may resist fiscally-generated administrative policies by challenging them but, unlike racial harassment, they cannot be avoided.

Non-whites are more likely to be undereducated, underemployed, and have less access to external support resources. Hispanics, especially, are vulnerable to language and other cultural barriers, which increase their isolation from other groups and decrease their ability to seek and obtain existing resources. Language barriers increase their cultural isolation and reduce the quantity and quality of services such as health care or recreation, and also increase the probability of disciplinary actions caused by misunderstandings. In Illinois, current hiring freezes make it virtually impossible to recruit specialized staff, and also make filling vacated positions extremely difficult, which further hampers delivery of even basic amenities.

Fiscal constraints, especially during the reduction of "superfluous" social and related programs during the Reagan/Bush Administrations, remove any possibility of developing programs or services that would address the specific needs of particular groups, such as literacy programs for functional illiterates[3]. By removing resources which make rehabilitative programs and services possible, fiscal constraints virtually assure that upon release from prison non-whites will be more likely to return to the environment from which they came. This increases the probability of recidivism by ignoring, and thus perpetuating, the problems faced by prisoners prior to incarceration.

In addition, fiscal cutbacks encourage the expansion of illicit prison economies and behavior by decreasing available licit opportunities for economic and other reward systems (e.g., work programs, vocational training). Cutbacks also decrease security and related functions which tend to increase the occurrence of certain illicit behaviors (e.g., prostitution, drug use, violence). Consequently, racial polarization and an inability to unite in economic interests causes the competition for scarce resources to take on racial overtones (Smith and Gibson 1988). This further polarizes inmates because of the ensuing conflicts that arise both between and within various groups.

Control Consequences

As bureaucratic structures, prisons exist to control, but this control is often influenced by staff discretion rather than formal rules (Thomas 1984, 1988; Thomas et. al. 1991). Guards are more than simple guardians of state power: they are also conduits of racial meaning that affect non-white staff. Like prisoners, guards may form tacit racial alliances with prisoners that shape how they control and whom they target for control. It is not uncommon for security personnel to subvert control along racially divided lines by trading favors, obtaining contraband, or even by establishing illicit economic partnerships. This creates conditions that not only neutralize state power but also reflect de facto tacit coalitions for racial resistance between the keepers and the kept. This does not mean that the two groups are consciously working together, but rather that the outcome of their activities operates to circumvent policies established by the state. Non-white prison guards may experience their condition in ways parallel to that of inmates; they, too, are stigmatized, brutalized, and must cope with elements of their existence (e.g., fear, frustration, hostility) in ways similar to inmates (e.g., Lombardo 1981; Jacobs and Retsky 1975). As one black cell-house supervisor complained, "In a black-white issue, I've never won." Racial distinctions within the ranks of prison staff heighten tensions inherent in a racially imbalanced form of social organization. Some researchers (e.g., Jacobs and Kraft 1978) have concluded that hiring more non-white staff might not effectively eliminate some forms of racial tension, because both black and white guards share similar attitudes of administrative control. However, although the so-called "guard mentality" is shared by both white and non-white staff, it is mediated dramatically by racial divisions, and racial codes shape staff discretion to favor whites. Ironically, even though white guards are perceived to be harder on non-whites than on whites, this does not mean that non-white staff are necessarily any easier on non-whites. Non-white staff may be perceived as treating non-whites more harshly because they have submitted to the codes of white culture. For some inmates, this fosters hostility and contempt toward them:

> That's all part of that hate process. Black guards tend to over-identify
> with whites to avoid being perceived as "part of them" [convicts]. I tend to
> think that that's not so with the European race, 'cause the European guards
> take care of the Europeans here. They have a camaraderie down here,
> really all over the U.S. I would prefer to have a European supervisor than
> one of my own complexion, as, well, just like the Asiatic police out there,
> they'll come down harder on him [an oriental] than on you. It's a psycho-
> logical thing that comes from being black in the U.S. Most brothers [non-
> white guards] thinks they's European. I don't know why anybody would
> want to be a European.

Examples of white guards favoring white inmates include special protection, favoritism in job assignments and other institutional activities and discretionary application of institutional policies. In a decade of prison research, I have heard of no instance from even the most biased whites complaining of racial harassment by non-whites. Non-white inmates, by contrast, continuously complain about this problem. In disciplinary hearings comprised of white officers, subtle allusions to non-whites as a category ("They" always stick together; "They" always lie) were heard far more often to justify attacking a nonwhite prisoner's credibility than a white's. One white prisoner explained how he planned to use the race game to transfer to a prison with an educational program he wanted by manipulating willingness to protect whites from blacks:

> Whites find it easy to get transferred if they say they are afraid for their lives from blacks. I'd like to go into some form of electrical or mechanical engineering when I get out, but they don't offer those kinds of courses...If I don't get parole, I'll have myself beat up by a couple of brothers and get put into protective custody, then transfer out to wherever I can get the math courses.

A white gay prisoner used staff animosity against blacks to secure a transfer when he wrote a document detailing gang activities and gave it to officials. He leaked his scheme to fellow prisoners to assure that he would be "marked" for a "hit," thus assuring the transfer. Whether true or not, this incident illustrates the perception that white guards will act in collusion with white prisoners in the race game. Such stories by whites who intentionally used the race game typify one subtle advantage whites possess which non-whites do not: *The images of non-whites as violent and predatory create a resource for manipulating staff that exploits and reinforces these images.* Racial meanings become a polarizing resource that makes doing time a bit easier for whites at the expense of non-whites.

The effects of racial tension on staff are not without consequences. For staff, racial problems contribute to absenteeism, high resignation rates, sabotage, insubordination or greater withdrawal of organizational commitment. Such staff responses, as Aronowitz (1973) has argued, reflect tacit subversive behaviors that mediate not only the social order of prisons, but the state's ability to control them as well. That is, the apparatus of the state is incapable of providing the means to directly or actively implement state power (as prison control) in an effective or efficient manner, thus contributing to prisons' racial "crisis." This mediates prison organization by subverting and neutralizing it as a means of control and regimentation, and intensifies tensions which state power must ultimately address. In short, the state's power is subverted by inmate and staff activity in which all participants are ultimately victimized.

Resisting Racial Meanings

Despite racial power imbalances, there exist forms of social organization and activity that reflect the antinomy between domination and struggle on one hand and security/control needs on the other. Two juxtaposed examples illustrate how racial meanings are translated into forms of accommodation and resistance: Gangs and prisoner litigation.

Gangs. The justifiably violent image of gangs depicted by the media obscures their function as an accommodation strategy to prison existence. In Illinois prisons, gangs are perceived as a "black thing." Consequently, the phenomenon is considered "racial" by definition[4]. Prisoners, staff, and some researchers (e.g., Camp and Camp 1985:134) are consistent in their estimates that gang membership in Illinois prisons ranges between 80 to 90 percent. Gang formation partially reflects street culture. However, those affiliated with gangs in Illinois and even some "independent critics" agree that gangs reflect more than the importation of urban social organization into the prison. Gangs are a survival mechanism that provide protection from other inmates and serve as a power resource that mediates what are often seen as "repressive" administrative policies and racial discrimination by white prisoners and staff. In this sense, gang membership becomes a way of doing time and self help (e.g., D. Black 1983).

As a response to prison conditions (e.g., Jacobs 1977; Thomas et. al. 1980, 1981), gangs challenge the basis upon which both the philosophy and implementation of punishment exists in contemporary society. The mythology of one of Illinois prisons' most powerful gangs connotes images of resistance in the liturgy of its origins as articulated by a leader:

> The [gang name] was born out of frustration and repression in 1959 in a
> juvenile correctional center. A group of young black man-children, having
> experienced the living conditions of the black ghetto compounded with
> their repressive experiences with Europeans and institutionalized racism,
> decided that some type of organization among themselves was necessary
> for their survival and growth. Thus in the womb of oppression and racism
> was born the [gang name]. In the beginning the [gang name] was merely a
> vehicle of survival and growth for those within its ranks. But as [gang
> name] evolved the survival and development of black people was incorpo-
> rated into our philosophy and principles. As man-child grew, so did his
> awareness and consciousness grow.

The point is not whether the account of this gang's genesis is factual, although evidence corroborates it. Rather, gang members, while often recognizing and justifying their illicit behaviors and acknowledging contradictions between rhetoric and action, nonetheless imbue their groups with an explicit set of ideological meanings that signify racial identity and resistance to oppression. A leader of another powerful gang provided a similar vocabulary of motive for the origins of his group:

> The gang structure is...a source of unity, a sense of solidarity, that would
> give us identification as a people....We are individuals who believe in
> organizing and assimilating ourselves into what is acceptable to us....
> [E]ducationally, we don't balance out. Financially, we don't balance

out....We know, and we accept without doubt or contradiction, that [the administration] will not allow us to evolve as credible individuals, related to what is offered to us as the American dream. We don't want the white man to put white paint over our black faces.

Administrators view gangs as threats to prison security, and even some gang members express strong ambivalence about their utility. Called "organizations" by prisoners, these groups reflect an antimony between predatory behavior on one hand and self-help on the other. The perception that white staff employ retaliatory violence on non-whites provides the rhetorical accounts justifying gang membership, which one inmate drew upon to explain his own affiliation:

> Guards will handcuff and whup a nigger over on segregation, which I have seen....[Gangs]...can get [you] away from that. [Staff violence on prisoners] happens on a regular... sometimes...daily basis. They made a daily habit out of whipping [prisoner's name] over on segregation. I...seen them whup studs...in segregation. They done killed a couple of studs since I been here, and got away with it. Whenever a situation rises where they want to go to the extreme and get somebody, they got the facilities and the capabilities to get away with it.

Although prison administrators do not formally acknowledge the existence of gangs, weight of numbers makes the reality otherwise, and for one high-placed gang leader, his organization functioned as a buffer that protected black inmates[5]:

> They have to acknowledge the gangs because we, without no apprehensions at all, none whatsoever, we! are here...I'm saying that the gangs function as a balance between the administration and the population. Things that took place [during a period when abuses occurred] don't take place now.

In addition to offering protection, gang affiliation makes life easier by providing resources to its members, by offering some relief from discretionary harassment, and by serving as a buffer between formal rules and their discretionary enforcement. However, gangs can control their members as vigorously and as physically as staff. Obedience is required and "chastisement" is often physical[6]:

> ...[W]e have ways...[to]...solve problems among ourselves. A few of us that has some influence,...control...[and] understanding,...deal with the administration and the residents [prisoners]....[W]e deal with things ourselves, we keep somebody from goin' in the hole [segregation], from losin' some good-time, but it don't happen again.... [W]ithout the administration's approval, we take them down in the basement, down in

the shower, you know, and, uh, "chastise" them (Stateville inmate, from TV. documentary "Hard Time").

In sum, gangs exist as a contradictory prison entity. On one hand, they provide solidarity for members, offer some protection against outsiders and staff and reduce some of the pangs of imprisonment. However, they constitute strong informal organizations within a formal one, which creates an element of instability as they formulate their own rules and control systems. On the other hand, and ironically, gangs also contribute to the stabilization of prison society by reducing random violence and other unacceptable behavior. Leaders tend to be conservative, and it is in their interests to "keep the lid on" disruptions that could undermine their status or enterprises.

This does not mean that prison gangs are necessarily desirable. They invoke their own form of discipline which tends to be violent, promote a variety of illicit enterprises and can pose a threat to the safety of guards and other prisoners. The goal here is not to romanticize the predatory behaviors of gangs or to criticize the excesses. Rather, it is to present an alternative meaning of their existence as seen by those who participate in them. To see them only through the eyes of prison administrators and "official definitions" perpetuates the misunderstandings of the racial experience.

Because gangs typify one form of resistance to social control, they challenge the political framework upon which prisons rest. This is not to suggest that such groups are politically conscious although some are exceptionally so. Such racial solidarity, however, does provide a means for resisting the power and authority of the prison administration while also contributing to the increase in the "crisis" atmosphere of prisons. In this sense, gang activity may be interpreted as historically-specific imported responses adapted to accommodate the prison experience. This, in turn, requires placating strategies by the state in the form of increased security, decreased amenities, informal and discretionary staff/inmate alliances, and a public relations campaign of spin control in which the problems of prison are redefined as a reflection of inmate "pathology" rather than, at least in part, as a product of administrative failures and societal factors. Gangs exist because neither prisons nor society at large are able to provide meaningful alternatives to meet needs or provide protection from racial and other predations.

Prisoner Litigation

In addition to strategies of accommodation, opportunities for emancipatory struggle against administrative policies of racial domination also exist. One of the most effective and productive of these alternatives is prisoner litigation, in which prisoners sue their captors in Federal court to challenge policies or prison conditions (Milovanovic and Thomas 1989; Thomas 1988, 1989; Thomas and

Mika 1988). Litigation falls at the opposite continuum of gang organizations because it is non-violent and tends to address specific problems in order to improve the prison environment. Further, the benefits are more tangible and acceptable (Thomas 1988), and some inmates see it as a better strategy for attacking racial and other forms of oppression than violence or separatism.

As a form of resistance, litigation has several basic characteristics. Prisons are an absurd environment (Milovanovic and Thomas 1989), and prisoner litigation provides a strategy to react meaningfully and rationally to resist it. About 75 percent of all inmate suits challenge conditions of confinement. Although less than one percent of all prisoner suits explicitly allege racism, perhaps as many as 15 percent have a racial component to the extent that they challenge policies or actions that were precipitated by discrimination. Suits challenging conditions are generally filed under various federal civil rights acts, and reasons for litigating include conditions, prison violence, and policies (Thomas 1988:117-119).

Contrary to the view of media and prison officials, most prisoners' civil rights suits are not frivolous and possess substantive and legal merit (Thomas 1988). Prisoners' suits are narratives of grievances, and these grievances detail the arbitrary and debilitating nature of prison life. Suits alleging violence, which account for about 18 percent of all prisoner civil rights suits, suggest that assaults by staff, deliberate or reckless failure of staff to protect inmates from gangs or other inmates, and, in one class action suit (*Calvin R. v. Lane* 82-C-1955 (N.D. Ill. 1982), failure to create an environment of safety, remain recurrent problems that contribute to prisoner polarization.

Litigation also reflects fiscal and budgetary limitations that intensify the punitive nature of prison conditions. Suits attacking prison conditions account for 16 percent of civil rights suits. Lack of adequate health care is a special problem, but other serious complaints include poor or dangerous facilities, lack of programs and overcrowding (Thomas 1988:117-119).

Prisoner litigation is an existential act of rebellion, of saying "no," that carries a political edge. Prisoner litigation has expanded civil rights and has also improved prison conditions, judicial procedures and correctional policies. It has been instrumental in imposing minimal standards of fairness on prison operations, and has also contributed to making prisons more visible:

> As social praxis, litigation displays the ways...law can be used to transform social existence....Litigation provides a type of slippage that mediates between the formidable power of state agents and those whom the agents...control. The drama of litigation and the performances that create it decrease the historically tightly coupled link between the rules and practices of an organization, and contributes to the dialectical tension between

freedom and constraint (Milovanovic and Thomas 1989:255).

In this context, prisoner litigation alerts staff that unacceptable forms of oppression or abuse of power may lead to consequences they would prefer not to face. Although litigation does not "solve" racism, it creates an avenue for resistance and redress that, in combination with other means of combating oppression, minimizes some of the harshest degradation and abuses of power. Unlike other forms of resistance, such as gangs, litigation is far less dramatic and changes are slow and incremental. Nonetheless, the opportunity to litigate remains a powerful weapon in the arsenal against policies and behavior that reflect racial and other discriminatory codes.

The possibility for resistance must not be construed to mean that prisoners construct a social order that allows for "easy time," for there is no easy time in any prison. It does mean, however, that racial tensions generate forms of resistance that contribute to the subversion of state power as it is embedded in the authority to impose rules, regulations and ideologically—embedded techniques of control over non-white inmates. The irony of resistance is that it both emancipates (by challenging racial hegemony) and constrains (by reinforcing polarization (Milovanovic and Thomas 1989)). The subsequent strains and tensions placed upon prison organizations reverberate throughout the entire criminal justice system (Thomas and Mika 1989).

Conclusion

I have argued that the prison experience is a racial experience for all who participate in prison culture. Not all prisoners experience it equally, however. Pre-patterned framing devises or codes provide a partial common stock of assumptions and knowledge that shape the formation of prison culture and the corresponding consequences. Racial codes offer tentative guidelines for action, rhetorical devices for accounting for actions and a preliminary set of precepts for doing time. Racial codes define what is expected of prisoners: the result is polarization that disproportionately penalizes non-whites.

The sign system embedded in racial identity is violent because it imposes metaphors that wrench prisoners out of their shared humanity and creates conditions that exacerbate qualities such as hostility, violence, distrust, and predation. If prisons are "colleges of crime," it is not because prisoners learn more efficient ways of committing crime, which they do not, but because they are socialized into an environment that reinforces characteristics unlikely to aid in readapting to society upon release. Racial codes promote this experience. Racial codes are violent because they trash reality. They create false images that correspond to ideologies of suppression for whites and oppression for blacks.

These ideological images, the simulacra, become the reality and form the icons that guide behavior. They disrupt the social fabric by creating racially-embedded symbols that can be manipulated at the expense of one group for the advantage of another.

Racial codes are violent because they create structural barriers that preclude some groups from the same access to resources available to other groups. Exclusionary systems of resource allocation influenced by racial factors add to the punitive sanctions of prison life. The symbols denoting and connoting racial meanings contribute to turmoil in prisons by shaping an inescapable aspect of culture that is debilitating for all inmates and staff and subverts administrative efforts to deliver parity in racial resources and assure a safe existence. Prison administrators argue that racial tension is largely a reflection of broader social problems over which they have no control, and, so they claim, they are powerless to ameliorate it. By shifting the focus of race in prisons away from the conceptual dichotomy of interaction or structure, and by including an examination of how race, as a system of significations, provides a language of behavior that shapes resource allocation, socialization, group formation and culture, its complexity may be more fully recognized. In so doing, creative social and administrative policies to address racial oppression in ways that make prison life more tolerable for all those who experience it must be devised.

NOTES

1. I use the term "white" to refer to prisoners of Euro-American ancestry. "Non-white" refers to prisoners of color, primarily Afro-Americans and Hispanics. Asians and native-American prisoners are rare in Illinois prisons.

2. The incident occurred in Chester, Illinois, and included myself and two other members of the John Howard Association.

3. Funds for many programs are in jeopardy, and other policies have removed some programs. Although there seem to be no studies assessing the functional literacy rate in Illinois prisons, it has been estimated in maximum security prisons at about 35-40 percent by educational personnel, although prisoners in Stateville's educational program have argued that it is closer to 60 percent in that institution. For further information see: *Insight* 1991:21-22.

4. The most powerful gangs in Illinois prisons are The Vice Lord Nation, the El Rukns, and the Disciples (or "Black Gangster Disciples), all Afro-American groups, and a Hispanic gang, the Latin Kings. The only white gangs are found in the state's southern prison. The Northsider's originated in Menard as a protective response to non-white organizations. The ideological basis of the group is described as "white nationalism" by some members, and it actively recruits white prisoners and discourages white "independents." A second

group, comprised primarily of "bikers," is not often categorized as a gang, but with the exception of recruitment, it meets the criteria that define other organizations as gangs. However, the overwhelming consensus of both staff and prisoners is that the biker organization bothers nobody unless first bothered.

5. In one prison, the warden was relieved from his position for colluding with gang members to resolve a variety of prison problems (Smith 1987a, 1987b).

6. For additional discussion of gang violence in Pontiac, see Gibson and Smith (1988).

Disparity in the Incarceration of Minorities in New York State, 1985-1986*

James F. Nelson**

IN 1988 FOUR out of every five inmates in New York State prisons were black or Hispanic. Yet only one out of every four persons in the state was black or Hispanic. This concentration of minorities in prisons has been cited as evidence of racism not only in New York State (Grossman 1987; Murphy 1989; Schulman and Gryta 1988), but across the United States (Christianson 1981).

Introduction

The finding that the majority of prisoners are minorities does not, in itself, demonstrate that the criminal justice system is racist. Differences in incarcera-

*Portions of this paper copyright, 1990, ©New York State Division of Criminal Justice Services.
**I would like to thank Seth Jacobs for developing the initial research proposal which lead to this study. I would also like to thank Bruce Frederick, Steven Greenstein, David van Alstyne, Vince Monti, Henry Brownstein, Donna Hall, William Wilbanks, Sherwood Zimmerman, Carl Pope, James Gilmer and Richard Dehais for helpful comments and critical reviews.

tion rates may be due to differences in offending rates, arrest practices, case processing decisions, and parole release decisions. Differences in incarceration rates might also be attributed to biases in the criminal justice system to the extent that arrest practices, case processing decisions, and parole decisions unfairly affect how minorities are treated.

Most of the research in the 1980s that estimated disparities in post-arrest case processing concluded that there were no disparities, that disparities were relatively small, or that disparities in some decisions were balanced by opposite disparities in other decisions (see Blumstein 1982; Hagan and Peterson 1984; Klein et al. 1990; Kleck 1981; Myers and Talarico 1987; Petersilia 1983; Pommershein and Wise 1989; Spohn et al. 1982; and Wilbanks 1987. For opposing views see: Crutchfield and Bridges 1985; Zimmerman and Fredrick 1983; and Albonetti et al. 1983).

The present study expands upon this literature and analyzes disparities in post-arrest case processing. It asks whether the concentration of blacks and Hispanics in New York State's prisons and jails can be partially accounted for by disparities in how often similarly situated minorities and whites were incarcerated following arrest. Statistical models are used to control for differences in arrest charges, prior criminal records and county of processing. The analysis demonstrates that minorities were incarcerated more often than similarly situated whites in almost all counties studied. However, it also suggests that removing disparities in post-arrest processing would not substantially reduce the concentration of minorities in jails and prisons.

Research Design

This study models incarceration following arrest for all counties in New York State. It combines all case processing decisions that occurred between arrest and final disposition into an incarceration outcome variable. Defendants sentenced to jail or to prison were classified as incarcerated. Defendants whose cases were dismissed or adjourned, or sentenced to probation, conditional discharge, time served, or probation were classified as not incarcerated.

This is not a sentencing study. Sentencing studies begin at conviction. In contrast, the present study begins at arrest. Disparities in incarceration outcomes reflect disparities in sentencing decisions as well as disparities in decisions that occurred between arrest and final disposition. A finding of no disparities in incarceration outcomes does not necessarily mean that minorities and whites were treated in the same manner at all processing stages. For example, minorities could have the same chances of being incarcerated as whites if they were less likely to be convicted, but were more likely to be incarcerated following conviction.

Disparity was measured as a residual variable. It represents all differences in how often white and minority defendants were sentenced to jail or prison that could not be explained by differences in arrest charges, prior criminal records, and county of processing.

The disparities estimated in this paper may not be the result of discriminatory actions based upon racial and ethnic prejudices. The disparities may be attributable to variables that were related to both minority status and case processing decisions. Racial and ethnic discrimination are just two possible causes. Unmeasured differences in economic status, charge severity, prior criminal records, evidence, demeanor, and community reputations are other possible causes.

The problem of equating disparities with prejudices was addressed by Gibson (1978). He demonstrated that prejudicial attitudes were not correlated with disparities in sentencing decisions made by eleven judges. Instead, disparities were correlated to differences in how judges viewed the importance of criminal records in making sentencing decisions. Judges who sentenced blacks more harshly than whites put more importance on prior criminal records than judges who did not sentence blacks more harshly than whites. Gibson's study shows that disparities are not necessarily due to prejudices. The only way to attribute disparities to prejudices is to measure prejudices directly and show that they are independently related to disparities.

The inability to identify the causes of disparity is not a problem for the purposes of this study. This study was designed to determine whether minorities were incarcerated more often than whites once differences in arrest charges, prior criminal records, and county of processing were taken into account. Regardless of cause, significant amounts of disparity suggest that there may be a problem with how minorities are processed by the criminal justice system; such findings would warrant additional research to investigate sources of disparity.

Disparity was estimated within counties to ensure that differences among counties in how often defendants were incarcerated were not confounded with differences in how often whites and minorities within the same county were incarcerated. To simplify discussion, Bronx, Kings, New York (Manhattan and Staten Island) and Queens counties are referred to as "New York City Counties," while the remaining 58 counties are referred to as "Upstate Counties," (this includes Nassau and Suffolk counties which are located on Long Island). The study does not explain why incarceration was used more often in some counties than in others.

The Data Set

Arrest and case processing data were obtained from the Computerized Criminal History/Offender-Based Transaction Statistics (CCH/OBTS) data system maintained by the New York State Division of Criminal Justice Services. This system recorded arrest information and defendant characteristics for all arrests of persons charged with fingerprintable offenses. The arrest information contained a description of each arrest offense and a summary of how each case was disposed. Fingerprints were used to identify the same defendant over time.

The study is based upon the population of defendants arrested between January 1, 1985 and December 31, 1986 and is limited to defendants whose cases were disposed by July of 1987. For defendants with more than one arrest during this period, the study is limited to the first arrest. Limiting the analysis to one arrest per defendant removed inconsistencies in the data system. In most jurisdictions, multiple charges were recorded as one arrest. In some jurisdictions, multiple charges were sometimes recorded as separate arrests. Limiting the analysis to one arrest per defendant ensured that multiple charges were treated as one arrest in all jurisdictions.

The Most Serious Arrest Charge

Arrest charge, prior criminal record, and extent of evidence are frequently cited as the most important legal or "legitimate" influences affecting case processing. These influences are called "legitimate" because they have a basis in law and because persons believe they should affect case processing (Hagan and Bumiller 1983). In contrast, race is called an extra-legal or "illegitimate" influence because there is no basis in law for treating minorities differently than whites.

The most serious arrest charge was selected to measure both the type of crime and its seriousness. Thirty-three arrest charges were analyzed. They ranged from Class B misdemeanor charges to Class B felony charges. Class A felonies were excluded from this study. Only 1 percent of arrest in the sample were class A felonies, and there were too few cases to analyze disparity. In addition, persons whose most serious charges were driving while intoxicated or prostitution were excluded. These charges were brought only in certain counties, making estimation of cross-county disparity effects for these crime charges infeasible[1].

The percentages of defendants who were incarcerated for each arrest charge by minority status are presented in Table 10.1. Black and Hispanic defendants are categorized as minority defendants. All other defendants are categorized as white. Seventy-nine percent of defendants (341,743 out of 430,998) were charged with one of the 33 arrest charges presented in this table. The data in this and subsequent tables are based upon the first arrest that occurred in 1985-1986.

The last column in Table 10.1 displays differences in incarceration for minorities and whites. It shows that minorities were incarcerated more often than whites for 14 out of 21 felony charges and for 11 out of 13 misdemeanor charges.

Table 10.1 also shows that incarceration percentages varied by crime type within class. Incarceration percentages for whites ranged from 18 to 41 percent for B felonies, from 12 to 25 percent for C felonies, from 8 to 23 percent for D felonies, and from 1 to 16 percent for E felonies. For minorities, they ranged from 21 to 38 percent for B felonies, from 16 to 30 percent for C felonies, from 8 to

Table 10.1
Number of Defendants and Percentage Incarcerated by Arrest Charge and
Minority Status, NYS, 1985-1986

Arrest Charge	Minorities		Whites		Difference
	Number of Defendants	% Incar- cerated	Number of Defendants	%Incar- cerated	% Minorities- % Whites
Felony Arrest Charges					
B Drug Poss'n	4,851	21%	491	18%	2%
B Drug Sale	11,690	38	1,258	41	-2
B Robbery	8,631	34	1,382	36	-1
C Assault	2,075	19	524	22	-3
C Burglary	5,426	30	4,018	25	4
C Drug Poss'n	1,076	18	341	13	4
C Weapons	1,480	16	302	12	4
C Robbery	7,912	22	1,171	21	0
D Assault	17,448	8	6,552	8	-0
D Burglary	5,519	31	4,816	23	7
D Drug Sale	2,986	26	511	16	9
D Forgery	1,842	14	1,781	16	-1
D Larceny	8,272	15	4,529	14	1
D Stln Property	1,997	19	1,210	17	2
D Weapons	4,515	16	1,224	14	2
D Robbery	1,990	25	401	19	6
E Mischief	1,666	13	2,407	5	7
E Gambling	3,425	1	265	1	0
E Larceny	9,294	21	5,118	11	10
E Stln Property	2,303	20	1,460	16	3
E Rkls Endngrt	1,094	15	870	14	1
All Felonies	105,492	21	40,631	16	4

Continued..

Table 10.1 Continued

Arrest Charge	Minorities		Whites		Difference
	Number of Defendants	% Incar- cerated	Number of Defendants	%Incar- cerated	% Minorities- % Whites
Misdemeanor Arrest Charges					
A Assault	14,849	4%	14,858	3%	0%
A Burglary	3,769	14	3,171	6	8
A Mischief	3,880	5	8,076	3	2
A Drug Possession	22,759	11	11,651	4	6
A Drug Sales	5,655	15	987	5	9
A Theft Transit	12,183	6	1,918	2	4
A Larceny	20,357	14	28,383	4	9
A Stolen Property	3,669	12	3,085	6	6
A Weapons	4,636	6	3,204	3	3
A Resist Arrest	5,831	9	5,830	6	3
B Burglary	2,603	7	2,980	2	4
B Drug Possession	4,776	5	2,751	0	4
B Personal	1,470	4	1,659	5	-0
All Misdemeanors	106,437	12	88,553	4	8
All Arrests	211,929	15	129,814	8	7

31 percent for D felonies, and from 1 to 21 percent for E felonies. These within-class variations suggest that the seriousness of arrest charge is not adequately measured by the class of the charge.

Prior Criminal Record

The arrests and convictions that occurred in the ten year period preceding the instant offense were combined into a criminal history score (see Nelson 1989). The score ranged from zero (no prior arrests) to ten (two or more prior felony convictions).

Criminal records are frequently based solely upon convictions. Arrests were included in the criminal record score because they influence incarceration decisions, even when the number and seriousness of prior convictions are taken into account (Nelson 1989). If blacks and Hispanics were arrested more often than whites, and if the number of prior arrests affected the chances of being incarcerated, then excluding arrests from the prior record score could introduce a spurious relation between minority status and incarceration.

Basing the criminal record score upon arrests and convictions alleviated some problems with missing dispositions. About 20 percent of all cases in the CCH/OBTS did not have final dispositions. These events would not have affected the criminal record score had the score been based solely upon convictions.

The percentage of defendants who were incarcerated by prior record score and minority status is presented in Table 10.2. The table shows that incarceration covaried with the criminal history score, and that minorities were incarcerated more often than whites for all but the highest criminal history score.

Table 10.2
Number of Defendants and Percentage Incarcerated by Prior Record Score
and Minority Status, NYS, 1985-1986

Prior Record Score	Minorities		Whites		Difference
	Number of Defendants	% Incarcerated	Number of Defendants	%Incarcerated	% Minorities-% Whites
0	111,000	6%	86,973	3%	2%
1	18,696	11	11,206	8	3
2	14,592	15	8,616	11	4
3	9,554	19	4,640	13	5
4	7,461	23	3,345	16	6
5	15,878	27	5,483	22	5
6	11,157	32	3,599	28	4
7	9,198	39	2,410	36	3
8	5,304	48	916	41	6
9	1,639	54	196	52	1
10	7,450	41	1,800	44	-3

The frequencies in Table 10.2 can be grouped to demonstrate that minorities had more extensive criminal records than whites. Overall, 48 percent of the minorities but only 33 percent of the whites were arrested one or more times in the ten year period preceding the instant offense. The average prior record score equalled 2.12 for minorities and 1.15 for whites. Among defendants with prior arrest records, minorities had more extensive records. The average prior record for minorities with prior arrests equalled 4.45; the average for whites equalled 3.52.

The County Unit

The post-arrest processing of defendants in New York State is organized on a county basis. Defendants are processed in county superior courts and in lower criminal courts within each county. Prosecution is directed by each county's district attorney's office.

Disparities were estimated separately for counties that processed at least 1,900 white and 1,900 minority defendants. These counties included the four most populous counties within New York City, the six most populous counties outside of New York City, and the 52 least populous counties aggregated into one county unit. The number and percentage of white and minority defendants who were incarcerated by county are presented in Table 10.3. The last column shows that minorities were incarcerated more often than whites in all counties. Differences in the percentage incarcerated exceeded 9 percent in half of the counties.

Table 10.3
Number of Defendants and Percentage Incarcerated by County
and minority Status, NYS, 1985-1986

County Defendants	Minorities		Whites		Difference
	Number of Defendants	% Incarcerated	Number of Defendants	%Incarcerated	% Minorities-% Whites
Bronx	33,248	17%	3,469	7%	10%
Kings	46,979	14	8,648	6	8
New York	71,305	13	15,986	6	7
Queens	19,706	19	7,596	9	10
Erie	6,276	9	9,092	4	4
Monroe	4,709	11	5,729	6	4
Nassau	5,929	21	7,728	9	11
Onondaga	1,939	13	4,018	7	6
Suffolk	3,895	18	10,077	8	10
Westchester	5,984	22	5,572	8	14
52 County	11,959	18	51,269	9	9

The frequencies in Table 10.3 can be grouped to show that most of the minorities (83.8%) were processed in one of the four largest counties of New York City. Most of the whites (72.4%) were processed in other counties. Almost forty percent of the whites but less than 6 percent of the minorities were processed in the 52 county aggregate.

Estimating disparities within counties made it easy to control for differences in how often similarly situated defendants were incarcerated in different counties. No attempt was made to explain why some counties incarcerated defendants more often than other counties.

Table 10.4
County, Prior Record, and Minority Logit Parameters by
Top Arrest Charge, New York State, 1985-1986

County***	County Parameter	Prior Record: 1+ Prior Arrest	Minority Status: No Prior Arrests	Minority Status: 1+ Prior Arrests
Top Arrest Charge: Felony Offense				
Westchester	1.41*	2.76*	2.35*	1.73*
Bronx	.73*	1.67*	2.15*	2.15*
Queens	1.23*	2.44*	2.00*	1.30*
Kings	.71*	2.22*	1.95*	1.46*
Suffolk	2.24*	1.65*	1.60*	1.63*
Nassau	2.78*	2.03*	1.35*	1.49*
Onondaga	1.33*	2.26*	2.01*	1.11
Other 52	2.78*	1.62*	1.40*	1.19*
New York	1.00**	1.73*	1.04*	1.09*
Monroe	2.24*	1.62*	1.58*	1.07
Erie	.86*	2.02*	1.29	.97
NY State		1.73*	0.96	.93*
Top Arrest Charge: Misdemeanor Offense				
Westchester	1.20*	5.94*	4.59*	2.82*
Bronx	2.18*	3.02*	2.32*	2.48*
Queens	1.88*	3.62*	3.05*	2.33*
Kings	1.92*	2.70*	1.98*	2.47*
Suffolk	1.69*	4.50*	2.91*	1.56*
Nassau	1.34*	5.04*	2.38*	1.89*
Onondaga	.68*	4.27*	1.63	1.49
Other 52	3.99*	2.43*	2.20*	1.40*
New York	1.00**	4.84*	2.12*	1.45*
Monroe	1.41*	3.90*	1.57	1.19
Erie	.83*	4.07*	1.41	1.15
NY State		3.08*	1.60*	1.53*

*Parameter was significantly different from 1.00 at the .05 level of significance.
**The County parameters estimate odds relative to New York County.
***Counties are ordered by the product of their minority parameters.

Estimating Disparity

1. Disparity Measured by Logit Parameters. Logit parameters that describe county, prior arrest record, and minority parameters are presented in Table 10.4. The parameters show multiplicative changes in the odds of incarceration that were associated with specific changes in each variable. The minority status parameters are equivalent to odds-ratios between minority status and incarceration[2].

The county parameters show how the odds of incarceration in each county differed from the odds of incarceration in New York County. For felony offenses, the county parameters ranged from .71 in Bronx County to 2.78 in the 52 county unit. For misdemeanor offenses, these parameters ranged from .68 in Onondaga County to 3.99 in the 52 county unit. In general, the odds of incarceration for a felony crime were particularly low in three of the four most populous counties of New York City (Kings, Bronx, and New York). A similar pattern did not occur for misdemeanor crimes.

The prior record parameters show how the odds of incarceration for persons having prior arrest records differed from the odds of incarceration for persons who were arrested for the first time. These parameters ranged by county from 1.04 to 2.35 for felony charges and from 1.41 to 4.59 for misdemeanor charges. In all counties, parameters were higher for misdemeanor than for felony charges.

The minority status parameters show how the odds of incarceration for minorities differed from the odds for whites. Separate parameters were estimated for defendants with and without prior arrest records because preliminary analyses (not presented here) demonstrated that there were significant interactions between minority status, incarceration, and prior arrest record. Most (34 out of 44) of the minority parameters were significantly greater than one, demonstrating that minorities were incarcerated more often than whites. In almost every comparison made within the same county, minority parameters were larger for misdemeanor than for felony charges, and were larger for defendants without than for defendants with prior arrest records.

The product of the four minority parameters (two for B felony offenses and two for misdemeanor offenses) was used to rank each county on disparity. The first six counties listed in Table 10.4 exhibited considerable disparity. The last five counties exhibited less disparity. The least disparity was measured in Erie County. None of its minority parameters were significantly greater than one.

The county labeled "NY State" displays parameters for a model that estimated disparities for the State as a whole. The minority parameters for this model give the misleading impression that for B felony charges minorities were incarcerated slightly less often than whites! Reasons for this unexpected relationship are discussed in the next section.

2. Disparity Measured by Standardized Percentages. While the logit parameters make it easy to compare how each variable affected the odds of incarceration, they do not show how each variable affected the percentage of defendants who were incarcerated. This effect was estimated from standardized incarceration percentages (see original report for details: Nelson 1991).

COUNTY EFFECTS CONFOUND STATEWIDE COMPARISONS. The last column in Table 10.5 displays the percentage of defendants who would be incarcerated in every county. The percentages demonstrate large differences in the use of incarceration by county. For B felony arrests, the percentages would range from 15.6 percent in Erie County to 33.2 percent in Nassau County. Relatively few defendants would be incarcerated in New York, Kings, and Bronx Counties. For misdemeanor arrests, the percentages would range from 3.6 percent in Onondaga County to 17.2 percent in Westchester County.

The large differences in the use of incarceration by county made disparity impossible to estimate from statewide totals. The problem with using statewide data is illustrated by the two averages in Table 10.5. The "Unweighted Average" is a simple average of the percentages in Table 10.5. These averages do not take into account the fact that most minorities were processed in the New York City area and most whites were processed in other areas. The "NY State Weighted Average" takes the distribution of minority status and arrest charges found within each county into account. These averages were obtained from logit models based upon statewide totals.

Differences between the weighted and unweighted averages are particularly striking for defendants arrested for felony crimes. The unweighted averages show that minorities would be incarcerated more often than whites. These averages reflect the fact that in 21 out of 22 comparisons, minorities with the same case characteristics as whites had higher incarceration percentages. Yet, the weighted averages show the opposite, namely that whites were incarcerated more often than minorities. The statewide pattern occurred because the county effect was slightly larger than the minority status effect. Incarceration percentages for whites outside of New York City were larger than incarceration percentages for minorities within New York City. *Yet in both areas, minorities were incarcerated more often than whites.* When averaged across counties, minorities appear to have lower incarceration percentages than whites because of overall differences between New York City and the rest of the state in how often defendants were incarcerated (for discussion see Blumstein 1982; Zimmerman and Frederick 1983).

ARREST CATEGORY AND PRIOR CRIMINAL RECORD EFFECTS. Table 10.5 demonstrates that incarceration was closely related to the category of the arrest charge and to the existence of an arrest record. Unweighted averages for whites ranged from 1 percent for persons arrested for misdemeanor charges without arrest records to 32 percent for persons arrested for felony charges with prior arrest records. For minorities the percentages ranged from 3 to 37 percent, respectively.

In many counties, prior record had a greater influence on incarceration than

Table 10.5
Standardized Percentages of Defendants Incarcerated and Percentage
Differences by Top Arrest Charge, County, Prior Arrest Record, and Minority
Status, New York State, 1985-1986

County	No Prior Arrests			At Least 1 Prior Arrest			All Cases
	Minorities	Whites	Minorities-Whites	Minorities	Whites	Minorities-Whites	
Arrest Category: Felony Charges							
Westchester	17.9	9.0	8.9	47.3	35.7	11.6	28.6
Bronx	10.0	5.1	4.9	33.5	20.5	13.0	18.5
Queens	14.3	8.1	6.2	39.1	33.8	5.3	24.0
Kings	8.9	4.9	4.0	28.9	22.5	6.4	16.7
Suffolk	19.0	13.3	5.7	45.7	35.3	10.4	29.1
Nassau	19.6	15.7	3.9	52.7	44.0	8.7	33.2
Onondaga	15.3	8.6	6.7	35.2	33.2	2.0	23.1
52 Counties	20.2	15.7	4.5	43.6	39.8	3.8	29.8
New York	6.9	6.7	.2	28.8	27.2	1.6	16.8
Monroe	18.8	13.3	5.5	30.3	29.0	1.3	23.0
Erie	7.4	5.9	1.5	25.8	26.2	-0.4	15.6
Unweighted Average	14.4	9.7	4.7	37.4	31.6	5.8	23.5
NYS Weighted Average	10.3	10.7	-.4	32.7	34.2	-1.5	20.8
Arrest Category: Misdemeanor Charges							
Westchester	6.2	1.4	4.8	45.1	25.7	19.4	17.2
Bronx	3.3	1.4	1.9	20.8	10.1	10.7	8.1
Queens	3.7	1.2	2.5	21.8	11.4	10.4	8.6
Kings	2.5	1.3	1.2	16.6	7.8	8.8	6.4
Suffolk	3.2	1.1	2.1	16.6	11.6	5.0	7.1
Nassau	2.1	.9	1.2	23.7	15.1	8.6	9.0
Onondaga	.7	.5	.2	9.2	6.5	2.7	3.6
52 Counties	5.5	2.6	2.9	19.6	15.2	4.4	9.5
New York	1.4	.7	.7	14.0	10.4	3.6	5.6
Monroe	1.5	.9	.6	10.0	8.7	1.3	4.5
Erie	.8	.6	.2	10.6	9.5	1.1	4.4
Unweighted Average	2.8	1.1	1.7	18.9	12.0	6.9	7.6
NYS Weighted Average	2.4	1.5	.9	17.1	12.2	4.9	7.2

arrest category. The unweighted averages show that defendants arrested for felony charges without prior arrests would be incarcerated less often than defendants arrested for misdemeanor charges with prior arrest records.

MINORITY STATUS EFFECTS. Differences in standardized percentages for minorities and whites are presented for defendants without prior arrest records in the 4th column and for defendants with prior arrest records in the 7th column of Table 10.5. Positive differences occurred in counties that would incarcerate minorities more often than whites, and negative differences occurred in counties that would incarcerate whites more often than minorities. Forty-three out of the 44 differences were positive, indicating that minorities would be incarcerated more often than whites. Differences were particularly large in the first six counties listed in each section.

Percentage differences depended upon the category of arrest charge and the extent of prior criminal record. Percentage differences were smallest for misdemeanor defendants with no prior record. Percentage differences were about as large for defendants arrested for felony crimes (regardless of arrest record) as they were for misdemeanor defendants with prior arrest records.

These findings demonstrate the importance of considering percentages when interpreting logit parameters. Using just the logit parameters, one might assume that the greatest decreases in disparities would be achieved by developing programs to reduce the largest minority parameters. This logic would suggest that programs should be designed to remove disparities for persons arrested for misdemeanor crimes who do not have prior arrest records. The problem with this logic is that removing disparities for these defendants would have the least impact on the number of defendants adversely affected by disparities, because few defendants arrested for misdemeanor crimes without prior arrest records are incarcerated.

The Impact Of Disparity on Incarcerated Populations

The standardized percentages presented in Table 10.5 suggest that the concentration of minorities in New York State jails and prisons might be reduced by removing disparities in post-arrest processing. In 1988, blacks and Hispanics represented 80 percent of the state's prison inmates and 67 percent of all persons who were held before trial or sentenced to jail. Yet, blacks and Hispanics represented less than 25 percent of the state's general population.

The effect that disparities had on the percentage of minorities among defendants sentenced to jail or prison was estimated by comparing the percentage of minorities among defendants sentenced to incarceration under two logit models. One model included minority effects and one did not. The one that excluded minority effects shows how defendants would be processed if incarceration were determined solely by arrest charges, prior criminal records, and county of processing. The observed distribution of arrest charges, prior criminal records, minority status and county were used to estimate probabilities under both models.

The percentages of defendants sentenced to jail or prison who were minorities are presented in Table 10.6. The table shows that removing disparities would not change the minority character of jails and prisons. The percentage of persons sentenced to incarceration who were minorities would be reduced from 77.2 to 74.5 percent for defendants arrested for B felony charges and from 73.6 to 66.7 percent for defendants arrested for misdemeanor charges. The larger reduction for misdemeanor arrests would not reduce the concentration of minorities in prisons because defendants who were convicted of misdemeanor crimes could not be sentenced to prison.

The largest reductions in the percentage of minorities would occur among defendants who did not have a prior criminal record. The percentage of minorities would decrease from 72.5 to 67.6 percent for defendants arrested for felony charges and from 60.0 to 46.7 percent for defendants arrested for misdemeanor charges. These decreases would have little impact on the percentages of incarcerated persons who were minorities because relatively few persons who were arrested for the first time were incarcerated.

Discussion

This study indicates that from 1985 through 1986, minorities were incarcerated more often than whites in New York State. *Disparities* were *least likely* to affect persons arrested for misdemeanor crimes who *did not have prior arrest records*. Disparities were about as likely to affect defendants arrested for misdemeanor crimes who had prior arrest records as they were to affect persons arrested for felony crimes.

Disparities varied by county. The smallest disparities occurred in New York and Erie Counties. The largest disparities occurred in Westchester County. The lack of disparity in New York County combined with above average levels of disparity in Bronx, Kings, and Queens Counties suggests that the counties of New York City should be analyzed separately when estimating disparities.

The finding that minorities were more likely to be incarcerated than whites is at odds with most research undertaken in the 1980s. This prior research, which was based primarily upon sentencing decisions for persons convicted of felony crimes, suggested that disparities have little if any effect on sentencing decisions. The present study would have supported this conclusion had the analysis been limited to aggregate state totals for felony arrest charges.

Table 10.6
Percentage of Minority Defendants Among Persons Sentenced to Jail or Prison for Logit Models that Include and that Exclude Disparities in Case Processing by Prior Record, Arrest Class, and County, New York State, 1985-1986

County	No Prior Arrests Model Includes Disparities			1+ Prior Arrests Model Includes Disparities			All Defendants Models Include Disparities		
	Yes	No	Differ-ence	Yes	No	Differ-ence	Yes	No	Differ-ence
Arrest Category: Felony Charges									
Westchester	69.9*	53.3	16.5	72.4*	66.2	6.2	71.8	63.1	8.7
Bronx	96.4*	93.1	3.3	96.6*	94.4	2.2	96.5	94.1	2.4
Queens	87.3*	79.4	7.9	82.4*	80.2	2.2	83.9	80.0	4.0
Kings	93.5*	89.0	4.5	92.7*	90.8	1.9	92.9	90.3	2.6
Suffolk	36.0*	28.1	7.9	52.0*	45.5	6.5	46.3	39.3	6.9
Nassau	51.4*	45.8	5.7	63.4*	59.2	4.1	60.1	55.4	4.6
Onondaga	49.0*	35.0	14.1	47.7*	46.3	1.5	48.3	43.6	4.7
52 Counties	27.7*	23.0	4.6	34.3*	32.4	1.9	32.1	29.2	2.9
New York	88.0	87.8	0.2	92.3	91.9	0.4	91.3	91.0	0.3
Monroe	52.0*	43.0	8.9	63.4	62.5	0.9	60.0	56.6	3.3
Erie	52.3	46.4	5.9	59.2	59.7	-0.5	57.9	57.2	0.7
Total	72.5	67.6	4.8	78.9	77.1	1.9	77.2	74.5	2.7
Arrest Category: Misdemeanor Charges									
Westchester	76.3*	43.2	33.2	78.2*	67.4	10.8	77.9	64.6	13.4
Bronx	94.2*	88.1	6.2	95.7*	91.6	4.2	95.5	91.0	4.5
Queens	85.3*	66.4	19.0	85.7*	76.0	9.7	85.6	74.3	11.3
Kings	87.7*	78.4	9.2	91.9*	84.3	7.6	91.2	83.4	7.9
Suffolk	42.9*	20.8	22.1	52.0*	43.6	8.5	50.4	39.4	11.0
Nassau	56.8*	36.5	20.3	70.4*	60.9	9.5	68.8	57.9	10.9
Onondaga	33.3	25.0	8.3	55.7	48.1	7.5	53.4	45.8	7.6
52 Counties	24.4*	13.1	11.3	32.4*	27.2	5.2	30.0	23.1	7.0
New York	84.7*	72.6	12.0	90.6*	87.8	2.8	90.0	86.3	3.7
Monroe	43.8	33.3	10.4	62.8	59.5	3.2	59.7	55.3	4.4
Erie	36.8	28.9	7.9	59.2	56.4	2.8	57.1	54.0	3.0
Total	60.0	46.7	13.3	76.3	70.7	5.6	73.6	66.7	6.9

*Minority parameter was significant at the .05 level of significance.

The absence of disparities based in statewide totals combined with the presence of disparities based upon county totals demonstrate that disparities should not be estimated from highly aggregated data. Disparities were impossible to estimate from state level totals because minority populations were concentrated in counties that incarcerated relatively few defendants. Once differences in the seriousness of arrest charges and the extent of prior criminal records were taken into account, the percentage of whites who were incarcerated for felony arrests outside of New York City exceeded the percentage of minorities who were incarcerated for felony arrests within New York City. Aggregated to the state level, whites were incarcerated more often than minorities even though the converse was true at the county level. Similar patterns may occur in other states that process most minorities in a few counties.

Like previous research, the present analysis suggests that the concentration of minorities in jails and prisons is more closely related to differences in arrest charges and prior criminal records than to disparities in post-arrest case processing. While it would not change the minority character of jails and prisons, *removing disparities would slightly decrease the concentration of minorities in jails and prisons.* The reduction would be larger for jail than for prison populations.

The total impact of removing disparities could be larger than the effect that was estimated in this paper. Removing disparities could reduce the seriousness of prior records for minorities, and this, in turn, could reduce their chances of subsequent incarcerations (see Farrell and Swigert 1978).

This research demonstrates that minorities were incarcerated more often than comparably situated whites. It does not provide enough detail about how defendants were processed to suggest what caused disparities or how they might be reduced.

NOTES

1. Felon DWI charges occurred mainly in upstate counties. Misdemeanor DWI charges primarily involved whites, and consequently the sample of these charges was not adequate for assessing disparity. Prostitution charges occurred primarily in New York City Counties, and thus a cross-county examination of disparity for these charges was not feasible.

2. The effect of prior record for defendants with arrest records was measured by employing a continuous score variable (see Nelson 1989). The separate coefficients estimated for each county demonstrated that prior record significantly affected incarceration outcomes. These coefficients, however, are not included in Table 10.4, and did not alter interpretations of this Table.

Racially Motivated Crimes in New York City

James Garofalo

T HE EXPRESSION of racial bias can take many forms. Everyday discourse can contain subtle expressions of bigotry that are deeply rooted in personalities and attitudes (van Dijk 1987). Opportunities for employment, housing, and other amenities can be limited by the conscious bias of individuals or by inequities that are embedded in the social structure. On occasion, people commit assault or even murder because of racial hatred.

In the United States today, a number of forms of racial discrimination — in education, housing, employment, public accommodations, and so forth — are prohibited under various federal, state, and local statutes. Although there are exceptions, most of these statutes provide for civil remedies, and enforcement is initiated by complaints to regulatory agencies or commissions. Local criminal justice systems have very limited roles with respect to these statutes.

It is true that there are criminal prosecutions for bias-motivated conduct under special statutes: omnibus "denial of civil rights" provisions in federal law, and parallel provisions in some states, as well as criminal laws pertaining to desecration of religious objects, cross-burning, and so forth (Padgett 1984; Washington D.C. Lawyers' Comm. 1986). But this chapter focuses on common street crimes — such as assault, harassment, and vandalism — that are routinely handled by local criminal justice agencies.

With few exceptions, the substantive criminal laws dealing with these common crimes are unconcerned with motivation. While individuals within the system may use their discretion and handle cases differently depending on their perceptions of motives, the law would have an assault arising from a dispute about a parking space handled the same way as an assault motivated by racial hate. Some states have changed this by enacting new statutes prohibiting behaviors such as "ethnic and religious intimidation" (see ADL 1988a). Other states have enacted provisions that increase the level of a crime or enhance the penalties for a crime when bias motivation is present (in Minnesota, for example, see Minn. Board 1990). But many states are reluctant to bring the vague notion of motivation into the substantive criminal law or to create laws that appear to provide different penalties for crimes against different categories of victims.

An alternative to changing the substantive criminal law is to establish new programs and policies within the criminal justice system in order to give special attention to bias-motivated crimes. Thus, the federal government and many states have begun to mandate the separate reporting and recording of "hate crimes" to highlight the problem of crimes motivated by bias. At the local level, special police, prosecutor, and victim services units have been formed (or, more often, advocated) as a means of directing additional attention and resources toward common crimes that are motivated by racial, religious, and other forms of bias (see ADL 1988b; NY Governor's Task Force 1988).

This chapter is based on data from a study of a New York City Police Department unit created to handle crimes motivated by bias against the race, ethnicity, religion, or sexual orientation of the victim. The research was funded by the National Institute of Justice. It involved data collection in two sites — NYC and Baltimore County, MD — but only the New York City data are used here.

The Bias Incident Investigating Unit

The New York City Police Department is the largest municipal police agency in the United States. Its 30,000 police officers handle staggering numbers of reported crimes and calls for service. When very serious hate crimes occur and capture the public's attention — as the December 1986 Howard Beach and August 1989 Bensonhurst incidents did — even the overburdened New York City criminal justice system is capable of focusing its attention and resources on the cases (for example, see the account of the investigation and prosecution of the Howard Beach crimes by Hynes and Drury 1990). But, as will be shown momentarily, most bias-motivated crimes are not very serious, in terms of their penal law categories. The crimes are overwhelmingly misdemeanors, or even lesser violations, rather than felonies. In an overburdened criminal justice system, such as New York City's, misdeeds of this magnitude tend to elicit minimal responses.

Thus, in late 1980, the New York City Police Department formed a Bias Incident Investigating Unit (BIIU) to give special attention to crimes motivated by racial, ethnic, and religious bias, regardless of the crime's seriousness under the penal law. In mid-1985, crimes motivated by the victims' sexual orientation were added to the unit's responsibilities. The BIIU is commanded by an Inspector who reports directly to the Chief of the Department. The Unit has about 18 investigators in addition to supervisory and administrative personnel.

When the first NYC police officer on the scene suspects that a crime was motivated by racial, ethnic, religious, or sexual orientation bias, he or she notifies the shift sergeant. If the sergeant confirms the suspicion, the precinct commander or duty captain is notified, responds to the scene, makes a final determination, and contacts the BIIU. Once this occurs, the BIIU is responsible for the case, and a special review is required to reclassify the crime as being not bias-motivated.

As the name implies, the BIIU is primarily an investigative unit, although the officers make special efforts to help victims as well. The unit does not handle non-criminal cases. When bias incidents that do not constitute crimes come to its attention, the unit refers the cases to the city's Commission on Human Rights, which maintains a Bias Prevention and Response Team. However, the BIIU maintains close contact with other, non-criminal justice agencies and organizations in the city, such as the NAACP, the Gay and Lesbian Task Force, and the Anti-Defamation League.

In a sense, the fact that this chapter is derived from a study of enhanced criminal justice responses to hate crimes makes the chapter somewhat unique in this book. Most discussions of minorities and criminal justice focus on the disadvantages that minorities face. Programs like the BIIU, on the other hand, have been criticized for giving privileged attention to minorities — for showing greater concern about crimes committed against minorities than about crimes committed against non-minorities.

The Data Set

The primary data set for the study of bias-motivated crimes in New York City consists of matched samples of bias and non-bias crimes.

All bias crimes assigned to the BIIU during 1987 and 1988, and not

subsequently reclassified, were used. A matched sample of non-bias crimes was
then selected. For each bias crime, a non-bias crime in the same general penal
law category (e.g., an assault, without regard to degree) that occurred in the same
police precinct on the same day was identified. If a relevant matching crime did
not occur on the same day, the prior day was searched, then one day after, two
days before, two days after, and so forth. The only exception to this procedure
was that domestic assaults and disturbances were eliminated from the potential
pool of non-bias comparison cases; bias crimes rarely involve domestic
relationships, while domestic cases are relatively common among non-bias
crimes. After adjusting for differences in how incidents are counted by the police
and eliminating a few cases because of missing data, the final numbers were
1,020 bias crimes and 1,015 non-bias comparisons.

The main data set was supplemented with interviews with BIIU investigators
and personnel in other relevant agencies and organizations, such as the Victim
Services Agency and the Human Rights Commission. Small samples of bias and
non-bias crime victims (50 of each) were also selected for telephone interviews
to explore the impacts of crimes on the victims and the service needs of victims.

Findings

There is a long history of racially motivated violence in America—not only
against blacks, but against native Americans and Asians as well (e.g., see Bailey,
this volume and Zatz et al., this volume). Violence motivated by ethnic and
religious hate is also well documented (e.g., Myers 1960; Newton and Newton
1991a). Today, it is recognized that most racial and ethnic minority groups bear
disproportionate burdens of common criminal victimization, regardless of the
motivations of the offenders, but there is a concomitant concern that crimes
motivated by racial hate may be on the increase (e.g., Flowers 1988, ch. 1).

When the topic of racially motivated crime is brought up, it is quite common
for people to think immediately of two kinds of events: (1) periodic major
crimes that receive national attention, such as mail bombing that killed civil
rights activist Robert Robinson in Georgia or the killing of black teenager Yusuf
Hawkins in the Bensonhurst section of Brooklyn, NY, or (2) the acts of organized
groups, such as the Ku Klux Klan.

It is true that racial hate generates a long list of severe assaults and even
murders in the United States (see Newton and Newton 1991a). It is also true that
the Klan is still active (although not as active as in the period between the Civil
War and World War II), and that newer groups, such as the white Aryan
Resistance and the Skinheads, have arisen to carry on the Klan's traditions (see
Newton and Newton 1991b; Ridgeway 1990). However, the everyday reality of
hate crime is much different.

1. Types of Crimes and Types of Bias. Hate crimes consist overwhelmingly
of minor crimes (in terms of their penal law categories, not necessarily their
effects on victims) committed by lone offenders or small groups of offenders
who do not claim membership in any racist organization. Less than 5 percent of
the racially motivated crimes in the New York City data contained any indication
of a connection to an organized hate group. The types of crimes, broken down
by the type of bias involved, are shown in Table 11.1.

Table 11.1
Type of Bias by Type of Crime, NYC, 1987-1988

Type of Crime	Racial	Ethnic	Religious	Sexual Orientation	Unclass-ified*
Assault	42%**	42%	6%	41%	33%
Menacing	6	3	1	2	3
Reckless Endangerment	1	2	0	2	0
Harassment	37	44	34	45	18
Criminal Mischief	7	6	55	8	33
Robbery	4	2	1	2	11
Burglary	1	0	2	0	0
Other	1	1	1	1	2
Number of Incidents	585	62	280	66	27

* In unclassified cases, multiple and sometime conflicting forms of bias were expressed.
** Column percentages may not sum to 100 because of rounding.

As indicated in Table 11.1, crimes motivated by bias against the victims'
race, ethnicity, or sexual orientation were primarily assaults and harassments.
Harassment can best be described as repeated and aggressive name-calling, and
as will be shown later, the assaults are mostly minor, rarely producing injuries
to the victims.

An exception to the type of crime pattern in Table 11.1 occurs for incidents
motivated by religious bias, which in this case, were primarily anti-Semitic
incidents. The majority of crimes motivated by religious bias were criminal
mischiefs (vandalisms); assaults were relatively uncommon. This difference is
also apparent when the targets of the bias crimes are examined. About 90 percent
of the racial, ethnic, and sexual orientation crimes were directed against
individuals, while this was the case for only about a third of the religious crimes.
Religious bias was much more commonly directed against objects than persons:
places of worship, schools, cemeteries, housing units, businesses.

The numbers of cases in Table 11.1 show quite clearly that racially motivated crimes were the most common — 585 of the 1,020 cases. However, a surprising finding emerges when the racially motivated crimes are examined further. Of the 585 racially motivated crimes, 57 percent (336 incidents) were anti-black in nature, while 36 percent (209) were anti-white. The remaining 7 percent (40) involved bias against other racial groups, primarily Asians. Apparently, common crimes involving racial hate include more than crimes against racial minorities.

Most of the incidents in which the victims saw the offenders contained information about the victim's perception of the offender's race and/or ethnicity. The New York City data has information about 908 offenders in bias-motivated crimes and 738 offenders in non-bias crimes (there are more offenders per incident in bias crimes). Table 11.2 presents the perceived race/ethnicity of offenders.

Table 11.2
Type of Bias by Perceived Race/Ethnicity of Offender
New York City, 1987-88

Perceived Race or Ethnicity	Type of Bias							
	Anti-Black	Anti-White	Anti-Other	Ethnic	Religious	Sexual Orientat.	Unclass.*	NonBias
White	88%**	5%	65%	82%	52%	57%	54%	40%
Black	1	84	19	13	25	8	12	41
Other Race	2	0	0	0	3	0	0	2
Hispanic	1	5	8	0	11	21	19	14
Unidentified	8	6	8	5	9	14	15	3
Number of Offenders	382	247	37	63	103	76	26	738

* In unclassified cases, multiple and sometimes conflicting forms of bias were expressed.
** Column percentages may not sum to 100 because of rounding.

The table indicates that blacks are over-represented as offenders (84 percent) in only one category of bias crimes: racial bias directed against whites. The percentage of offenders perceived to be black was 41 percent in the comparison (non-bias) crimes. Using the comparison crimes as a point of reference, blacks were under-represented as offenders in crimes involving bias against "other" racial groups, ethnicity, religion, and sexual orientation, while whites are over-represented as offenders. This is at least somewhat surprising in the New York

City context, given the substantial publicity about conflicts between blacks and Jews (more than 90 percent of the religious bias crimes were anti-Semitic) and blacks and some Asian groups (particularly Korean owners of small businesses).

The data suggest that racially motivated street crimes against blacks and whites are reciprocal, to a great degree. Reciprocity does not appear in the crimes motivated by ethnic bias which, in this case, are directed almost exclusively against Hispanics. Whites comprised 82 percent of the offenders in the ethnic bias crimes, versus 40 percent of the offenders in the comparison (non-bias) crimes. But Hispanics accounted for only 5 percent of the offenders in the racial crimes directed against whites, versus 14 percent in the comparison crimes (see Table 11.2). The issue of bias crime reciprocity between whites and blacks will be discussed in the conclusions of this chapter.

Earlier, in Table 11.1, the distributions of crime types for various categories of bias motivation were presented. Within the category of racial bias, crimes against blacks and whites were similar, in the sense that they were overwhelmingly direct-contact, personal crimes, rather than vandalisms or burglaries. However, the racially motivated crimes directed against blacks and whites do show some differences, as shown in Table 11.3.

Table 11.3
Type of Racial Bias by Type of Crime,
NYC, 1987-1988

| Type of Crime | Racially Motivated | |
	Against Blacks	Against Whites
Assault	34%*	57%
Menacing	8	3
Reckless Endangerment	1	1
Harassment	45	26
Criminal Mischief	8	1
Robbery	2	9
Burglary	1	0
Other	1	2
Number of Incidents	336	209

* Column percentages may not sum to 100 because of rounding.

The important points about Table 11.3 are that, in comparison to the racial crimes against whites, the crimes directed against blacks contain fewer assaults and robberies (and concomitantly, more harassments and menacings) and more vandalisms (criminal mischief). This suggests that, in expressing racial hate through street crimes, blacks tend to be more direct and more aggressive than whites.

2. The Nature of Racially Motivated Crimes. Since the overwhelming majority of racially motivated crimes, against blacks and whites, were direct-contact, personal crimes, the remainder of the chapter excludes crimes types other than these.

Racially motivated crimes against blacks and whites were similar to each other, and to the comparison crimes, in time of occurrence. Most took place in the evening (3 p.m. to 8:59 p.m.) or late night (9 p.m. to 2:59 a.m.). Both kinds of bias crimes were also similar to each other in place of occurrence. About 78 percent of the bias crimes against blacks and 83 percent of the ones against whites occurred in public places, such as sidewalks/streets, subways/buses, parks/playgrounds (other than school); only small percentages occurred in or immediately around private dwellings. In contrast, the comparison crimes were more likely to take place at private dwellings (28 percent) and were less likely to be committed in public places (48 percent).

The place of occurrence finding is consistent with the finding that victims of comparison crimes were much more likely than victims of racially motivated crimes to know the offenders. In the racially motivated crimes, nearly 60 percent of the victims said that the offender was definitely a stranger, and another 30 percent were not sure whether the offender was a stranger or someone they knew. The comparable figures for the non-bias, comparison crimes were 37 percent and 25 percent. Stated another way, more than a third of the victims in the non-bias crimes identified the offender as someone they knew, but the same was true in only about 10 percent of the racially motivated crimes.

Victims of racially motivated crime were younger and more often male than was the case in the non-bias comparison crimes. About half of the victims in the race bias crimes were less than 20 years old, compared to a quarter of the victims in the non-bias crimes. About three-quarters of the victims of racially motivated crimes were male, compared to 60 percent of the non-bias crimes. There were only small age and gender differences between the bias crimes directed at blacks and those directed at whites.

Similar patterns are evident with respect to the ages and genders of offenders. Although somewhere between 80 and 90 percent of the offenders in both types of racially motivated crimes and in the comparison crimes were perceived by victims to be 30 years old or younger, offenders in the bias crimes tended to be younger. About two-thirds of the offenders in both kinds of racially motivated crimes were perceived to be less than 21 years old, in comparison to about 45 percent in the non-bias crimes. Likewise, the offenders in the bias and non-bias crimes were overwhelmingly males, but the proportions of male offenders were slightly higher in the racially motivated crimes against blacks (94 percent) and whites (88 percent) than in the non-bias, comparison crimes (81 percent).

In addition to being younger and more often male, the offenders in racially motivated crimes were more numerous. Almost two-thirds of the non-bias, comparison crimes were committed by a lone offender, and almost all of the rest were committed by two or three offenders. In contrast, the majority of racially motivated crimes were committed by more than two offenders, a pattern that holds for racial crimes committed against both blacks and whites.

Not surprisingly, the disproportionate appearance of multiple offenders in racially motivated crimes was matched by a disproportionate presence of multiple victims in those crimes. Almost all (92 percent) of the non-bias, direct-contact personal crimes involved a lone victim. Lone victims characterized most of the racially motivated crimes too, but the proportion (72 percent) was much lower than in the comparison crimes. The distributions of numbers of victims was virtually identical for racial crimes against blacks and racial crimes against whites.

The pattern with respect to use of weapons is a bit ambiguous, as shown in Table 11.4. Weapons were used in a little more than a third of the direct-contact, racially motivated crimes against blacks, but in only about a quarter of both the racially motivated crimes against whites and the comparison crimes. However, the racially motivated crimes do differ substantially from the comparison crimes in terms of the *types* of weapons used. When offenders did use weapons, the weapons were more likely to be guns — and less likely to be "other" weapons such as clubs and rocks — in the comparison crimes than in the racially motivated crimes.

There is no ambiguity about the most direct effect on the victim, namely physical injury. The rate of victim injury was much higher in the non-bias, comparison crimes (54 percent of the victims) than in either kind of racially motivated crime (38 percent in crimes against blacks; 36 percent in crimes against whites).

3. The BIIU Response. As mentioned earlier, the Bias Incident Investigating Unit of the New York Police Department is just what its name implies: an investigative unit. The unit's formal purpose is to give enhanced investigative attention to bias-motivated crimes.

The New York City police are required to file a follow-up investigative report on virtually any type of follow-up work they conduct on their cases, after the initial incident report. As the data for this study were being coded by the researchers, the difference in amount of investigative effort applied to cases was

Table 11.4
Weapon Use in Direct-Contact Racially Motivated
and Comparison Crimes, New York City, 1987-1988

	Racially Motivated		Comparison Crimes (nonbias)
	Against Blacks	Against Whites	
Offender had a Weapon			
No*	64%**	76%	76%
Yes	36	24	24
Number of Incidents	(289)	(200)	(772)
Type of Weapon Used			
Gun	14%**	13%	23%
Knife	17	25	26
Other	66	60	47
Unidentified***	3	2	3
Number of direct Contact Incidents in which Offender had a Weapon	(104)	(48)	(148)

* Includes incidents in which the victim did not know whether or not the offender has a weapon.
** Column percentages may not sum to 100 because of rounding.
*** Incidents in which the offender has a weapon, but the type of weapon was not specified.

evident from the sheer sizes of the case folders: case folders in the BIIU were usually stuffed with documentation, while non-bias case folders, in the general department records area, were very slim. This difference is documented systematically in Table 11.5.

As shown in Table 11.5, about three-quarters of the non-bias, comparison cases received no follow-up investigative activity. This is not surprising in the criminal justice system for a place like New York City; recall that virtually all of these incidents were misdemeanors or lesser violations. In marked contrast, two or fewer follow-up investigative reports were filed in less than 10 percent of the racially motivated cases. Six or more follow-up reports were filed in nearly three-quarters of the racial crimes against blacks and in 60 percent of the racial crimes against whites. And the reports do not reflect simply "paper" effort. The researchers had substantial opportunities to observe the BIIU investigators at work, and many of the follow-up reports described substantial activities, such as canvassing dozens of addresses in searches for witnesses.

The enhanced follow-up attention evidently produces some results, at least in terms of the proportions of cases that resulted in an arrest. At least one arrest was made in 11 percent of the non-bias, comparison cases. The arrest rates for

Table 11.5
Number of Follow-up Investigative Reports Filed
In Direct-Contact Racially Motivated and Comparison Crimes
New York City, 1987-1988

Number of Reports Filed	Racially Motivated		Comparison Crimes (nonbias)
	Against Blacks	Against Whites	
None	1%*	1%	76%
1 or 2	4	8	16
3 to 5	22	32	6
6 to 10	30	28	1
> 10	42	32	0
Number of Direct-Contact Incidents	289	200	772

* Column percentages may not round to 100 because of rounding.

racially motivated crimes were two to three times as high: 31 percent for crimes committed against blacks, and 26 percent for crimes committed against whites.

Discussion

Major crimes of racial hate receive national media attention; they generate debate and calls for action. But there is another reality to racially motivated hate crime: the relatively minor assaults, harassments, vandalisms, and other street crimes that occur daily. This chapter has focused on that second reality through data accumulated by a police unit formed to investigate hate crimes.

A substantial portion of the chapter examined the characteristics of racially motivated, direct-contact, personal crimes in relation to a comparison sample of non-bias crimes of the same penal law types that occurred during the same time periods, in the same precincts. The results were not too surprising. The racially motivated crimes were committed by offenders who tended to act in groups, to be younger, and to be more often male than the offenders in the comparison crimes. Victims of racially motivated crimes showed the same patterns vis-a-vis the victims of comparison crimes: more often multiple victims who were younger and more likely to be male. The victim-offender relationship in racially motivated crimes was more likely to be one of stranger-to-stranger than was the case in the non-bias crimes. Correspondingly, the racially motivated crimes more often occurred in public places — sidewalks, parks, subway stations — than did the comparison crimes, which often took place in, or immediately about, private dwellings.

Comparing racially motivated and non-bias crimes on weapon use did not produce clear findings, except that, among incidents in which a weapon *was* used by the offender, the weapon was more likely to be a gun in the non-bias crimes than in the racially motivated crimes. This probably reflects the fact that the non-bias crimes were more likely to occur in or near someone's home, where a gun might be more readily available.

Physical injuries to victims occurred more often in the non-bias, comparison crimes than in the racially motivated crimes. However, there are some indications from the interviews with small samples of victims of bias and non-bias crimes that the victims of racially motivated crimes suffered greater and more long-lasting stress and anger. The interviews were exploratory, and most of the interesting aspects of the interview data derive from responses to open-ended questions. However, preliminary analyses suggest that, when compared to other victims, the victims of racially motivated crimes are more likely to feel that their whole world has been attacked. And, ominously, there are strong indications that racial resentments are heightened by their experiences.

The New York City Police Department unit established to handle bias crimes — the BIIU — does devote substantial attention to the cases that come to its attention. This attention appears to pay off in higher arrest rates than would be expected, given the types of crime involved. However, interviews with the BIIU investigators revealed that investigation and arrest do not constitute the sole reasons for the unit's existence. The investigators are very attuned to an expectation that they will provide additional, caring attention to the victims of bias crime. They are also quite aware that the unit serves a political purpose — not in any cynical sense, but in the sense of representing part of the city's political statement that bias-motivated crimes are a special concern and will not be ignored or dealt with routinely.

But the most surprising and intriguing finding was presented, with little comment, early in the chapter: the racially motivated crimes were not restricted to ones committed against minority racial groups. Excluding crimes directed against racial groups other than black and white, nearly 40 percent of the racially motivated crimes were directed against whites. This suggests that the city streets are a context for a more balanced form of racial conflict than is played out in the realms of employment, housing, education, and so forth. Basically, blacks are at less of a disadvantage in face-to-face encounters on the streets than they are in the various institutional spheres of American life.

A reasonable parallel can be drawn with the situation in the nation's prisons. Prison inmates face each other on a somewhat level playing field, and whites have become a minority group in many state prisons (e.g., see Thomas, this volume). As Jacobs concluded more than a decade ago, "prison, ironically, may be the one institution in American society which blacks 'control'" (1979: 24; for similar observations with respect to juvenile facilities, see Bartollas and Sieverdes 1981).

Biased behavior by whites against blacks is nothing new, but the streets provide blacks with a more level playing field — just as the prison does — to act on their resentments toward whites. The power disadvantages that blacks face in the employment, housing, and other markets are not as relevant on the streets. Of course, some disparity remains in racially motivated street crimes; after all, a higher proportion of the racially motivated crimes in the New York City data were committed against blacks than against whites. This remaining disparity probably reflects residential segregation and the differential placement of amenities — such as shopping and recreational opportunities — in predominantly white areas. In New York City, for example, whites do not often venture into Harlem or Bedford-Stuyvesant for shopping and entertainment, but blacks are less able to avoid going into predominantly white areas.

This discussion is not meant to cast a favorable light on the finding that bias-motivated street crimes represent a more balanced form of racial conflict than what is found in other spheres. The finding is important because it helps us to understand the depth of racial bias and resentment in the United States. Racial hate is not unidirectional; it reaps what is sows.

References

Achen, G.H. 1986. *The Statistical Analysis of Quasi-experiments*. Berkeley: University of California Press.

Adamson, C. 1984. Toward a Marxian Penology: Captive Criminal Populations as Economic Threats and Resources. *Social Problems* 31(4): 435-458.

Adamson, C. 1983. Punishment After Slavery: Southern State Penal Systems, 1865-1880. *Social Problems* 30(5): 555-569.

Albonetti, C.A., R.M. Hauser, J. Hagan, and I.H. Nagel. 1989. Criminal Justice Decision Making as a Stratification Process: The Role of Race and Stratification Resources in Pretrial Release. *Journal of Quantitative Criminology* 5: 57-82.

Ansari, Z. 1990. The Muddled Methodology of the Wilbanks NDT Thesis. In *Racism, Empiricism and Criminal Justice*, edited by B. MacLean and D. Milovanovic. Vancouver, Canada: Collective Press.

Anti-Defamation League. 1988a. *Hate Crime Statutes: A Response to Anti-Semitism, Vandalism, and Violent Bigotry.* NY: Anti-Defamation League of B'nai B'rith.

Anti-Defamation League. 1988b. *Hate Crimes: Policies and Procedures for Law Enforcement Agencies.* NY: Anti-Defamation League of B'nai B'rth.

Arkin, S.D. 1980. Discrimination and Arbitrariness in Capital Punishment: An Analysis of Post-Furman Murder Cases in Dade County, Florida, 1973-1976. *Stanford Law Review* 33: 75-101.

Arnold W. R. 1971. Race and ethnicity relative to other factors in juvenile court dispositions. *American Journal of Sociology* 77: 221-222

Aronowitz, S. 1973. *False Promises: The Shaping of American Working Class Consciousness.* New Brunswick, NJ: Transaction.

Ayers, E. L. 1984. *Vengeance and Justice: Crime and Punishment in the 19th Century American South.* NY: Oxford.

Azicri, M. 1981-1982. The Politics of Exile: Trends and Dynamics of Political Change among Cuban Americans. *Cuban Studies* 11(2)/12(1): 55-73.

Bach, R. L. 1980. The New Cuban Immigrants: Their Background and Prospects. *Monthly Labor Review* (October): 39-46.

Bach, R. L., J. B. Bach, and T. Triplett. 1981-1982. The Flotilla 'Entrants': Latest and Most Controversial. *Cuban Studies* 11(2)/12(1): 29-48.

Baldus, D.C., C. Pulaski, and G. Woodworth. 1983. Comparative Review of Death Sentences: An Empirical Study of the Georgia Experience. *Journal of Criminal Law and Criminology* 74: 661-753.

Baldus, David C. 1986. Arbitrariness and Discrimination in the Administration of the Death Penalty: A Challenge to State Supreme Courts. *Stetson Law Review* 15: 133-261.

Baldus, D.C., G. Woodworth, and C.A. Pulaski. 1985. Monitoring and Evaluating Contemporary Death Sentencing Systems: Lessons from Georgia. *University of California-Davis Law Review* 18: 1375-1407.

Barnow, B.S., G.G. Cain, and A.S. Goldberger. 1980. Issues in the Analysis of Selection Bias. In *Evaluation Studies Review Annual,* edited by E.W. Stromsdorfer and G. Farkas. Beverly Hills, CA: Sage.

Baro, A. 1988. The Loss of Local Control Over Prison Administration. *Justice Quarterly* 5(3): 457-473.

Bartollas, C. and C. M. Sieverdes. 1981. The Victimized White in a Juvenile Correctional System. *Crime and Delinquency* 27(4): 534-543.

Bayley, D. H., and H. Mendelsohn. 1969. *Minorities and The Police: Confrontation in America.* NY: Free Press.

Beck, E.M. and S.E. Tolnay. 1990. The Market for Cotton and the Lynching of Blacks, 1882-1930. *American Sociological Review* 55(4): 526-539.

Bedau, H. A. (ed.). 1982. *The Death Penalty in America* 3rd edition. NY: Oxford University Press.

Berger, M. 1967. *Equality by Statute*. Garden City, NY: Doubleday.

Berger, P.L. 1967. *The Sacred Canopy*. Garden City, NY: Doubleday

Bernard, Thomas J. 1983. *The Consensus Conflict Debate: Form and Content in Social Theories*. NY: Columbia University Press.

Bernstein, I. N., E. Kick, J. T. Leung, and B. Schulz. 1977. Charge reduction: An intermediary stage in the process of labelling criminal defendants. *Social Forces* 56: 362-84.

Bienen, L. B., N. A. Weiner, D. W. Denno, P. D. Allison, and D. L. Mills 1988 The Reimposition of Capital Punishment in New Jersey: The Role of Prosecutorial Discretion. *Rutgers Law Review* 41: 27-372.

Bishop D.M., and C.Frazier. 1988. The Influence of Race in Juvenile Justice Processing. *Journal of Research in Crime and Delinquency* 25: 242-263.

Black, Donald. 1983. Crime as Social Control. *American Sociological Review* 48 (February): 34-45.

Black, D. 1980. *The Manner and Customs of the Police*. NY: Academic Press.

Black, D. 1976. *The Behavior of Law*. NY: Academic Press.

Black, D., and A. Reiss. 1967. *Studies in Crime and Law Enforcement in Major Metropolitan Areas*. Washington, D.C.: U.S. Government Printing Office.

Black, M. 1962. *Models and Metaphors: Studies in Language and Philosophy*. Ithaca, NY: Cornell University Press.

Blauner, R. 1972. *Racial Oppression in America*. NY: Harper and Row.

Blumstein, A. 1982. On the Racial Disproportionality of United States' Prison Populations. *Journal of Criminal Law and Criminology* 73: 1259-1281.

Bohm, Robert M. 1991. American Death Penalty Opinion, 1936-1986: A Critical Examination of the Gallup Polls. In *The Death Penalty in America: Current Research*, edited by R.M. Bohm. Cincinnati: Anderson.

Bohm, R.M., L.J. Clark, and A.F. Aveni. 1991. Knowledge and Death Penalty Opinion: A Test of the Marshall Hypotheses. *Journal of Research in Crime and Delinquency* (forthcoming).

Bonger, W. 1943. *Race and Crime*. NY: Columbia University Press.

Bosarge, B.B. 1987. FBOP: Awaiting Results of NIC's After Action Studies of Two Prison Riots. *Corrections Digest* 18(26): 1, 6-8.

Bosswell, T. D. and J. R. Curtis. 1983. *The Cuban American Experience: Culture, Images and Perspectives*. Totawa, NJ: Rowman and Allenheld, Publishers.

Bourdieu, P. and J. Passeron. 1979. *The Inheritors: French Students and their Relation to Culture*. Chicago: University of Chicago Press.

Bowers, W.J., G.L. Pierce and J.F. McDevitt. 1984. *Legal Homicide: Death As*

Punishment in America, 1864-1982. Boston: Northeastern University Press.

Bowers, W.J. and G.L. Pierce. 1982. Racial Discrimination and Criminal Homicide under Post-Furman Capital Statutes. In *The Death Penalty in America* 3rd edition, edited by H. Bedau. NY: Oxford University Press.

Box, S. 1981. *Deviance, Reality and Society.* NY: Holt, Reinhart and Winston.

Box, S. and C. Hale. 1983a. Liberation and Female Criminality in England and Wales Revisited. *British Journal of Criminology* 22: 35-49.

Box, S. and C. Hale. 1983b. Liberation or Economic Marginalization: The Relevance of Two Theoretical Arguments to Female Crime Patterns in England and Wales, 1951-1980. *Criminology* 22,4: 4773-497.

Brown, R. H. 1977. *A Poetic for Sociology: Toward a Logic of Discovery for the Human Sciences.* NY: Cambridge University Press.

Bullington, Bruce. 1977. *Heroin Use in the Barrio.* Lexington, Mass: Lexington Books.

Burke, P. and A. Turk. 1975. Factors Affecting Post Arrest Disposition: A Model for Analysis. *Social Problems* 22: 213-232.

Bynum, Tim 1981. Parole Decision Making and Native Americans. In *Race, Crime, and Criminal Justice,* edited by R.L. McNeely and Carl E. Pope. Beverly Hills: Sage.

Bynum, T. S. and R. Paternoster. 1984. Discrimination Revisited: An Exploration of Frontstage and Backstage Criminal Justice Decision Making. *Sociology and Social Research* 69: 90-108.

Camp, G. M. and C. G. Camp. 1985. *Prison Gangs: Their Extent, Nature and Impact on Prisons.* Washington: U.S. Department of Justice.

Carliner, D. 1977. *The Rights of Aliens: The Basic ACLU Guide to an Aliens Rights.* NY: Avon Books.

Carlson, R.A. 1975. *The Quest for Conformity: Americanization Through Education.* NY: John Wiley and Sons.

Carroll, L. 1977a. Humanitarian Reform and Bi-racial Sexual Assault in a Maximum Security Prison. *Urban Life* 5(January): 417-437.

Carroll, L. 1977b. Race and Three Forms of Prison Power: Confrontation, Censoriousness, and the Corruption of Authority. In *Contemporary Corrections: Social Control and Conflict,* edited by C. R. Huff. Beverley Hills: Sage. 40-54

Carroll, L. 1988. *Hacks, Blacks, and Cons: Race Relations in a Maximum Security Prison.* Prospect Heights, IL: Waveland Press.

Chambliss, W. 1969. *Crime and the Legal Process.* NY: McGraw-Hill.

Chambliss, W. and R. Seidman. 1982. *Law, Order, and Power.* Reading, Mass.: Addison-Wesley.

Chiricos, T. and G. Waldo. 1975. Socioeconomic Status and Criminal Sentencing: An Empirical Assessment of a Conflict Proposition. *American Socio-logical Review* 40: 753-72.

Christianson, S. 1981. Our Black Prisons. *Journal of Crime and Delinquency* 27(3).

Clark, J. M. 1975. *The Exodus From Revolutionary Cuba (1959-1974): A Sociological Analysis.* Ph.D Dissertation. University of Florida.

Clark, J.M., J.I. Lasaga, and R.R. Reque. 1981. *The 1980 Mariel Exodus: an Assessment and Prospect.* Washington, D.C.: Council for Inter-American Security.

Cohen, A.W. and E.C. Viano (eds.). 1976. *Police Community Relations: Images, Roles, Realities.* Philadelphia: J. B. Lippincott Company.

Colvin, M. 1981. The Contradictions of Control: Prisons in Class Society. *Insurgent Sociologist* 9/10 (Summer/Fall): 33-45.

Colvin, M. 1982. The 1980 New Mexico Prison Riot. *Social Problems* 25(June): 449-463.

Corrections Today. 1988. Lessons Learned: After the Riots. 50(3): 16-20.

Crites, L. 1978. Women in the Criminal Court. In *Women in the Courts* edited by W. Hepperle and L. Crites. Williamsburg, VA: National Center for State Courts.

Crutchfield, R.D. and G.S. Bridges. 1985. *Racial and Ethnic Disparities in Imprisonment: Final Report.* Institute for Public Policy and Management, University of Washington, Seattle, WA.

Curtis, L. A. 1975. *Violence, Race and Culture.* Lexington, MA: Lexington Books.

Datesman, S., and F. Scarpitti. 1980. Unequal protection for males and females in the Juvenile Court. In *Women, Crime and Justice,* edited by S. Datesman and F. Scarpitti. N.Y.: Oxford University Press.

Death Row, U.S.A. 1990. NY: NAACP Legal Defense and Educational Fund, Inc. (September 21).

Deloria, V. Jr. and C. M. Lytle. 1983. *American Indians, American Justice.* Austin: University of Texas Press.

Dannefer, D. and R.Schutt. 1982. Race and Juvenile Justice Processing in court and Police Agencies. *American Journal of Sociology* 87: 1113-1132.

DiIulio, J. J., Jr. 1987. *Governing Prisons: A Comparative Study of Correctional Management.* NY: The Free Press.

DiMarzio, N. Rev. Msgr. 1988. The Marielitos: Another Chance for Freedom. *Migration World* 16(2): 38-39.

Ellsworth, P. C. and L.Ross. 1983. Public Opinion and Capital Punishment: A Close Examination of the Views of Abolitionists and Retentionists. *Crime and Delinquency* 29: 116-169.

Espinosa, R. 1982. *Report on the Los Angeles Unified School District: A Comparison of School Finance and Facilites between Hispanic and Non-Hispanic Schools During Fiscal Year 1980-81*. Los Angeles: Mexican-American Legal Defense and Education Fund.

Fagan, J. A., Slaughter, and E. Harstone. 1987. Blind Justice? The Impact of Race on the Juvenile Justice Process. *Crime and Delinquency* 33: 224-258.

Farnworth, M. and . M. Horan. 1980. Separate Justice: An analysis of race differences in court processes. *Social Science Research* 9: 381-99.

Farrell, R. and V. Swigert 1978 Prior Offense record as a Self-Fulfilling Prophecy. *Law and Society Review* 12: 427-453.

Federal Bureau of Prisons. 1988. *A Report To The Attorney General On The Disturbances At The Federal Detention Center, Oakdale, Louisiana And The U.S. Penitentiary, Atlanta Georgia*. United States Department of Justice.

Feimer, S., F. Pommersheim, and S. Wise. 1990. Marking Time: Does Race Make a Difference? A Study of Disparate Sentencing in South Dakota. *Journal of Crime and Justice* 13: 86-102.

Fernandez, G. A. 1981-1982 Comment: The Flotilla Entrants: Are They Different? *Cuban Studies* 11(2)/12(1): 49-53.

Fernandez, G.A. 1982. The Freedom Flotilla: A Legitimacy Crisis of Cuban Socialism, *Journal of Inter-American Studies and World Affairs* 24(2): 183-209.

Fernandez, G.A. 1984. Conflicting Interpretations of the Freedom Flotilla Entrants, *Cuban Studies* 14(1): 49-51.

Fernandez, G.A. and L. Narvaez. 1987 Research Note: Refugees and Human Rights in Costa Rica: The Mariel Cubans. *International Migration Review* 21(2): 406-415.

Flakser, D. 1971. *Marxism, Ideology and Myth*. NY: Philosophical Library.

Flanigan, D.J. 1987. *The Criminal Law of Slavery and Freedom*. NY: Garland.

Fleisher, M.S. 1989. *Warehousing Violence*. Newbury Park, CA: Sage.

Florida Department of Corrections. 1983. *Research Report: Cubans, Mariel Boatlift Cubans, and Haitians Committed to the Florida Department of Corrections*. Bureau of Planning, Research and Statistics 81-R-10.

Flowers, R. B. 1988. *Minorities and Criminality*. NY: Praeger.

Foote, C. 1954. Compelling Appearance in Court: Administration of Bail in Philadelphia. *University of Pennsylvania Law Review* 102: 1031-79.

Fragomen, A. T., A. J. Del Rey, and S. C. Bell 1989 *Immigration Procedures Handbook*. NY: Clark Boardman Company, Ltd.

Friedland, M. 1965. *Detention Before Trial*. Toronto: University of Toronto Press.

Fyfe, J.J. 1981. *Police Use of Deadly Force*. Washington, D.C.: Police Foundation.

Gallup Report 1989 Public Support for Death Penalty is Highest in Gallup Annals. Princeton, NJ: The Gallup Report.

Garber, S., S. Klepper and D. S. Nagin. 1983. The Role of Extralegal Factors in Determining Criminal Case Disposition. In *Research in Sentencing: The Search for Reform*, vol. II, edited by A.Blumstein et al. Washington, D.C.: National Academy Press.

Georges-Abeyie, D. 1990. Criminal Justice Processing of Non-White Minorities. In *Racism, Empiricism and Criminal Justice*, edited by B. D. MacLean and D. Milovanovic. Vancouver, Canada: Collective Press.

Georges-Abeyie, D. 1984a. The Criminal Justice System and Minorities: A Review of the Literature. In *The Criminal Justice System and Blacks*, edited by D.Georges-Abeyie. NY: Clark Boardman and Company.

Georgies-Abeyie, D. (ed.). 1984b. *The Criminal Justice System and Blacks*. NY: Clark Boardman Company.

Gibson, R. and W. Smith. 1987. Gangs Lock Pontiac in a Web of Violence. *Chicago Tribune*. July 18: 1, 2.

Goldstein, M. 1987. Toward Community-oriented Policing: Potential, Basic Requirements and Thresholds Requirements. *Crime and Delinquency* 33 (1): 6-30.

Goodell, W. 1971. *Views of American Constitutional Law in its Bearing Upon American Slavery*. Freeport, NY: Books For Libraries Press.

Governor's Task Force on Bias-Related Violence. 1988. Douglas A. White, Chair. *Final Report*. March, State of New York.

Greenberg, D. and D. Humphries. 1980 The co-optation of fixed sentencing reform. *Crime and Delinquency* 26: 206-225.

Greene, J. R., and C. Klockars. 1991. What Police Do. In *Thinking About Police*: *Contemporary Readings*, edited by C. B. Klockars and S. Mastrofski. NY: McGraw-Hill.

Greene, J. R., and S. D. Mastrofski (eds.). 1988. *Community Policing: Rhetoric or Reality*. NY: Praeger.

Gross, S. R. and R. Mauro. 1989. *Death and Discrimination: Racial Disparities in Capital Sentencing*. Boston: Northeastern University Press.

Grossman, E. 1987. Prison Study Raises Concern. *Poughkeepsie Journal* 4(March): 38.

Groves, W.B. and G.R. Newman. 1987. *Punishment and Privelege*. NY: Harrow and Heston.

Gruhl, J., S. Welch, and C. Spohn. 1984. Women as Criminal Defendants: A Test for Paternalism. *Western Political Quarterly* 37: 456-467.

Gusfield, J. 1963. *Symbolic Crusade: Status Politics and the American Temperance Movement*. Urbana: University of Illinois Press.

Hagan, J. 1974. Extra-Legal Attributes and Criminal Sentencing: An Assessment of a Sociological Viewpoint. *Law and Society Review* 8: 357-383.

Hagan, J., and C. Albonetti. 1982. Race, Class, and the Perception of Criminal Injustice in America. *American Journal of Sociology* 88: 329-355.

Hagan, J., and K. Bumiller. 1983. Making Sense of Sentencing: A Review and Critique of Sentencing Research. In *Research in Sentencing: The Search for Reform* vol. II, edited by A. Blumstein et al. Washington, D.C.: National Academy Press.

Hagan, J. and R.D. Peterson. 1984. Changing Conceptions of Race: Towards an Account of Anomalous Findings of Sentencing Research. *American Sociological Review* 49: 56-70.

Hagan, J., and M. S. Zatz. 1985. The Social Organization of Criminal Justice Processing Activities. *Social Science Research* 14: 103-125.

Hall, A. 1984. *Pretrial Release Program Options*. Washington, D.C.: NIJ.

Hall, E. L. and A. A. Simkus. 1975. Inequality in the Types of Sentences Received by Native Americans and Whites. *Criminology* 13: 199-222.

Harris, Carl V. 1973 Reforms in Government Control of Negroes in Birmingham, Alabama, 1890-1920, *The Journal of Southern History* 38(4): 567-600.

Headly, B. 1990. What Really Lies Behind the Myth of 'No Discrimination' in the Criminal Justice System. In *Racism, Empiricism and Criminal Justice*, edited by B. D. MacLean and D. Milovanovic. Vancouver, Canada: Collective Press.

Hepburn, J. R. 1978. Race and the Decision to Arrest: An analysis of Warrants Issued. *Journal of Research in Crime and Delinquency* 15 (January): 54-73.

Henri, F. 1975. *Black Migration: Movement North, 1900-1920*. Garden City, NY: Anchor Press.

Higginbotham, A.L. 1973. Racism and the Early American Legal Process. *The Annals of the American Academy of Political and Social Science* 407: 1-17

Hill, G.D., A.R. Harris and J.L. Miller. 1985. The Etiology of Bias: Social Heuristics and Rational Decision Making in Deviance Processing. *Journal of Research in Crime and Delinquency* 22(2): 135-162.

Himmelstein, Jerome L. 1983 *The Strange Career of Marijuana: Politics and Ideology of Drug Control in America*. Westport, CT: Greenwood Press.

Hindus, Michael S., 1980. *Prison and Plantation: Crime, Justice, and Authority in Massachusetts, 1767-1878*. Chapel Hill: The University of North Carolina Press.

Hindelang, M. 1978. Race and Involvement in Common Law Personal Crimes.

American Sociological Review 43: 93-109.

Hoebel, E. Adamson 1969 Keresan Pueblo Law. In *Law, Culture and Society*, edited by L. Nader. Chicago: Aldine.

Holmes, M. D., H.C. Daudistel and R. A. Farrell. 1987. Determinants of charge reductions and final dispositions in cases of burglary and robbery. *Journal of Research in Crime and Delinquency* 24(3): 233-54.

Holmes, M.D. and H.C. Daudistel. 1984. Ethnicity and justice in the Southwest: The sentencing of Anglo, black, and Mexican origin defendants. *Social Science Quarterly* 65(2): 265-277.

Hunt, E.H. 1980. Castro's Worms. *National Review* 32(12): 722-724.

Huizinga, D. and D.Elliott. 1987. Juvenile Offenders: Prevalence, Offender Incidence and Arrest Rates by Race. *Crime and Delinquency* 33: 206-223.

Hynes, C. J. and B. Drury. 1990. *Incident at Howard Beach*. NY: G.P. Putnam's Sons.

Insight Into Corrections. 1991 *Insight*. (April). Illinois Department of Corrections, Springfield.

Irwin, J. and D. R. Cressey. 1962. Thieves, Convicts, and the Inmate Culture. *Social Problems* 10 (Fall): 142-155.

Jackson, G. 1970. *Soledad Brother: The Prison Letters of George Jackson*. NY: Bantam Books.

Jacobs, D. 1978. Inequality and the Legal Order: An Ecological Test of the Conflict Model. *Social Problems* 25: 515-25

Jacobs, J. B. 1974. Street Gangs Behind Bars. *Social Problems* 21(3): 395-409.

Jacobs, J. 1977. *Stateville: The Penitentiary in Mass Society*, Chicago: University of Chicago Press.

Jacobs, J. B. 1979. Race Relations and the Prisoner Subculture. In *Crime and Justice: An Annual Review of Research*, edited by N. Morris and M. Tonry. Chicago: University of Chicago Press.

Jacobs, J.B. 1983. *New Perspectives on Prisons and Imprisonment*. Ithaca: Cornell University Press.

Jacobs, J.B., and L.J. Kraft. 1978. Integrating the Gatekeepers: A Comparison of Black and White Prison Guards in Illinois. *Social Problems* 25(February): 304-318.

Jacobs, J.B., and H.G. Retsky. 1975. Prison Guard. *Urban Life* 4(April): 5-29.

Jacoby, J. E. and R. Paternoster. 1982. Sentencing Disparity and Jury Packing: Further Challenges to the Death Penalty. *Journal of Criminal Law and Criminology* 73: 379-87.

Jaffee, A. J., R. M. Cullen, and T. D. Boswell. 1980. *The Changing Demography of Spanish Americans*. NY: Academic.

Jenkins, P. 1984. *Crime And Justice: Issues and Ideas*. Belomont, CA: Brooks/

Cole.

Johnson, R. and H. Toch. 1988. *The Pains of Imprisonment*. Prospect Heights, Ill.: Waveland.

Jolly, R. and E. Sagarin. 1984. The First Eight Executed After Furman: Who Was Executed with the Return of the Death Penalty? *Crime and Delinquency* 30: 610-23.

Jones, W. R. 1991. *Theory and Dynamics of Racism and Oppression*. Florida State University.

Joseph, J. D. 1987. *Black Mondays: Worst Decisions of the Supreme Court*. Bethesda: National Press.

Keil, T. J. and G. F. Vito. 1990. Race and the Death Penalty in Kentucky Murder Trials: An Analysis of Post-Gregg Outcomes. *Justice Quarterly* 7: 189-207.

Kennedy, S. 1959. *Jim Crow Guide to the U.S.A*. London: Lawrence and Wishart Ltd.

Kerr, J. R. 1969. Constitutional Rights, Tribal Justice, and the American Indian. *Journal of Public Law* 18: 311-338.

Klimko, F. 1986. Atlanta's Cuban Crisis. *Corrections Compendium* 11(2): 1-7.

Kleck, G. 1981. Racial Discrimination in Criminal Sentencing: A Critical Evaluation of the Evidence with Additional Data on the Death Penalty. *American Sociological Review* 46: 783-805.

Kleck, G. 1985. Life Support for Ailing Hypotheses: Modes of Summarizing the Evidence for Racial Discrimination in Sentencing. *Law and Human Behavior* 9: 271-285.

Klein, S.P., S. Turner, and J. Petersilia. 1988. *Racial Equity in Sentencing*. Rand Corporation, Santa Monica, CA.

Klepper, S., D.S. Nagin and L. Tierney. 1983. Discrimination in the Criminal Justice System: A Critical Appraisal of the Literature. In *Research in Sentencing: The Search for Reform*, vol. II, edited by A.Blumstein et al. Washington, D.C.: National Academy Press.

Krisberg, B. et al. 1987. The Incarceration of Minority Youth. *Crime and Delinquency* 33: 171-205.

Kuhn, T. 1970. *The Structure of Scientific Revolutions*. London: Chicago Press.

LaFree, G. 1989. *Rape and Criminal Justice: The Social Construction of Sexual Assault*. Belmont, CA: Wadsworth.

LaFree, G. 1985. Official Reactions to Hispanic Defendants in the Southwest. *Journal of Research in Crime and Delinquency* 22: 213-237.

LaFree, G. 1980. The effect of sexual stratificaton by race on official reactions to rape. *American Sociological Review* 45: 842-854.

Lakoff, G. and M. Johnson. 1980. *Metaphors We Live By*. Chicago: University of Chicago Press.

Lauren, P. G. 1988. *Power and Prejudice: The Politics and Diplomacy of Racial Discrimination*. Boulder: Westview Press.

Lefcourt, R. 1971. *Law Against the People*. NY: Random House.

LeVine, R.A. 1973. *Culture, Behavior, and Personality*. Chicago: Aldine Publishing Company.

Levy, J. E., S.J. Kunitz, and M. Everett. 1969. Navajo Criminal Homicide. *Southwestern Journal of Anthropology* 25: 124-152.

Loftin, C. and D. McDowall. 1988. The Analysis of Case-Control Studies in Criminology. *Journal of Quantitative Criminology* 4: 85-98.

Lodge, D. 1988. *The Modes of Modern Writing: Metaphor, Metonymy, and the Typology of Modern Literature.* Chicago: University of ChicagoPress.

Logan, R.W. 1957. *The Negro in the United States*. Princeton: Nostrand Company, Inc.

Lombardo, L. X. 1981. *Guards Imprisoned: Correctional Officers at Work*. NY: Elsevier.

Louisiana Slave Codes of 1852. The Consolidation and Revision of the Statutes of the State, 1852 . New Orleans.

Lujan, C. C. 1986. *American Indians and Imposed Law: The Impact of Social Integration on Legal Perceptions Among Two Southwestern Tribes*. Doctoral dissertation, Department of Sociology, University of New Mexico.

Lujan, C. C. 1990a. American Indian Women and the Law. Paper presented at the International Sociological Association meetings, Madrid, Spain.

Lujan, C.C. 1990b. Census Underenumeration Among the American Indians and Alaskan Natives. Unpublished manuscript.

Lynch, M.J. 1990. Racial Bias and Criminal Justice: Definitional and Methodological Issues. In *Racism, Empiricism and Criminal Justice*, edited by B. MacLean and D. Milovanovic. Vancouver, Canada: Collective Press.

Lynch, M. J. and W. Byron Groves. 1989. *A Primer in Radical Criminology* 2nd ed. NY: Harrow and Heston.

Lynch, M.J. and M.K. Nalla. 1989. The Correlates of Crime: A Critique of Causal and Methodological Issues. Paper presented at the Annual Meeting of the American Society of Criminology, November, Reno, Nevada.

Lynch, M.J. and E.B. Patterson. 1990. Racial Discrimination in the Criminal Justice System: Evidence from Four Jurisdictions. In *Racism, Empiricism and Criminal Justice*, B. MacLean and D. Milovanovic. Vancouver, Canada: Collective Press.

MacLean, B. and D. Milovanovic. 1990. An Anatomy of the 'No Discrimination Thesis.' In *Racism, Empiricism and Criminal Justice*, edited by B. MacLean and D.Milovanovic. Vancouver, Canada: The Collective Press.

MacLean, B. and D. Milovanovic. 1990. *Racism, Empiricism and Criminal*

Justice. Vancouver, Canada: The Collective Press.

Manning, P. K. 1979. Metaphors of the Field: Varieties of Organizational Discourse. *Administrative Science Quarterly* 24(December): 660-672.

Manning, P.K. (Forthcoming) Strands in the Postmodernist Rope: Ethnographic Themes. In *Studies in Symbolic Interaction* vol. 13, edited by N. Denzin, Greenwich (Conn.): JAI.

Mastrofski, S. 1983. The Police and Non-Crime Services. In *Evaluating Performance of Criminal Justice Agencies*, edited by G. Whitaker and C. Phillips.Beverly Hills, CA: Sage.

McCarthy, B. R., and B.L. Smith. 1986. The conceptualization of discrimination in the juvenile justice process: the impact of administrative factors and screening decisions on juvenile court dispositions. *Criminology* 24: 41-64.

McLemore, D. S.1980. *Racial and Ethnic Relations in America*, 2nd Edition. Boston: Allyn and Bacon.

McNeely, R.L. and C.E. Pope. 1981. *Race, Crime and Criminal Justice.* Beverly Hills, CA: Sage.

Messerschmidt, J. 1986. *Capitalism, Patriarchy and Crime.* Totowa, NJ: Rowman and Littlefield.

Michalowski, R. 1985. *Order, Law and Crime.* NY: Random House.

Miethe, T. and C.A. Moore. 1985. Socioeconomic Disparities Under Determinante Sentencing Systems. *Criminology* 23: 337-363.

Milovanovic, D. 1988. *A Primer in the Sociology of Law.* Albany, NY: Harrow and Heston.

Milovanovic, D., and J. Thomas. 1989. Overcoming the Absurd: Prisoner Litigation as Primitive Rebellion. *Social Problems* 36(February): 48-60.

Minnesota Board of Peace Officer Standards and Training. 1990. *Bias Motivated Crimes: A Summary Report of Minnesota's Response.* St. Paul: Minnesota Post.

Mirande, A. 1987. *Gringo Justice.* Nortre Dame: University of Notre Dame Press.

Montagu, A. 1964. *The Concept of Race.* NY: MacMillian.

Moore, J. 1978. *Homeboys: Gangs, Drugs, and Prison in the Barrios of Los Angeles.* Philadelphia: Temple University Press.

Morse, W., and R. Beattie. 1932. Survey of the Administration of Criminal Justice in Oregon, Report No. 1: Final Report on 1771 Felony Cases in Multnomah County. *Oregon Law Review* 11(4): 86-117.

Muir, W. K. 1977. *Police: Streetcorner Politicians.* Chicago: University of Chicago Press.

Murphy, J. 1989. *A Question of Race: Minority/White Incarceration in New York State.* Center for Justice Education, Albany, NY.

Musto, D. F. 1973. *The American Disease: Origins of Narcotic Control.* New Haven: Yale University Press.

Myers, G. 1960. *History of Bigotry in the United States.* NY: Capricorn Books.

Myers, M.A., and S. Talerico. 1987. *The Social Context of Criminal Sentencing.* NY: Springer-Verlag.

Myrdal, G. 1969. *Objectivity in Social Research.* NY: Pantheon.

Nagel, S. 1969. *The Legal Process from a Behavioral Perspective.* Homewood, Il: Dorsey.

Nakell, B. and K. A. Hardy. 1987. *The Arbitrariness of the Death Penalty.* Philadelphia: Temple University Press.

Nam, C.B. and M.G. Powers. 1968. Changes in the relative status level of workers in the United States, 1950-1960. *Social Forces* 47(2):158-170.

Nelson, J.F. 1989. An Operational Definition of Prior Criminal Record. *Journal of Quantitative Criminology* 5: 333-352.

Newton, M. and J. A. Newton. 1991a. *Racial and Religious Violence in America: A Chronology.* NY: Garland.

Newton, M. and J. A. Newton. 1991b. *The Ku Klux Klan: An Encyclopedia.* NY: Garland.

New York Governor's Task Force on Bias-Related Violence. *Final Report.* Albany, NY.

Nichols, N. 1982. Castro's Revenge. *The Washington Monthly* 14(1): 38-42.

Nowicki, E. 1987. The Cuban Connection. *Police* (April): 38-69.

Office of Juvenile Justice and Delinquency Prevention (OJJDP). 1989. *Juvenile Court Statistics, 1985.* Washington, D.C.: USGPO.

Orfield, G. et al. 1984. *The Chicago Study of Access and Choice in Higher Education: A Report to the Illinois Senate Committee on Higher Education.* Chicago: University of Chicago.

Padgett, G.L. 1984. Racially-Motivated Violence and Intimidation: Inadequate State Enforcement and Federal Civil Rights Remedies. *Journal of Criminal Law and Criminology* 75 (1): 103-138.

Paternoster, R. 1991. Prosecutorial Discretion and Capital Sentencing in North and South Carolina. In *The Death Penalty in America: Current Research*, edited by R.M. Bohm. Cincinnati: Anderson.

Paternoster, R. 1984. Prosecutorial Discretion in Requesting the Death Penalty: A Case of Victim-Based Racial Discrimination. *Law and Society Review* 18: 437-478.

Paternoster, R. 1983. Race of Victim and Location of Crime: The Decision to Seek the Death Penalty in South Carolina. *Journal of Criminal Law and Criminology* 74: 754-785.

Passel, J.S. and P.A. Berman. 1986. Quality of 1980 Census Data for American

Indians. *Social Biology* 33: 163-182.

Peak, K. and J. Spencer. 1987. Crime in Indian Country: Another 'Trail of Tears.' *Journal of Criminal Justice* 15: 485-494.

Pedraza-Bailey, S. 1981-1982 Cubans and Mexicans in theUnited States: The Functions of Political and Economic Migration. *Cuban Studies* 11(2)/12(1): 79-95.

Pedraza-Bailey, S. 1985. *Political and Economic Migrants in America: Cubans and Mexicans*. Austin, Texas: University of Texas Press.

Pepinsky, H. and P. Jesilow. 1984. *Myths that Cause Crime*. Cabin John, MD: Seven Locks.

Pepper, S.C. 1948. *World Hypotheses: A study in Evidence*. Berkeley: University of California Press.

Petersilia, J. 1983. *Racial Disparities in the Criminal Justice System*. Santa Monica, CA: Rand.

Petersilia, J. and S. Turner. 1987. Guideline-based Justice: Prediction and Racial Minorities in D.M. Gottfredson and M. Tonry. *Prediction and Classification*. Chicago: University of Chicago Press.

Peterson, M.F. 1984. Work Attitudes of Mariel Boatlift Refugees. *Cuban Studies* 14(2): 1-19.

Pindyck, R., and D. Rubinfeld. 1981. *Economic Models and Economic Forecasts*. NY: McGraw-Hill.

Platt, T. 1979. The Triumph of Benevolence: The Origins of the Juvenile Justice System in the United States. In *Law and Order in American History*, edited by J. M. Hawes. Port Washington, NY: Kemikat Press.

Pollack, O. 1950. *The Criminality of Women*. Philadelphia: University of Pennsylvania Press.

Pommersheim, F,. and S. Wise. 1989. Going to the Penitentiary. A Study of Disparate Sentencing in South Dakota. *Criminal Justice and Behavior* 16: 155-165.

Portes, A. and R. L. Bach. 1985. *Latin Journey: Cuban and Mexican Immigrants in the United States*. Berkeley, California: University of California Press.

Portes, A., and A. Stepick. 1985. Unwelcome Immigrants: The Labor Market Experiences of 1980 (Mariel) Cuban and Haitian Refugees in South Florida. *American Sociological Review* 50: 493-514.

Portes, A., J.M. Clark, and R.D. Manning. 1985. After Mariel: A Survey of the Resettlement Experiences of 1980 Cuban Refugees in Miami. *Cuban Studies* 15(2): 37-59.

Possley, M. 1981. 5 ex-Prison Guards get 2 to 5 years for Beatings. *Chicago Sun Times*, 21 February: S2-2.

Quinney, R. 1979. *Criminology*. Boston: Little, Brown.

Quinney, R. 1974. *Criminal Justice in America*. Boston: Little, Brown.

Rabinowitz, H. N. 1978. *Race Relations in the Urban South, 1865-1890*. NY: Oxford University Press.

Radelet, M. L. 1981. Racial Characteristics and the Imposition of the Death Penalty. *American Sociological Review* 46: 918-927.

Radelet, M.L., and G.L. Pierce. 1985. Race and Prosecutorial Discretion in Homicide Cases. *Law and Society Review* 19: 587-621.

Ragsdale, F. 1985. Personal interview. University of New Mexico Law School.

Raspberry, W. 1991. Strict Laws, Not High Crime to Blame. *Washington Post, Tuesday, Jan.9: 5a.*

Reiman, J. H. 1985. Justice, Civilization, and the Death Penalty: Answering Van den Haag. *Philosophy and Public Affairs* 14: 115-148.

Reiman, J.H. 1990. *The Rich Get Richer and the Poor Get Prison: Ideology, Class, and Criminal Justice*. NY: Wiley.

Reiss, A.J. 1971. *The Police and the Public*. New Haven: Yale University Press.

Ridgeway, J. 1990. *Blood in the Face*. NY: Thunder's Mouth Press.

Robbins, S. P.1984. Anglo Concepts and Indian Reality: A Study of Juvenile Delinquency. *Social Casework*. 65: 235-241.

Robertson, J. O. 1980. *American Myth, American Reality*. NY: Hill & Wang.

Rusche, G. and O. Kirchheimer. 1968. *Punishment and Social Structure*. NY: Russell and Russell.

Sarat, A. and N. Vidmar. 1976. Public Opinion, The Death Penalty, and the Eighth Amendment: Testing the Marshall Hypothesis. *Wisconsin Law Review* 17: 171-206.

Schneider, V. and J.O. Smykla 1991 A Summary Analysis of Executions in the United States, 1608-1987: The Espy File. In *The Death Penalty in America: Current Research*, edited by R.M. Bohm. Cincinnati: Anderson.

Schulman, S. and M. Gryta. 1988. Poverty's Legacy is a Plague of Crime. *Buffalo News*, Nov. 15: 35-38.

Schur, Edwin. 1984. *Labelling Women Deviant*. NY: Random House.

Schur, E.M. 1971. *Labeling Deviant Behavior: Its Sociological Implications*. NY: Harper and Row.

Schwartz, D. 1984. Update: On Minimum Competency Testing. *Newsnotes*. Cambridge: Center for Law and Education.

Shepardson, M. and H. Blodwen. 1970. *The Navajo Mountain Community: Social Organization and Kinship Terminology*. Berkeley, CA: University of California Press.

Sherman, L. W. 1986. Policing Communities: What Really Works? in *Communities and Crime*. vol. 8, edited by A. J. Reiss and M. Tonry. Chicago: University of Chicago Press, 343-386.

Simon, D.R. and D.S. Eitzen. 1982. *Elite Deviance*. Boston: Allyn & Bacon.

Skolnick, J. and E. Currie. 1973. *Crisis in American Institutions*. Boston: Little, Brown.

Skolnick, J. H., and D.H. Bayley. 1986. *The New Blue Line: Police Innovation in Six American Cities*. NY: Free Press.

Smaka, F., G. Nicol, and T. Keller. 1983. *The Cuban Freedom Flotilla: From Mariel Harbor to Las Vegas*. Las Vegas Metropolitan Police Department.

Smith, D. A. 1986. The Neighborhood Context of Police Behavior, in *Communities and Crime*, vol. 8, edited by A. J. Reiss and M. Tonry.Chicago: University of Chicago Press.

Smith, D. A. 1987. Police Response to Interpersonal Violence: Defining the Parameters of Legal Control. *Social Forces* 3: 767-782.

Smith, D. A., and C.A. Visher. 1982. Street-level justice: Situational determinants of police arrest decisions. *Social Problems* 29: 167-177.

Smith, D.A., C.A. Visher, and L.A. Davidson. 1984. Equity and discretionary justice: The influence of race on police arrest decisions. *The Journal of Criminal Law and Criminology* 75: 234-249.

Smith, M. Dwayne 1987 Patterns of Discrimination in Assessments of the Death Penalty: The Case of Louisiana. *Journal of Criminal Justice* 15: 279-286.

Smith, T.W. 1975 A Trend Analysis of Attitudes toward Capital Punishment, 1936-1974. In *Studies of Social Change Since 1948*, vol. II, edited by J. E. Davis. University of Chicago: National Opinion Research Center.

Smith, W. 1987a. Minutes of Warden's Gang Meeting Told. *Chicago Tribune*, November 19: S2-3.

Smith, W. 1987b. Pontiac Warden Met with Gangs in the Past. *Chicago Tribune*, November 22: S2-1, 2.

Smith, W. 1988. Pontiac Guards Search Cells for Weapons. *Chicago Tribune*, February 2: S2-3.

Smith, W. and R. Gibson. 1988. Drugs are Lifeblood of Pontiac Gangs. *Chicago Tribune*, July 19: 1, 6.

Southern Regional Council. 1969. *Race Makes the Difference*. Atlanta, GA: Southern Regional Council.

Spohn, C., J. Gruhl, and S. Welch. 1982. The Effect of Race on Sentencing: A Reexamination of an Unsettled Question. *Law and Society Review* 16: 71-88.

Spohn, C., J.Gruhl, and S. Welch 1987 The impact of the ethnicity and gender of defendants on the decision to reject or dismiss felony charges. *Criminology* 25(1): 175-91.

State of California. 1988. *Projected Total Population for California by Race/Ethnicity*. Sacramento, CA: Population Research Unit, Department of

Finance.

State Urged to Revamp Sentencing. *Chicago Tribune*, May 16, S2: 2.

Steel, R. D. 1985. *Steel on Immigration Law. NY: The Lawyers.* Co-operative Publishing Company.

Stewart, O. 1964. Questions Regarding American Indian Criminality. *Human Organ* 23: 61-66.

Stratton, J. 1973. Cops and Drunks: Police Attitudes and Actions in Dealing with Indian Drunks. *International Journal of the Addictions.* 8: 613-621.

Swift, B. and G. Bickel. 1974. *Comparative Parole Treatment of American Indians and Non-Indians at U.S. Federal Prisons.* Washington, D.C.: Bureau of Social Science Research.

Sykes, G. M. 1958. *The Society of Captives.* Princeton: Princeton University Press.

Symanski, A. and T. G. Goertzel. 1979. *Sociology.* NY: Van Nostrand.

Thomas, Jim 1984 Some Aspect of Negotiated Order, Mesostructure and Loose Coupling in Maximum Security Prisons. *Symbolic Interaction* 7(Fall): 213-231.

Thomas, J. 1988. *Prisoner Litigation: The Paradox of the Jailhouse Lawyer.* Totowa, NJ: Rowman and Littlefield.

Thomas, J. 1989. The 'Reality' of Prisoner Litigation: Re-packaging the Data. *New England Journal of Civil and Criminal Confinement* 15(1): 27-53.

Thomas, J., R.R. Chaka, E. Clemons, C. Secret, M. Clark, D. Nichols, R. Smith, J. Barksdale and A. Sanders. 1980. The Ideology of Prison Research: A Critical View of Stateville: The Penitentiary in Mass Society. *Crime and Social Justice* 14(Winter): 45-50.

Thomas, J., R.R. Chaka, E. Clemons, C.Secret, M. Clark, D. Nichols, R. Smith, J. Barksdale and A. Sanders. 1981. Prison Conditions and Penal Trends. *Crime and Social Justice* 15(July): 49-55.

Thomas, J., and H. Mika. 1988. The Dialectics of Prisoner Litigation: Reformist Idealism or Social Praxis? *Social Justice* 15(1:) 48-71.

Thomas, J., H. Mika, A. Aylward and J. Blakemore. 1991. Exacting Control Through Disciplinary Hearings: 'Making Do' with Prison Rules. *Justice Quarterly* 7: 37-57.

Thornberry, T.P. 1973. Race, socioeconomic status and sentencing in the juvenile justice system. *Journal of Criminal Law and Criminology* 64: 90-98.

Thornberry, T.P. 1979. Sentencing disparities in the juvenile justice system. *Journal of Criminal Law and Criminology* 70: 164-171.

Tifft, L. L. 1982. Capital Punishment Research, Policy, and Ethics: Defining Murder and Placing Murderers. *Crime and Social Justice* 17: 61-68.

Time. 1981. Trouble in Paradise. *Time*, November 23: 23.

Trends and Issues' 89: Criminal and Juvenile Justice in Illinois. 1989. Chicago: Illinois Criminal Justice Authority.

Unger, R. 1980. 'Get Tough' Attitude puts Strain on Prisons. *Chicago Tribune*. 22 September: S2-3.

U.S. Bureau of the Census. 1991. Personal interview. Racial Statistics Branch, Population Division, April.

U.S. Bureau of the Census. 1983,1980. *Census of Population and Housing: Census Tracts Pensacola, Florida Standard Metropolitan Statistical Area*. Washington, D.C.: USGPO.

U.S. Bureau of the Census. 1963. *Methodology and Scores of Socio-Economic Status*. Working Paper No. 15. Washington, D.C.: USGPO.

U.S. Commission on Civil Rights. 1970. *Mexican Americans and the Administration of Justice*. Washington, D.C.: USGPO.

U.S. Immigration and Naturalization Service. 1987. *Statistical Yearbook of the Immigration and Naturalization Service*. 1986. Washington, DC: USGPO.

Unnever, J. D. 1982. Direct and Organizational Discrimination in the Sentencing of Drug Offenders. *Social Problems* 30(2): 212-25.

Unnever, J. D., and L.A. Hembroff. 1988. The Prediction of Racial/Ethnic Sentencing Disparities: An Expectation States Approach. *Journal of Research in Crime and Delinquency* 25(1): 53-82.

van Dijk, T. A. 1987. *Communicating Racism: Ethnic Prejudice in Thought and Talk*. Newbury Park, CA: Sage.

Van Valkenburgh, R. 1937. *Navajo Law and Justice*. Museum Notes, Museum of Northern Arizona 9: 51-54.

Vidmar, N. and T. Dittenhoffer. 1981. Informed Public Opinion and Death Penalty Attitudes. *Canadian Journal of Criminology* 23: 43-56.

Violet, J.C. 1990. Immigration and Refugees. *Migration World* 18(1): 27-33.

Visher, C.A. 1983. Gender, Police Arrest Decisions, and Notions of Chivalry. *Criminology* 21: 5-25.

Vito, G.F. and T.J. Keil. 1988. Capital Sentencing in Kentucky: An Analysis of the Factors Influencing Decision Making in the Post-Gregg Period. *Journal of Criminal Law and Criminology* 79: 301-321.

Vold, G. and T. Bernard. 1986. *Theoretical Criminology*. NY: Oxford.

Ware, G. 1976. *From the Black Bar*. NY: G.P. Putnam's Sons.

Washington Crime News Services. 1988a. Atlanta, Oakdale Riots: FBOP Study Analyzes What Went Wrong. *Corrections Digest* 19(10): 1-6.

Washington Crime News Services. 1988b. Atlanta Uprising Could Have Been Prevented, Rep. Lewis Says. *Corrections Compendium* 19(3): 9.

Washington Crime News Services. 1988c. House Rejects Cuban's Plea. *Corrections Digest* 19(21): 4.

Washington D.C. Lawyers' Committee for Civil Rights Under Law. *1986. Striking Back at Bigotry: Remedies Under Federal and State Law for Violence Motivated by Racial, Religious, and Ethnic Prejudice.* Baltimore: National Institute Against Prejudice and Violence.

Weber, S. R. 1982. Native Americans Before the Bench: The Nature of Contrast and Conflict in Native-American Law Ways and Western Legal Systems. *The Social Science Journal* 19: 47-55.

Welch, S., J.Grulh, and C. Spohn. 1984. Dismissal, Conviction and Incarceration of Hispanic Defendants: A Comparison with Anglos and Blacks. *Social Science Quarterly* 65(2): 257-64.

White, H. 1978. *Tropics of Discourse: Essays in Cultural Criticism.* Baltimore: Johns Hopkins University Press.

White, W. S. 1987. *The Death Penalty in the Eighties: An Examination of the Modern System of Capital Punishment.* Ann Arbor, MI: University of Michigan Press.

Wideman, J. E. 1984. *Brothers and Keepers.* NY: Holt, Rinehart, and Winston.

Wilbanks, W., 1990a. The Myth of a Racist Criminal Justice System. In *Racism, Empiricism and Criminal Justice,* edited by B. MacLean and D. Milovanovic. Vancouver,Canada: Collective Press.

Wilbanks, W. 1990b. Response to the Critics of the Myth of A Racist Criminal Justice System. In *Racism, Empiricism and Criminal Justice,* edited by B. MacLean and D. Milovanovic. Vancouver, Canada: Collective Press.

Wilbanks, W. 1987a. *The Myth of a Racist Criminal Justice System.* CA: Wadsworth.

Wilbanks, W. 1987b. Are Female Felons Treated More Leniently by the Criminal Justice System? *Justice Quarterly* 3,4: 517-529.

Wilson, A. N. 1990. *Black on Black Violence: The Psychodynamics of Black Self-Annihilation in Service of White Domination.* NY: Afrikan World InfoSystems.

Wilson, J.Q. 1968. *Varieties of Police Behavior: The Management of Law and Order in Eight Communities.* Cambridge: Harvard University Press.

Wilson, W. J. 1990. *The Truly Disadvantaged.* Chicago: University of Chicago Press.

Wolfgang, M.E. and M. Riedel. 1975. Rape, Race, and the Death Penalty in Georgia. *American Journal of Orthopsychiatry* 45: 658-68.

Wolfgang, M.E. and M.Riedel. 1973. Race, Judicial Discretion, and the Death Penalty. *Annals of the American Academy of Political and Social Science* 407: 119-33.

Woodiwiss, M. 1988. *Crime Crusades and Corruption: Prohibition in the United States, 1900-1987.* Totawa, NJ: Barnes and Noble.

Wright, B. 1987. *Black Robes, White Justice*. Secaucas, NJ: Lyle Stuart Inc.

Zahn, M. A. 1989. Homicide in the Twentieth Century: Trends, Types, and Causes. In *Violence in America, vol. 1: The History of Crime*, edited by T. R. Gurr. Newbury Park, CA: Sage.

Zatz, M. 1987. The Changing Forms of Racial/EthnicBiases in Sentencing. *Journal of Research in Crime and Delinquency* 24(1): 69-92.

Zatz, M. 1985. Pleas, Priors and Prison: Racial/Ethnic Differences in Sentencing. *Social Science Research* 14: 169-193.

Zatz, M. 1984. Race, Ethnicity and Determinate Sentencing: A New Dimension to an Old Controversy. *Criminology* 22: 147-171.

Zatz, M. and J. Hagan. 1985. Crime, Time and Punishment: An Exploration of Selection Bias in Sentencing Research. *Journal of Quantitative Criminology* 1: 103-126.

Zeisel, H. 1981. Race Bias in the Administration of the Death Penalty: The Florida Experience. *Harvard Law Review* 95: 456-68.

Zimmerman, S.E. and B.C. Frederick. 1983. *Discrimination and the Decision to Incarcerate*. NY Division of Criminal Justice Services, Albany, NY.

Zion, J. W. 1983. The Navajo Peacemaker Court: Deference to the Old and Accomodation to the New. *American Indian Law Review* 11: 89-109.

CASES CITED

Baldwin v. Alabama 105 S.Ct. 2727 (1985)

Brown v. Board of Education 347 U.S. 483 (1954)

Calvin R. v. Lane 82-C-1955 (N.D.Il1) (1982)

Coker v. Georgia 433 U.S. 584 (1972)

Duro v. Reina 100 S.Ct. 2053 (1990)

Ex Parte Crow Dog 109 U.S. 556 (1883)

Furman v. Georgia 408 U.S. 238 (1972)

Gregg v. Georgia 428 U.S. 153 (1976)

Jurek v. Texas 428 U.S. 262 (1976)

Korematsu v. United States 323 U.S. 214 (1944)

McClesky v. Kemp 107 S.Ct. 1756 (1987)

Plessy v. Ferguson 163 U.S. 537 (1896)

Proffitt v. Florida 428 U.S. 242 (1976)

Pugh v. Rainwater 557 F 2nd 1189 (1977)

Pugh v. Rainwater, rehearing 557 F 2nd 1189 (1978)

United States v. Kagama 118 U.S. 375 (1886)

Village of Arlington Heights v. Metro Housing Dev. Corp. 429 U.S. 252, 266 (1977)

Zant v. Stephens 103 S.Ct. 2733 (1983)

About the Authors

Bonnie Adams obtained her B.A. in Criminology from the University of South Florida and is currently pursuing a Ph.D. in Criminology at the University of Maryland. In addition, she is a research associate at the Center for Substance Abuse Research at the University of Maryland.

Frankie Bailey is Visiting Assistant Professor/Research Fellow in the Michael J. Hindelang Criminal Justice Research Center, School of Criminal Justice, State University of New York at Albany. She is author of *Out of the Woodpile: Black Characters in Crime and Detective Fiction* (1991). She is currently at work on a research project dealing with images of victims and offenders in the mass media. Her areas of interest include crime history and cultural diversity.

Robert Bohm is an Associate Professor in the Department of Criminal Justice at the University of North Carolina at Charlotte. He has written extensively on the death penalty in the United States, especially on death penalty opinion. His edited volume, *The Death Penalty in America: Current Research*, has recently been published by Anderson.

David Clark is currently assigned to the Research Unit of the New York State Department of Correctional Services. His duties there include research into the Mariel Cuban population incarcerated in the New York State Prison system. Dr. Clark received his Ph.d from the School of Criminal Justice, the State University of New York at Albany in 1988. His research interests include victimology and issues related to incarceration.

Billy R. Close is currently a doctoral student in the School of Criminology and Criminal Justice at Florida State University, where he is a McKnight Doctoral-Fellowship recipient. He recruits, counsels, and co-directs orientation programs for Florida State University's Black Studies Program with Dr. William R. Jones. He has worked for several commissions investigating racial and ethnic bias in the Florida criminal justice system.

Margaret Farnworth is an Associate Professor of Criminal Justice at Sam Houston University. Her areas of interest include the implications of social stratification for criminal behavior, for criminal justice processing, and for criminological theory.

Daniel Georges-Abeyie is Associate Dean of the School of Criminology and Criminal Justice and Professor in the Program in Criminal Justice at the Florida State University. He has published widely on race, crime and criminal justice, geography and crime, as well as terrorism, and is a nationally recognized expert in these areas.

James Garofalo is Professor and Director of the Center for the Study of Crime, Delinquency, and Corrections at Southern Illinois University (and disputed holder of the Lombroso Cup). He has conducted research and published widely in the areas of victimization and policing, in such leading journals as Criminology, the Journal of Research in Crime and Delinquency, the Journal of Criminal Law and Criminology, Quantitative Criminology, and Victimology. He has recently completed a major study funded by the National Institute of Justice on Bias motivated crimes.

Nanette Graham received her M.A. in Criminal Justice from the University of South Carolina and is currently pursuing a Ph.D. in Criminology at the University of Maryland. Her research interests include: drug abuse and delinquency prevention and evaluation research.

Carol Chiago Lujan is an Assistant Professor of Justice Studies, Arizona State University, and is currently on loan to the Bureau of Indian Affairs as Director of the Office of Alcohol and Substance Abuse Prevention in Washington, D.C.. A member of the Navajo tribe, her research interests focus on injustice issues concerning American Indians, including child abuse and neglect, census underenumeration and perceptions of law and legal agents.

Michael J. Lynch is an Assistant Professor in the Program in Criminal Justice at the School of Criminology and Criminal Justice, Florida State University. He received his Ph.D. in 1988 from the SUNY Albany's School of Criminal Justice. His recent work includes publications in race and criminal justice, penology and criminological theory. His books include *A Primer in Radical Criminology* (with W. Byron Groves), *Corporate Crime, Corporate Violence* (with Nancy Frank, forthcoming), and *Discovering Criminology* (with D. Galaty and G.R. Newman, forthcoming).

James F. Nelson is a Research Specialist at the Division of Criminal Justice Services, Albany, New York. He is currently studying disparities based upon felon arrest charges. He has published methods for measuring the seriousness of prior criminal record and for analyzing repeated events. He is an amateur limnologist and avid windsurfer. He received the Columbia County "Good Earth Keeping Award" for his environmental work in 1983.

E. Britt Patterson is an Assistant Professor in the Program in Criminal Justice in the School of Criminology and Criminal Justice, Florida State University. He received his Ph.D. from the University of Maryland in 1988. His areas of interest include race, crime and criminal justice, the ecology of crime and research methods, and has published in the Journal of Research in Crime and Delinquency and Journal of Quantitative Criminology.

Douglas Smith is a Professor at the University of Maryland Institute of Criminal Justice and Criminology and past editor of *Criminology*, the official journal of the American Society of Criminology. His current research involves decision-making and recidivism in juvenile justice and methodological and theoretical interpretations of the criminal career paradigm. His recent articles have appeared in American Sociological Review, Social Forces, Law and Society Review, Journal of Quantitative Criminology, and Journal of Research in Crime and Delinquency.

Zonna K. Snyder-Joy is a doctoral candidate in Justice Studies at Arizona State University. She is currently researching the perceptions of federal Indian policy held by Indian women involved in education, law and tribal government.

Raymond H.D. Teske Jr. is a Professor of Criminal Justice at Sam Houston State University. His interests include comparative criminal justice procedures and sentencing, with an emphasis on the Federal Republic of Germany, criminological theory and victimology.

Ted Tollett is currently the Program Administrator of the Research and Development Unit for the Children, Youth and Families Program Office located in the Florida Department of Health and Rehabilitative Services. He has worked for the Children, Youth and Families Program since 1984. He has also worked for Florida's Division of Youth Services for seven years as a Planner and Evaluator.

Gina Thurman is a doctoral fellow in Criminal Justice at Sam Houston University. Her interests include jail population trends, the impact of state level policies on local governments and criminal justice system analyses.

Jim Thomas is Professor of Sociology and Criminology at Northern Illinois University. His research interests include prisons, prison culture and computer culture. He has been performing observational research and interviews in the Illinois prisons system since 1980. He has recently published articles on prison culture and prisoner litigation.

Marjorie Zatz is an Associate Professor of Justice Studies at Arizona State University. She has published widely in the area of racial and ethnic discrimination in court processing and discrimination in processing and sanctioning, and is currently conducted a National Science Foundation funded study of social and legal change in Cuba and Nicaragua.

Index

LEGAL CASES CITED

Situational Crime Prevention:
Successful Case Studies
Edited by Ronald V. Clarke
Rare collection of studies demonstrating the effectiveness of the situational approach to crime prevention. Tremendously useful for classroom discussion. CONTENTS (Tentative): 1. Curbside Deterrence/Decker. 2. Steering Column Locks and Car Theft /Mayhew, Clarke and Hough. 3. Preventing Post Office Robberies in London / Ekblom. 4. Preventing Burglary on a British Public Housing Estate/ Pease. 5. Crime Prevention and Commercial Burglary/Griswold. 6. Exact Fare on Buses /Chaiken, Lawless and Stevenson. 7. Operation Identification or the Power of Publicity? /Laycock. 8. The British Columbia Transit Fare Evasion Audit /Deschamps, Brantingham and Brantingham. 9. Psychological Deterrence of Electronic Security /Scherdin. 10. Thefts from Vehicles in Shipyard Parking Lots /Eck and Spelman. 11. Video Cameras and Bus Vandalism /Poyner. 12. Situational Crime Prevention in Two Car Parks /Poyner. 13. Preventing Convenience Store Robbery/Hunter and Jefrey. 14. Cheque Gurantee Cards and Prevention of Fraud / Knutsson and Kulhorn. 15. Deterring Obscene Phone Callers /Clarke. 16. Developing More Effective Strategies for Curbing Prostitution/Matthews. 17. Say "Cheese!": The Disney Order that is not so Mickey Mouse/Shearing and Stenning. 18. Burmingham Markets: Reducing Theft from Shopping Bags /Poyner. 19. Less Telephone Vandalism: How did it Happen? /Challinger. 20. Subway Graffiti in New York City /Sloan-Howitt and Kelling. Approx. 220 pages. ISBN hard/soft: 091157722X/211. Price: $49.50/17.50. **AVAILABLE JANUARY 1992.**

A Primer in the Sociology of Crime
by S. Giora Shoham and John Hoffmann
With depth, clarity and erudition, this primer covers all the classic theory and research on the sociology of crime. CONTENTS: 1. Criminology and Social Deviance. 2. Theoretical and Methodological Issues in Criminology. 3. Ecological Theories of Crime and Delinquency. 4. Anomie and Social Deviance: Strain Theories. 5. Differential Association and its Progeny. 6. Control Theories of Crime and Delinquency. 7. Social Reaction to Crime: Stigma and Interaction. 8. Conflict and Radical Perspectives on Crime. 9. Recent Developments in the Sociology of Crime. References. Index. 179 pages .ISBN: 091157719X. Paperback. $15.50

A Primer in the Sociology of Law
by Dragan Milovanovic
The vagaries of the sociology of law made accessible to all! Places criminal justice in true perspective. Use in courses on sociology of law, social problems, law and social control, nature of crime, introduction to criminal justice, introduction to sociology, theoretical criminology. CONTENTS: *I. Basic Concepts and Origins of the Sociology of Law. II.The Classical Theorists.* 1. Durkheim. 2. Weber. 3. Marx. *III. Modern Perspectives* 4. Legal Realism. 5.Critical Legal Studies. 6. Structural Theories of Law. 7. The Semiotic Approach to Law .*IV. Conclusion.* 8. Essay Questions. 160 pages. Prices: Hardbound (ISBN: 0-911577-13-0.): $32.00. Paperbound: (ISBN 0911577122) : $17.50.

Punishment and Privilege
Edited by W. Byron Groves and Graeme Newman
A collection of original articles by outstanding scholars in criminal justice. CONTENTS: 1.Introduction/Groves and Newman. 2. Physician Immunity from Prosecution and Punishment /Jesilow, Pontell and Geis. 3. Sanctions Against Corporations: Economic Efficiency or Legal Efficacy? /Fisse. 4. Retributivism, Punishment and Privilege/ Braithwaite. 5.Punishment, Privilege and Structured Choice /Groves and Frank. 6. On Sentencing /van den Haag. 7. Power Concentration and Penal Severity /Killias. 8. This Can't be Peace: A Pessimist Looks at Punishment /Pepinsky. 9. Punishment and Social Structure: What Does the FutureHold? /Bernard. 170 pages, paper. Price: (0-911577-106): $17.50.

A Primer in Radical Criminology: Second Edition
by Michael J. Lynch and W. Byron Groves
Substantially revised and expanded. The most popular and widely adopted text in radical criminology. The **Journal of Criminal Law and Criminology** said of the First Edition: ``*...remarkably comprehensive and thorough in its coverage of radical, as well as much 'traditional' literature...*" 158 pages. Price: (Paper: 0911577157): **$12.99.**

Crimes Against Health and Safety
by Nancy Frank
Covers criminal pollution of all kinds, and questions the effectiveness of health and safety regulation. Carefully reviews corporate behavior,and recommends changes in criminal prosecution. Widely adopted for courses in white collar crime, safety management, private security, regulatory justice, and sociology of law. 95 pages. Price (Paperback 0-911577-05-X): $9.99.